Phenomenology
and the
Theory of Science

Northwestern University
STUDIES IN *Phenomenology &*
Existential Philosophy

Aron Gurwitsch

Edited by

Phenomenology and the Theory of Science

LESTER EMBREE

Northwestern University Press

1 9 7 4   Evanston

ARON GURWITSCH

Phenomenology and the Theory of Science

EDITED BY LESTER EMBREE

The essays in this volume—written between 1936 and 1973, and taken from unpublished as well as published sources—reflect the author's lifelong concern with perceptual experience and scientific thought. Following Husserl, Professor Gurwitsch shows how the natural and the human sciences are founded upon the world encountered in everyday life and how both scientific theories and the life-world itself find their ultimate elucidation and grounding in acts and streams of phenomeno- logically reduced consciousness. This position is presented in historical connection with such figures and movements in modern thought as Galileo, Descartes, and existentialism. While efforts to refine some phenomenological theories are included, all of the contents were ad- dressed to non-phenomenologists. In short, this book is an introduction to the phenomenology of science.

Lester Embree is Assistant Professor of Philosophy at Northern Illinois University.

ISBN 0–8101–0446–6

STUDIES IN PHENOMENOLOGY AND EXISTENTIAL PHILOSOPHY

Contents

Editor's Preface

THE WRITINGS OF ARON GURWITSCH brought together in this volume were composed on a variety of occasions. They date from as early as 1937 and as late as 1973. Some were journal articles or critical studies, some appeared previously in books along with the work of others, some have been assembled out of smaller pieces, and some have been taken from unpublished manuscripts. Nevertheless, they all flow from a long-standing and central concern, which is reflected in the title chosen for the collection. The contents of this volume were all written for nonphenomenologists, and as a rule their phenomenological contents are presented in historical connection with figures and movements in modern philosophy, e.g., Descartes and existentialism.

Science for Gurwitsch is *Wissenschaft*. This differs from science in the current ordinary English sense in two important respects. First, even though technology is acknowledged to have its basis in science, it is separate from *Wissenschaft*. In the second place, *Wissenschaft* is not merely or even mainly natural science, for it also includes the human sciences (especially psychology, history, and sociology) and the formal sciences (logic and mathematics). The theory of science is the philosophical discipline in which the fields, relations, methods, categories, presuppositions, and grounds of the sciences are examined.

The style of the authentically Husserlian theory of science is reflected in the first part of this volume. Two contentions are basic to this theory: (1) the theories produced by scientists derive from and ultimately refer back to the life-world; and (2) both the sciences and the life-world find their ultimate clarification and grounding when considered as intentional correlates of acts and streams of consciousness. To recognize this, however, one must have performed the phenomenological epochē. The phenomenological theory of science is thus part of constitutive phenomenology. While the first part of this volume is devoted to phenomenological theory of science, the second is devoted to transcendental phenomenology as oriented toward problems arising in the theory of science.

The contents of this volume, the title, and the principles of the edition were established with the author before he died. As editor, I have tried to make the terminology and style uniform throughout the book. The notes and the titles of chapters and sections have undergone the greatest changes, but there are minor changes on almost every page. Some of the naturally many repetitions have been eliminated. However, without the author to approve radical changes, I have been conservative.

A biographical sketch of the author and a list of his writings through 1971 are included in *Life-World and Consciousness: Essays for Aron Gurwitsch,* ed. Lester Embree (Evanston, Ill.: Northwestern University Press, 1972).

I thank Dr. Bethia Currie and Dr. Jorge García-Gómez for their translations. I thank the Department of Philosophy of Northern Illinois University, Dr. David Seligman, Chairman, for time released from teaching and material support, both of which hastened the completion of my work.

LESTER EMBREE

DeKalb, Illinois
January, 1974

Abbreviations

Titles frequently referred to in this book will be cited in footnotes and between parentheses in the text by the following abbreviations.

Aron Gurwitsch

FC   *The Field of Consciousness.* Pittsburgh: Duquesne University Press, 1964.

SPP   *Studies in Phenomenology and Psychology.* Evanston, Ill.: Northwestern University Press, 1966.

Edmund Husserl

CM   *Cartesian Meditations.* Translated by Dorion Cairns. The Hague: Martinus Nijhoff, 1960.

Crisis *The Crisis of European Sciences and Transcendental Phenomenology.* Translated by David Carr. Evanston, Ill.: Northwestern University Press, 1970.

EJ   *Experience and Judgment.* Translated by James S. Churchill and Karl Ameriks. Evanston, Ill.: Northwestern University Press, 1973.

FTL   *Formal and Transcendental Logic.* Translated by Dorion Cairns. The Hague: Martinus Nijhoff, 1969.

Ideas *Ideas: General Introduction to Pure Phenomenology.* Translated by W. R. Boyce Gibson. New York: The Macmillan Company, 1931.

LI   *Logical Investigations.* Translated by J. N. Findlay. New York: Humanities Press, 1970.

FOR RAJA

PART I

The Project of the Phenomenological Theory of Science

1 / The Life-World and the Phenomenological Theory of Science

As EARLY AS THE *Ideen zu einer reinen Phänomenologie und phänomenologischen Philosophie,* Husserl had designated the descriptive and analytical study of the world of common experience or—as it came to be denoted in the terminology of his later writings—the *Lebenswelt* (life-world) as an urgent desideratum. What is meant is the world as it is encountered in everyday life and given in direct and immediate experience—especially perceptual experience and its derivatives, memory, expectation, and the like—independent of and prior to scientific interpretation.

At every moment of our life, we find ourselves in the world of common everyday experience. We have a certain familiarity with this world which is not derived from what science may teach us; within this world we pursue all our goals and carry on all our activities, including scientific ones. As the universal scene of our life, the soil, so to speak, in which all human activities, productions, and creations are cultivated, the world of common experience is the foundation of the latter as well as of whatever may result from them. Insofar as the construction of the scientific universe as well as the elaboration of science in the specifically modern or "Galilean" style is concerned, the perceptual world underlies the world of common experience and is presupposed by it in a still further sense, in that it serves as a

This essay originally appeared as "Problems of the Life-World," in *Phenomenology and Social Reality: Essays in Memory of Alfred Schutz,* ed. Maurice Natanson (The Hague: Martinus Nijhoff, 1970).

[3]

point both of departure and of reference for that construction which is to provide a mathematical explanation of events and occurrences in the world of perceptual experience.[1] Accordingly, Husserl postulated the all-encompassing description of that world, pursuing it in all its dimensions and considering it under the totality of its aspects, as a scientific task of the first order of importance. At the time Husserl wrote (1913), this task had hardly been embarked upon or even seen as a task by others.

In the more than fifty years that have passed since the publication of the *Ideas,* what Husserl had denoted as a desideratum has found at least partial fulfillment.[2] Husserl himself, in his later writings, especially in his last work, *Die Krisis der europäischen Wissenschaften und die transzendentale Phänomenologie,*[3] but also in *Phänomenologische Psychologie,*[4] went far beyond the first general delineations of the world of everyday experience that he had presented in the *Ideas* (§§ 27 ff.). What in *Crisis* Husserl came to denote as the life-world has also been dealt with by writers, both German and French, whom it has become customary to classify as "existentialists," namely, Heidegger, Sartre, and Merleau-Ponty.[5] Finally, we have to mention the work of Schutz, who endeavored to lay philosophical foundations of the social sciences and to provide a clarification, by means of phenomenological analysis, of their basic notions.[6] It

1. It must be noted that the term "scientific" has to be construed here in the broad sense of its German equivalent, *wissenschaftlich,* that is, it is not restricted to natural science and does not have technological connotations.

2. Hereafter we shall refer to Husserl's *Ideas* by this abbreviation of the English title. Full bibliographic data on this and other works and the abbreviations by which they are cited are given in the list of abbreviations on p. xi.

3. See the author's report on this text, "The Last Work of Edmund Husserl," reprinted in *Studies in Phenomenology and Psychology* (Evanston, Ill.: Northwestern University Press, 1966).

4. See "Edmund Husserl's Conception of Phenomenological Psychology," chap. 4, below.

5. Heidegger, *Being and Time,* trans. John Macquarrie and Edward Robinson (London: SCM Press, 1962); Sartre, *Being and Nothingness,* trans. Hazel E. Barnes (New York: Philosophical Library, 1956); and Merleau-Ponty, *Phenomenology of Perception,* trans. Colin Smith (New York: Humanities Press, 1962).

6. *Collected Papers,* 3 vols. (The Hague: Martinus Nijhoff, 1962–66), and *The Phenomenology of the Social World,* trans. George Walsh and Frederick Lehnert (Evanston, Ill.: Northwestern University Press, 1967).

is Schutz who has seen the life-world as primarily a social world and has done more than anyone else to advance its study and elucidation from the point of view of its social aspect, which is obviously of primordial importance.

In present-day philosophical discussions, outside the several trends of what is summarily called "analytic philosophy," the life-world occupies a central and focal position. Its discovery must be reckoned among the most momentous accomplishments of contemporary philosophical thought, an accomplishment and acquisition, we submit, of enduring value which will prove to be of significant consequence for the future development of philosophy.

Still, certain problems arise with respect to the very notion of the life-world, and the time has come to formulate these problems. To do so appears particularly urgent in view of the fact that the main writings of the existentialist thinkers are, on account of the available translations, better known in the English-speaking world or, at least, more easily accessible than the works of Husserl, which are only beginning to be adequately translated. Among the problems we have in mind, let us mention first the methodological significance of the notion of the life-world, the role it is to play, and the function it is destined to fulfill within the systematic context of philosophical and especially phenomenological theory. Closely related thereto is the question of whether, with the discovery of the life-world, philosophy has found its definitive field and domain of work—its permanent resting place, so to speak. Is philosophy from now on to be nothing other than a complete, all-encompassing, and systematic exploration of the life-world? Or is it perhaps that, even with the discovery of the life-world, notwithstanding the paramount importance of that discovery, the ultimate philosophical dimension has yet to be reached? If such should prove to be the case, one can further ask whether the importance of the discovery in question does not consist, among other things, in its being a phase of the journey toward the ultimate philosophical dimension.

EXISTENTIAL PHILOSOPHY AND
PHILOSOPHICAL ANTHROPOLOGY

FOR OUR PURPOSE it is opportune to glance at the intentions of the existentialist writers as these intentions have found realization in their actual work. It appears that in dealing with the life-world they do not so much concern themselves with *the world of common experience, the world of daily life,* as they do with *man and his existence, his ways of existing in the life-world.* This distinction is more than merely a matter of emphasis. It defines the line of demarcation which separates Husserl's work from that of the existentialists of every persuasion.

Husserl, to be sure, confronts the world as directly and immediately given in human experience, in contradistinction to the universe of science which is not experienced in direct immediacy but constructed for purposes of explanation (*Crisis*, § 34d). The world of common experience, as it is given prior not only to specific scientific interpretation but also to logical operations of all sorts which may be performed on the several items it contains, undoubtedly has human significance. From the outset Husserl has stressed that, among the things and objects encountered in the world of common experience, there are those essentially characterized by human significance in a preeminent sense, for example, tools, instruments, utensils of every description, works of art, literary documents, objects of cultural value, and the like (*Ideas*, § 27). By their very sense, such objects refer to their having been produced and their being for the use of human beings. In his account of the life-world Husserl sets himself the task of providing a complete and systematic description of such objects and others which are not man-made as they are directly experienced, and of analyzing the different ways in which they present themselves in experience. Concerning the life-world as a whole, he endeavors—as we shall see later—to lay bare its general style along various dimensions.

Man is encountered within the life-world and as inserted into it. Each one of us is aware both of himself and of his fellow men, the likes of him, as mundane existents among other mundane existents, the sense of mundanity being defined by the above-mentioned insertion. Man, to be sure, is characterized by distinctive features. Hence problems of a particular and highly specific nature arise with respect to man and human existence. Along the lines of Husserlian phenomenology, man and human existence would have to be considered within the frame, and against the background, of the life-world, as, so to speak, a secondary theme to be treated with reference to the primary one. We have used the grammatical form of the conditional because, as a matter of fact, Husserl has not dealt with the specific problems of human existence, except for a few occasional remarks which are not very significant and are rather in the nature of promissory notes (see, e.g., *CM*, p. 142). He has instead concerned himself with the problem of the constitution of the cultural world—a world made by men in the various forms of their mutual cooperation, and on whose objects sense and meaning are bestowed by virtue of intellectual and mental functions. As we shall see later, he conceives of the cultural world, or rather worlds, as arising on the basis of the "natural world"—"natural" now to be construed as not man-made but still as given in direct perceptual experience. Just because they deal with what is accomplished by man and the conditions of its being accomplished, these investigations pertain to a philosophy of culture rather than to a philosophy of human existence, as that term has come to be understood.

The preceding remarks should suffice to dissipate the erroneous opinion, all too often encountered, that Husserl is a forerunner of existentialism and that the main value of his work consisted in preparing the way for existentialist philosophy and has been superseded by the latter's advent. Certainly, existentialist philosophers have learned a great deal from Husserl; they have availed themselves of a great many results arrived at in his analysis of consciousness, and most of them have not failed to acknowledge their indebtedness to him. Still, they have not espoused his radical philosophical intentions, about which we shall say more in the subsequent section.

Our initial statement that existentialist philosophy is concerned with human existence in the world requires some elaboration. Most of all, *that man exists in the world means that he is involved in it.* Such involvement and the various modes and forms it assumes are of central interest in existential philosophy, where man is considered with regard to his conduct in his environment and the different ways in which he comes to terms or tries to come to terms with it, especially with his fellow men, and where he is confronted with certain situations of vital

importance in which he has to make decisions, to assume respon-
sibilities, and to enter into commitments. Man is viewed as
planning his future and as living toward it in his multifarious
endeavors to realize his projects. In a word, man is seen as fash-
ioning his ambiance as the scene of his committed life. Needless
to say, interhuman relations of all kinds hold a preeminent place
in considerations of this sort.

Thus, to approach the study of man means to consider him
in the full concreteness of his existence. This point has been
emphasized by the existentialist writers as well as by their
commentators. Consequently, the emphasis can no longer be
mainly, and certainly not exclusively, on man's mental and conscious life, on his intellectual functions, and on what is accomplished and produced by them. Taken in full concreteness,
man proves to be a psychosomatic unity. Each one of us has his
body or—as one often finds it expressed—each one *is* his body.
It is perfectly in keeping with the logic of the existentialist orientation that both Sartre and Merleau-Ponty (though not Heidegger) have devoted much attention to the somatic aspect of
human existence and have presented extensive and fruitful
analyses of it.[7] In speaking of the body, of course, they do not
have in view that which is described and studied in anatomy,
physiology, and the other biological sciences, which take the
standpoint of a detached observer; rather, they concern themselves with the somatic body as it is experienced and "lived" by
us in our very involvement with it.

Human existence taken in full concreteness furthermore has
a sociohistorical aspect. Man is born into a certain cultural group
whose language he speaks and whose interpretation of and out-
look on the world have been conveyed to him and are accepted by
him as a matter of course. He lives in a particular society at a
given period of its history. In this society he occupies a particular
place, either assigned to him by birth, as in a society of rigid
social stratification, or defined by his profession, function,
wealth, influence, etc. Once again, what is in question here are
not social and historical facts and the connections between them
as they are or may be ascertained and formulated by an im-

7. Sartre, *Being and Nothingness*, pt. III, chap. 2; Merleau-
Ponty, *The Structure of Behavior*, trans. Alden L. Fisher (Boston:
Beacon Press, 1963). See also the exposition of their views in
Richard M. Zaner, *The Problem of Embodiment* (The Hague:
Martinus Nijhoff, 1964).

partial observer, but as they appear to and enter the consciousness (in whatever mode) of those whose historical and social
conditions they define and determine and who are involved in
that situation, again to the point of saying that they *are* their
situation. Hence the Hegelian strain which may be discerned in
all existential philosophers and, in the case of French existentialists and writers influenced by them, the interest in and preoccupation with the thought of Marx, especially the early Marx.
Sartre's relinquishment of his earlier existentialist philosophy
and his espousal of Marxism appear as the logical outcome of
this earlier existentialism.[8]

However superficial, the preceding survey makes it clear that
existentialism is not so much an exploration of the life-world as
it is a *philosophical anthropology* whose theoretical procedures
have to a considerable extent been borrowed from Husserlian
phenomenology. This characterization also holds for the work of
Heidegger, his strong protestations to the contrary notwithstanding.[9] The term "anthropology" is not to be construed in the technical sense as synonymous with "ethnology" but must be given
the broader meaning of a general preoccupation with man and
his existence.

We are far from challenging the legitimacy of a philosophical
anthropology and equally far from denying the fruitfulness of
the insights into the forms and modes of human involvement and
the somatic and social aspects of human existence that have
resulted from the existentialist enterprise which, as we readily
grant, holds out the promise of still further valuable insights to
be attained. Nor do we overlook the many fruitful applications
which, understandably enough, the existentialist approach to
man and existential thought has found in the contemporary
psychological sciences, especially psychiatry. Since, as already
mentioned, the existentialist philosophers have made ample use
of Husserl's results and ideas, the latter have penetrated, at
least by way of mediation, into the work of contemporary psychologists and psychiatrists, some of whom, incidentally, have
sought further stimulation from immediate, direct acquaintance
with Husserl's work. It is most gratifying to see that phenomenological theory has proved valuable and fruitful in fields of research other than that in which it was originally developed.

8. *Critique de la raison dialectique* (Paris: Gallimard, 1960).
9. *Being and Time*, § 10.

Still, we must not permit ourselves to become fascinated by the fruits which the tree of phenomenology has borne to the point of neglecting its roots, for this could perhaps jeopardize the growth of further fruits which the tree could yield in the future, were its roots cultivated with the utmost care. Apart from such "pragmatic" considerations, we have to face the question of whether to accept the transformation of philosophy into anthropology, its dissolution into psychology, however widely the latter is conceived. If we grant the legitimacy of philosophical anthropology—even, for the sake of the discussion, the correctness of whatever results have been achieved thus far —does it follow that the ultimately radical philosophical dimension has been reached?

The Primacy of Consciousness

From the Husserlian point of view, we have now to raise the problem of access. Whether we concern ourselves with the universe as constructed and interpreted in the sciences of modern style or, for that matter, of any style, or with the life-world as directly experienced, or with whatever else, it is through acts of consciousness and through such acts alone that what we deal with is given and presented and thus becomes accessible to us. In the case of the life-world and whatever it comprises, the acts in question pertain to perceptual consciousness in both its originary and derivative modes (*Ideas*, § 99). As regards the scientific universe, allowance must be made not only for perceptual experience but also for specific acts of conceptualization, idealization, and formalization which presuppose perceptual experience, because they are founded on it in a way we shall discuss later.

In raising the problem of access to "reality"—in whatever sense the term is understood—we come to discern the pre-eminent role played by perceptual consciousness. It is required as an avenue of access to reality; it is, in fact, even the only avenue. On the other hand, by its very nature, perceptual consciousness does yield that access. Existential philosophy is often credited with having accounted for the immediacy of our contact with the world and mundane existence, for our being "at" the world. Such immediacy of contact, however, follows from Husserl's theory of the intentionality of consciousness, especially perceptual intentionality.[10] The novelty which is original with existentialism consists in the emphasis on involvement and commitment. However, for involvement in any of its forms and modes to be a possible topic of discussion and even to be experienced or "lived," acts of consciousness are required through which the involved subject becomes aware of his being involved and of the specific form and sense which his involvement assumes in a particular situation.[11]

Correspondingly, the same holds for the sociohistorical aspect of human existence. Even if a social or historical situation is taken as an objective fact, i.e., as it is ascertained by a historian or a social scientist, it refers to, and in that sense presupposes, acts of consciousness on the part of the objective observer through which he gains access to the subject matter of his investigation. In existentialism and philosophical anthropology, however, sociohistorical situations, as previously mentioned, are not considered as they are seen by a detached and impartial observer but, rather, as to what they mean to the subjects concerned and involved. Obviously, we are again referred to acts of consciousness (different, of course, from those of the scientific observer) through which the sociohistorical subjects and agents conceive of and interpret the society in which they live and their respective social roles, functions, situations, and positions.

In principle, the case is not different with regard to the somatic aspect of human existence. Undoubtedly, it is a great

10. G. Funke, *Phänomenologie—Metaphysik oder Methode* (Bonn: H. Bouvier & Co., 1966), p. 44, maintains that, for Descartes, consciousness is consciousness of objects (*Objektbewusstsein*) such that there is no gulf separating and isolating man as a self-sufficient subject from a world of equally self-sufficient objects. We have dealt with this problem in Descartes, but have come to a somewhat different conclusion. (See below, chap. 9, especially pp. 216 ff.)

11. H. L. Dreyfus, "Why Computers Must Have Bodies in Order To Be Intelligent," *Review of Metaphysics*, XXI (1967), 15 f., maintains that transcendental phenomenology is based on the "assumption" that "everything can be understood from the point of view of a detached objective thinker." Against this "assumption," he emphasizes "the crucial role of human involvement," which, he points out in following Merleau-Ponty (pp. 19 f.), can be understood only in terms of "the body which confers the meanings discovered by Husserl." At this point we ask whether involvement as experienced does not refer to consciousness experiencing it. Presently we shall raise the same question with respect to somatic experience.

merit of the existentialist philosophers to have called attention to the body with which we live and as we live it. But again the problem of access arises. We could not speak of somatic existence, in the sense in question, if it were not for acts of consciousness through which we become aware both of our being embodied in general and of particular postures, motions, motor tendencies, and the like. To be sure, the acts of consciousness which yield access to our embodied or somatic existence are of a specific nature. Yet for all their specificity, they are still acts of consciousness.[12]

Whether we concern ourselves with the life-world along the lines of Husserl's orientation or, following the direction of existentialism and philosophical anthropology, we deal with human existence within the life-world, in raising the problem of access we are led to consider consciousness and its acts. These include the acts through which the life-world presents itself to us and is interpreted in the sense it has for the sociohistorical group to which we belong (the life-world, as we shall show in the subsequent section, is essentially a cultural world) and the acts through which we conceive of ourselves as mundane existents, as human beings in a sense which is congruous with that in which we interpret our life-world.[13] Acts of consciousness are in play in all our conduct—in all our doings, involvements, commitments, hopes, fears, actions, and projects.

This is not the place to enter into a description of those acts and generic differences among them, or to analyze their systematic groupings and concatenations of a sometimes high degree of complexity, or, finally, to study the relations of foundation in which certain acts may stand to others. What alone matters in the present context is the *reference to consciousness as the universal and sole medium of access.* Granting, as we did at the outset, the significance of the disclosure of the life-world as an accomplishment of permanent value, we must not over-

12. See *FC*, pp. 303 ff.; and Zaner, *The Problem of Embodiment*, pt. III, chap. 3, § 2a.

13. Husserl, "Phänomenologie und Anthropologie," *Philosophy and Phenomenological Research*, II (1941), 8: "Sich als Mensch nehmen, das ist schon die Weltgeltung voraussetzen"; see also p. 9. This article, which reproduces a lecture given in Berlin on June 10, 1931, is Husserl's reply to the anthropological tendencies of Heidegger—whose name, however, is not mentioned. See also Husserl's "Nachwort," in *Ideas III, Husserliana* V (The Hague: Martinus Nijhoff, 1952), pp. 138 ff.

look another no less definitive accomplishment which philosophy achieved more than three centuries ago: the discovery by Descartes, in the second of his *Meditations on First Philosophy*, of the privilege and primacy of consciousness not only because of its indubitability but also because it is the universal medium of access to whatever we may be dealing with.

When consciousness is considered under that perspective, it must not be taken, as it was by Descartes, for a part of the world, a series or set of mundane events alongside other mundane events with which the former are interwoven and to which they stand in multifarious relations of causal or functional dependency. Such an approach would be beset by the absurdity of regarding the medium of access as forming part of that to which it yields access. Hence a special methodological device is required by means of which consciousness is stripped of the sense of mundanity or, as it may also be put, one which permits us to consider consciousness exclusively under the aspect of its presentational or presentifying function, that is, as opening up access to objects and entities of every kind, including those which pertain to the life-world. This device is the phenomenological or transcendental reduction. It is not possible to consider it here.[14]

Recognizing its legitimacy does not mean granting that philosophical anthropology is autochthonous in the sense of being in no need of radical clarification and justification. It does not mean that philosophical anthropology stands on its own legs in the sense of having no presuppositions. In inquiring into its foundations by raising the problem of access, we discovered consciousness as required for our apprehension of ourselves as mundane human beings, hence as a presupposition of philosophical anthropology, a presupposition most often taken for granted and, therefore, overlooked. By this token, *the life-world and all that it comprises, man as a mundane existent, all his modes of existing and conducting himself in the life-world, reveal themselves as correlates of acts and operations of consciousness and of multifarious concatenations, syntheses, and systematic organizations of those acts and operations.* With respect to the life-world as well as with regard to any domain of being, the task then arises of setting forth and so analyzing the corresponding

14. It has been treated by Husserl in almost all of his writings since *Ideas*. The second part of *Erste Philosophie, Husserliana* VIII (The Hague: Martinus Nijhoff, 1959), is entirely devoted to this topic.

and correlated "equivalent of consciousness" (*Bewusstseins-äquivalent*), an expression which may well serve as a succinct formulation of the program of Husserl's constitutive phenomenology.[15]

Recently the idea of the correlation between that which is given to consciousness and the consciousness of it has been stressed by Funke both in general and with special reference to the life-world.[16] Funke goes still further. In his thoroughgoing critical discussion of Heidegger's philosophy and of the attempts made in Germany in the twenties at a "revival" of metaphysics, Funke insists on the profound difference between *simply existing* and *formulating a philosophy of existence*. For the latter, acts of a specific kind of reflection, i.e., specific acts and operations of consciousness, are required by means of which mere existing is articulated and rendered explicit, hence, in a sense, transcended.[17] Heidegger's "fundamental ontology" (*Fundamentalontologie*), to mention a particularly striking point, deals with the facticity of Dasein as such, not with a particular factual existent, with the fact of *this* ego, *this* man; he does not write "eine Biographie dieses und nur dieses besonderen Lebens."[18] Rather, the particular de facto existence is seen as an exemplar of facticity, i.e., from a certain point of view. This requires specific acts of ideation and conceptualization. Philosophy, existentialist and other, must be recognized as a mental product and accomplishment and must be referred to the processes and operations of consciousness in which it originates. Differently expressed, every philosophy—constitutive phenomenology being no exception—stands under the obligation of accounting in its own terms for its very possibility.

This amounts to nothing less than a reassertion of the supreme law under which philosophy stands, the law which Plato formulated in the expression λόγον διδόναι, "render accounts." Husserl has this law in view when he repeatedly speaks of radicality as the task of philosophy and of the intellectual responsibility and self-responsibility of the philosopher. Throughout his book, Funke, with whom we find ourselves in agreement on a great many points, stresses that philosophy has the essential and even

15. *Ideas*, § 152; in *Crisis*, §§ 46, 48, Husserl speaks of "universales Korrelationsapriori" and "Korrelationssystem."
16. Funke, *Phänomenologie*, pp. 99, 139 ff., 168 ff.
17. *Ibid.*, pp. 30, 41 ff., 67 f., 17 ff., 234 ff.
18. *Ibid.*, p. 236.

the sole function of providing grounds and foundations (*Begründungen* and *Begründungszusammenhänge*). Adopting and appropriating the supreme law of philosophy, we are led to consciousness as the ultimate ground of all our awareness and knowledge, of all validation and invalidation, of all founding and grounding.

As a result of our discussion, the discovery of the life-world cannot be considered as the disclosure of the ultimate philosophical dimension but, at the most, as a steppingstone on the way toward that disclosure. We may say that with the discovery of the life-world the penultimate but not the ultimate philosophical dimension is reached, the ultimate dimension being consciousness under the aspect of its transcendental function. This view is borne out by the literary organization of *Crisis* which, very significantly, like two other books by Husserl (*Ideas* and *CM*), bears the subtitle *An Introduction to Phenomenological Philosophy*. After having rehabilitated the life-world by an analysis of the origin and the presuppositions of modern physics, physics of the Galilean style (in the subsequent section we shall briefly deal with that analysis), Husserl embarks on the treatment of the life-world with a view to opening an avenue of approach to transcendental phenomenology.[19] We point this out in order to dissipate some misunderstandings. In certain quarters *Crisis* is considered to be Husserl's most important book and his works in logic, or, rather, philosophy of logic, are disregarded. Moreover, the importance of *Crisis* is seen as demonstrating that Husserl has broken with his own past, has somehow relinquished the idea of constitutive phenomenology, and has moved in the direction of existentialist philosophy.[20] However, a close and thorough study of *Crisis* does not justify making a distinction, in the sense of an opposition, between the philosophy of the late and that of the early Husserl. Rather, such a study makes clear the intrinsic connection between Husserl's last work and his

19. The title of *Crisis*, pt. III A, is, "The Way into Phenomenological Transcendental Philosophy by Inquiring back from the Pregiven Life-World."

20. Funke, *Phänomenologie*, pp. 156 f. Even Suzanne Bachelard believes that in *Crisis* Husserl has not remained faithful to himself but has made concessions "to the tastes of the day, to the philosophies of existence" (*A Study of Husserl's Formal and Transcendental Logic*, trans. Lester Embree [Evanston, Ill.: Northwestern University Press, 1968], p. 141, n. 19): see below, n. 41.

earlier writings and testifies to the remarkable continuity in the development of his thought.[21]

In concluding our discussion of the idea and program of existentialist philosophy and philosophical anthropology, we wish to note that our criticism does not apply—at least, not without qualification—to the work of Alfred Schutz, whose significance for the elucidation of the social aspect of the life-world we mentioned earlier. Throughout all his writings, Schutz has deliberately abided by the "natural" as contrasted with the transcendental attitude, the latter being contingent on the performance of the phenomenological reduction. His analyses fall under the purview of mundane phenomenological psychology rather than transcendental phenomenology; they may be said to be parts and fragments of a philosophical anthropology which he had planned to write but which it was not given to him to work out.[22] In proceeding in this manner, Schutz has made use of the right of every scholar—a right of which, as he has pointed out himself, no scholar can fail to avail himself—namely, the right to define his field of inquiry and to indicate lines of demarcation which he does not intend to transcend in his research. Such a circumscription of a delineated field is at the same time a recognition of a domain beyond the lines of demarcation. With respect to Schutz's work, this means that, by deliberately confining his analyses within the limits of phenomenological psychology, he has taken notice of the transcendental problematics, a recognition of which numerous explicit formulations appear in his writings. He never claimed philosophical finality for his theories. He was well aware of their being capable of receiving a transcendental-phenomenological underpinning, though he himself did not enter into the transcendental dimension.[23]

21. This view is also maintained by J. M. Broekman, *Phänomenologie und Egologie, Phaenomenologica* XII (The Hague: Martinus Nijhoff, 1963), pp. 5 f., 27.

22. See Schutz's programmatic statement in "Husserl's Importance for the Social Sciences," *Collected Papers*, I, 149; see also Maurice Natanson's Introduction to that volume, pp. xlvi f. See also Alfred Schutz, *Reflections on the Problem of Relevance*, ed. Richard M. Zaner (New Haven: Yale University Press, 1970); and Alfred Schutz and Thomas Luckmann, *The Structures of the Life-World*, trans. Richard M. Zaner and H. Tristam Engelhardt, Jr. (Evanston, Ill.: Northwestern University Press, 1973).

23. It is in this light that our discussion of his essay "On Multiple Realities" (*Collected Papers*, I, 249 ff.) must be understood (*FC*,

THE LIFE-WORLD AS A CULTURAL WORLD

TO APPROACH THE LIFE-WORLD from a different angle, we recall that Husserl was led to its discovery by an analysis of Galilean physics and the disclosure of its presuppositions (*Crisis*, § 9). By Galilean physics Husserl does not mean the work of the historical Galileo but the science inaugurated by Galileo, the science of physics of the specific modern style. The universe, as it has come to be conceived in the course of the history of modern science (a conception entertained at every period of that history), is a construction, a system of constructs resulting from, and being the correlates of, conceptualizations of a specific sort, namely, idealizations, mathematizations, algebraizations, formalizations. Such processes—which, of course, are mental in nature—require materials on which to operate. Those materials, which must be pregiven, can be nothing other than the objects of everyday common experience. The life-world is defined as comprising all items and objects which present themselves in prescientific experience and as they present themselves prior to their scientific interpretation in the specific modern sense. As thus understood, the life-world proves to be a most essential presupposition or "foundation of sense" (*Sinnesfundament*) of the science of physics, insofar as the scientific universe is constructed on the basis of the manifold experiences of the life-world.

However, this foundation of sense has been obscured, obfuscated, and forgotten. Since the beginning of the modern development, the life-world has been concealed under a "tissue of ideas" (*Ideenkleid*) which has been cast on it like a mask, the ideas in question pertaining to mathematics and mathematical natural science. Something that in truth is a method—more precisely, the result and product of a method—has come to be taken for "true being" (*Crisis*, p. 51), while the life-world, which for us is the only truly real world, has been relegated to the inferior status of a merely subjective phenomenon. On account of our historical situation as heirs to the modern scientific tradition,

---

pp. 394–403); see also Maurice Natanson's remarks in his very sympathetic and appreciative review of the French version of our book in *Philosophical Review*, LXVIII (1959), 538.

the world presents itself to us, including those of us who are not professional scientists or even are ignorant of the details of scientific theories, with reference to and in the light of its possible mathematical idealization (*EJ*, § 10). The world is apprehended as indicating and pointing to an "objective reality", i.e., a reality once and for all determined in itself and hence the same for everyone. The task of the scientist is the disclosure of that objective reality which is hidden beneath the varying subjective appearances. We may likewise say that his task consists of specifying in detail the general scheme of our comprehension and interpretation of the world as it has historically developed.

To clarify the presuppositions and the sense of modern natural science, we must turn to the life-world as given in direct experience. According to Husserl (*Crisis*, §§ 33, 34 f.), the life-world may and must be made a topic of investigation in its own right and independent of the foundational problems of modern science. To restore the life-world in its original form, the sediment of sense which has accrued to it in the course of and because of the development of modern science must be removed. More is required than no longer basing oneself on, no longer starting from, no longer accepting, or no longer even taking notice of, particular scientific interpretations of the world, like the physics of Newton or of Einstein, contemporary quantum physics, etc. *What is in question is the very sense of objectivity which belongs to our comprehension of the world.* Reinstating the life-world in its original and authentic shape requires not merely turning away from every specific interpretation, relinquishing the idea of the universe as already scientifically determined—as already disclosed as to what it is in itself—but also, and above all, *removing and eliminating the very sense of scientific explicability as such and at large. To find access to the life-world, our experience of the world must be stripped of the reference to possible scientific explanation, of the component of sense by virtue of which the world is apperceived and apprehended as lending itself to scientific interpretation,* whatever that interpretation may be in detail. Another way of expressing it is to say that the reference to an ideal mathematical order must be eliminated from our experience of the world and that the latter must no longer be seen from the perspective of the former.

What do we have left, after this subtractive operation has been performed? Perceptual experience is reinstated in its own right. The yellow color of the chair over there is considered as a property of the thing itself and is not taken for a subjective sensation provoked by processes describable in mathematicophysical terms which impinge on our sense organs. The same holds for all "secondary" qualities, while the "primary" ones must be taken as they present themselves in perceptual experience, without reference to geometrical idealization.

However, the things encountered in the life-world are not adequately and certainly not completely characterized when they are described in terms only of their primary and secondary qualities. The chair has not only a certain shape and color but is also perceived as something on which to sit. Things present themselves as suitable and serviceable for certain purposes, to be manipulated and handled in certain ways, as instruments and utensils, in a word, with reference to actions to be performed or performable on them.[24] They appear in the light of schemes of apperception and apprehension which belong to what Schutz calls the "stock of knowledge at hand." That stock comprises, among other things, a set of more or less loosely connected rules and maxims of behavior in typical situations, recipes for handling things of certain types so as to attain typical results.[25] The elements composing the "stock of knowledge at hand" are socially approved and socially derived.[26] Social approval does not mean explicit promulgation or any kind of legal or formal sanction but rather the fact that, in a given society, certain modes of conduct are tacitly and as a matter of course accepted and taken for granted as behavior appropriate and, in this sense, "natural" in typical situations. The "stock of knowledge at hand" is socially

24. Heidegger's notions of "equipment" (*Zeug*) and "readiness-to-hand" (*Zuhandenheit*) are applicable here; see *Being and Time*, pp. 98 ff. On other grounds and in an entirely different context, Bergson, in chap. 1 of *Matter and Memory* (trans. Nancy Margaret Paul and W. Scott Palmer [London: George Allen & Unwin, 1911]), insisted on the intimate connection between perception and action. Challenging the traditional "postulate" that "*perception has a wholly speculative interest; it is pure knowledge*" (p. 17), Bergson maintains on the contrary that "the objects which surround my body reflect its possible action upon them" (p. 7). "Perception . . . measures our possible action upon things, and thereby, inversely, the possible action of things upon us" (p. 57).

25. Schutz, "Some Structures of the Life-World," *Collected Papers*, III, 120 f.

26. Schutz, "The Stranger" and "The Well-Informed Citizen," *Collected Papers*, II, 95 f., 133.

derived because only a comparatively small part of it originates in the personal experience of the individual; the bulk is transmitted to him by his parents, teachers, other persons in authority, and by all kinds of associates.

Going beyond Schutz, who has not dealt with this problem, we must stress that the perception of a thing from the perspective of the "stock of knowledge at hand" is not to be understood as though a sense or meaning were superveniently bestowed or imposed on a mere corporeal object which, prior to that imposition, was devoid of all sense and was to be described in terms of both primary and secondary qualities, but in those terms alone.[27] On the contrary, *the schemes of apperception and apprehension* play a determining role in and for perception; they *contribute essentially toward making the things encountered such as they appear in perceptual experience.* As a result of eliminating the reference to scientific explicability and an ideal mathematical order, we are not reduced to perceptual experience in its pristine purity, that is, to primary and secondary qualities only. Rather *the things perceived present themselves* as defined by the purpose they serve, the use that can be made of them, the manner in which they are to be handled, and so on—briefly, as *determined by schemes of apprehension.* Accordingly, the lifeworld, to which we gain access by the subtractive procedure in question, does not consist of mere corporeal objects in the sense just mentioned. On the contrary, it is a world interpreted, apperceived, and apprehended in a specific way. In a word, it is a *cultural world,* more precisely, the cultural world of a certain sociohistorical group, that of our society at the present moment of history.

Husserl emphasizes that the cultural sense of an instrument, a utensil, a machine, and also of a garden, a building, a work of art, a literary document, etc., is not externally attached to or associated with a mere corporeal thing.[28] Rather its sense is incorporated into and impressed (*eingedruckt*) on the cultural object and thus proves to be a character proper to that object. To be sure, all cultural objects as defined by the sense embodied and embedded in them refer to mental life, to the plans, projects, designs, intentions, and the life of makers and users.[29] However,

27. Cf. Heidegger, *Being and Time,* p. 101.
28. *Phänomenologische Psychologie,* ed. Walter Biemel, *Husserliana* IX (The Hague: Martinus Nijhoff, 1962), § 16.
29. In this connection, we refer to the very important distinc-

the cultural sense must not, because of that reference, be mistaken for a psychological event of a special kind. Such a misconception would entail the interpretation of a cultural object in terms of the perception of a mere corporeal thing accompanied by a special psychological occurrence.

Although a cultural object exhibits its sense as a property pertaining to it and essentially determining and defining it, an abstraction is possible through which cultural senses can be disregarded. By virtue of this abstraction, cultural objects are reduced to mere corporeal things (*pure dingliche Realitäten*); and, accordingly, the life-world, originally a cultural world, becomes a world of mere things (*Dingwelt*).[30] Though it is attained by an abstraction, the thing-world has, according to Husserl, priority with respect to the cultural world.[31] That is, the cultural world presupposes the thing-world as a substratum. It arises by virtue of specific acts of a "higher order" which are founded on acts of "pure" perceptual experience (yielding mere corporeal things in the sense just referred to) and whose intentional or noematic correlates are the several cultural senses impressed in the corporeal things, whereby the latter are transformed into cultural objects exhibiting their cultural senses as properties of their own.[32] In other words, the phenomenological account of

---

tion between the "subjective" and the "objective" sense of artifacts, actions, etc., which Schutz has established in *Phenomenology of the Social World*, § 27.

30. Husserl, *Phänomenologische Psychologie*, § 17. This abstraction still leaves human beings and animals as psychosomatic entities intact. A further abstraction is required for the disclosure of "Natur im prägnanter Sinne der physischen Natur," i.e., which leads to corporeal things defined by merely spatiotemporal extendedness, between which relations of physical causality obtain. In passing, we note that no mention is made in *Phänomenologische Psychologie* of the mathematization of nature, i.e., the reference to an ideal mathematical order, which plays a preeminent role in *Crisis* (§§ 8 ff.).

31. *Phänomenologische Psychologie*, p. 119.

32. Similarly, Schutz refers to "appresentational functions . . . which *transform* things into cultural objects, human bodies into fellow men, their bodily movements into actions or significant gestures, waves of sound into speech, etc." ("Symbol, Reality, and Society," *Collected Papers*, I, 328; emphasis added). The term "transform" seems to imply that, prior to the operations of the "appresentational functions," the items mentioned are "things," i.e., "outer objects, facts, and events."

cultural objects takes its departure from the thing-world and traverses the same path as the abstraction just indicated—but in the opposite direction. This view is in line with Husserl's account of intersubjectivity on the basis of the perceptual experience of corporeal things, allowance being made, of course, for the specific experience everyone has of his somatic body.[33]

It is not possible to enter here into a systematic presentation and critical discussion of Husserl's theory of the constitution of the cultural world, urgent though this task seems to us to be. Suffice it to point out that while the transition, by means of the abstraction from the cultural object to the corporeal thing, appears intelligible, it is difficult to see how the cultural object can be reconstructed or constituted on the basis of and starting from the corporeal thing. We confine ourselves to stating the following thesis—which, of course, requires more substantiation than we are able to present here: As the result of the removal or elimination of the historically accrued sediment of sense owing to which the world appears under the perspective of an ideal mathematical order, hence as determined in itself and amenable to scientific explanation of the specific modern style, we are not confronted with a world of mere corporeal things as given in "pristinely pure" perceptual experience. In other words, we do not encounter *the* "perceptual world," [34] the same for all human beings and all sociohistorical groups, on whose basis the several cultural worlds arise subsequently by means of acts of apprehension, apperception, and interpretation. Rather, we are confronted with *our* life-world, a world apperceived, apprehended, and interpreted in a specific way. To corroborate our thesis, we refer to the conclusion at which Piaget arrives in the course of his studies of the intellectual development of the human child, namely, that on no level of the development is there "direct experience either of the self or of the external environment. There only exist 'interpreted' experiences." [35] What holds for the development of the individual is certainly true with regard to different sociohistorical groups.

33. *CM*, Fifth Meditation, especially § 58. See Schutz's penetrating critical analysis, "The Problem of Transcendental Intersubjectivity in Husserl," *Collected Papers*, Vol. III.
34. Husserl uses this term in *Phänomenologische Psychologie* rather than the expression "life-world."
35. *The Origins of Intelligence in Children*, trans. Margaret Cook (New York: International Universities Press, 1952), p. 136.

Sociohistorical Relativism

HISTORICAL REFLECTIONS strip any cultural world of the matter-of-course character which it has for those who simply live in it.[36] In the light of such reflections, our cultural world appears as one among a great many others, for instance, the world of the ancient Egyptians, that of the ancient Mesopotamians, indeed, the numerous cultural worlds corresponding to the numerous sociohistorical groups that have existed in the course of history or still exist. Funke goes so far as to maintain that the notion of the life-world has meaning and especially unity only with regard to the scientific universe and the specific experiences of which that universe is the correlate.[37] Prior to and apart from the constitution of that universe, there are only the innumerable experiences of the individual subjects, their "topico-doxic apprehensions" and positions which hardly have anything in common, but all of which differ from and in a sense are opposed to the scientific universe. According to Funke, the concept of the life-world is a counterconcept with respect to that of the scientific universe and hence presupposes the latter. It seems to us that, in establishing his thesis, Funke has failed to make due allowance for the social dimension. Every sociohistorical group has its cultural world, which, to be sure, appears to *each* member of the group from his point of view and from a special perspective related to that point of view. The latter is to be understood in both the spatial and figurative senses, in such a way that each member takes it for granted that the world in which he finds himself is the same for him as for his fellow men whom he encounters, and that they apprehend it as a matter of course, in the way he does, as one and the same for all.[38]

In view of our earlier exposition of the correlation between that which is given to consciousness and the consciousness of it, there arises the task of setting forth in detail the specific form which this correlation assumes in the case, to state it in Funke's terminology, of a special "topico-doxic position" with respect to

36. Funke, *Phänomenologie*, pp. 48 f.
37. *Ibid.*, pp. 153 ff., 178 ff.
38. Cf. in this regard Schutz's detailed analysis in "Common-Sense and Scientific Interpretation of Human Action," *Collected Papers*, I, 5 ff.

what he calls the corresponding "Bewusstseinslage." [39] In terms of the thesis here maintained, the problem can be formulated as follows: Given a certain cultural world as the life-world of a sociohistorical group, the task is to find and to lay bare the acts of consciousness which in their systematic concatenation and intertexture make this specific world possible as their correlate. Answering this question for a particular cultural world amounts to understanding that world from within by referring it to the mental life in which it originates. Inasmuch as cultural worlds evolve in historical continuity with one another, investigations of this kind lead to a study of consciousness itself in its historical development. Along such lines it is possible to realize some of the profound intentions of Dilthey.

In granting the legitimacy and stressing the significance of historical studies along the lines just mentioned, we must face the *problem of relativism* which arises at this point. Not only are we confronted with a multiplicity of different cultural worlds or life-worlds but we find that all of them are on a par with one another. *From a historical point of view, there is no justification for assigning a privilege to any particular life-world, e.g., our own.* However, this statement can be made only on the level of a historical reflection, that is, it presupposes relinquishing the attitude of simply living in the life-world and taking it for granted. It requires adopting a point of view outside of or beyond our own life-world, from which we may look at the latter as well as at other life-worlds. In any event, *one cannot avoid the question of whether the main and, perhaps, only task of philosophy consists in understanding and accounting for the various cultural worlds which have made their appearance in history.* Just as, in consequence of existentialist trends, philosophy is in danger of being transformed into anthropology or psychology, so it is now threatened with being dissolved into a series of historical studies which, however legitimate and significant in themselves, cannot but lead to sociohistorical relativism.

Husserl dealt with historical relativism in his early discussion with Dilthey.[40] Against the historical relativization of philosophical systems Husserl upholds the idea of philosophy as a rigorous

39. Besides the passages cited above, n. 16, see pp. 50 ff., 146, 157.
40. Husserl, "Philosophy as a Rigorous Science," in *Phenomenology and the Crisis of Philosophy*, trans. Quentin Lauer (New York: Harper & Row, Torchbooks, 1965), pp. 122 ff.

science (*strenge Wissenschaft*), "objectively" valid, i.e., valid for everybody, because philosophy is built on unassailable foundations and proceeds in a cogent manner.[41] This idea found an incipient realization in Husserl's transcendental or constitutive phenomenology, which is a universal theory of consciousness considered under the aspect of the correlation between objects of any kind whatever and the acts of consciousness through which those objects present themselves. On the basis of this general correlation, the relativism is overcome. Whatever differences may obtain among the several cultural worlds and, correspondingly, among the several particular forms of conscious life in which the cultural worlds originate and of which they are the correlates, the general reference of every such world to the corresponding consciousness, which underlies all relativities, is not itself relative.[42] The task arises of setting forth and elucidating the universal structures of consciousness which make possible *any* cultural world as the life-world of a sociohistorical group. Only on the basis of a general theory of consciousness, as developed by Husserl in his several writings under the heading of intentionality, can the aforementioned program of understanding the various cultural worlds by referring each one of them to the corresponding mental life be realized and carried out, since all particularizations of consciousness here in question are variations within an invariant framework as delineated and defined by the essential and universal structure of consciousness.

The Perceptual World and Its Methodological Significance for a Phenomenological Theory of the Natural Sciences

There remains the question of whether relativism cannot be overcome in still another way. Husserl has formulated

41. Husserl's phrase in *Crisis* (p. 389), "*the dream is over,*" is often misinterpreted to mean that in his late period Husserl abandoned the idea of philosophy as a rigorous science. As Herbert Spiegelberg, *The Phenomenological Movement*, 2d ed., *Phaenomenologica* V (The Hague: Martinus Nijhoff, 1965), p. 77, has shown, referring both to the context of the phrase in question and to further corroborating evidence, it must rather be understood as a characterization of the intellectual climate of the time and not as an expression of Husserl's own position.

42. Funke, *Phänomenologie*, pp. 102 ff.

the problem of relativism as it arises in connection with the diversity of cultural worlds (*Crisis*, § 36). While living in our life-world, we hold certain truths which we share with fellow men who belong to the same sociohistorical group, that is, we share with them a certain cultural world common to all of us, however such agreement may have been brought about. When we come to another sociohistorical group, e.g., to Chinese peasants or to Negroes in the Congo, we find that their truths are not the same as ours. Is it possible—asks Husserl—to establish a body of truths valid for all subjects, truths about which normal Westerners, normal Hindus, normal Chinese can agree, all relativities and divergencies notwithstanding? Differently expressed, the question concerns a stratum or core common to all life-worlds and truths holding for that core. The truths sought are to refer to the life-world or to what has just been called a stratum of it, not to the scientific universe of objective science in the specific modern sense. As mentioned before, the scientific universe is an ideal mathematical construction superseding and substituted for the life-world. Presently we shall see that a radical philosophical account of the very possibility of the construction and constitution of the scientific universe is contingent on providing an answer to the question raised.

To that end, Husserl points to the universal invariant structure exhibited by every life-world. However they are interpreted and apprehended, things encountered in the life-world—any life-world—have spatial shapes. Trees, for example, have a cylindrical shape. Of course, they are not cylinders in the strict geometrical sense; rather, their shape is of a cylindrical type or, as we may say, they present a cylindrical physiognomy. Spatial shapes must be taken as they are given in perceptual experience, without being referred to ideal geometrical figures, even without being conceived as approximating the latter. In perceptual experience, the spatial shapes of things are determined only as to type—a margin of latitude is left for variations, deviations, and fluctuations (*Crisis*, p. 25). Things endure in time, whether changing or remaining unchanged. Change may be faster or slower, as in the case of motion. Fastness and slowness of motion must again be understood in conformity with the nature of perceptual experience, not in terms of velocity and acceleration as defined mathematically.

None of the things encountered in any life-world presents itself in isolation. The house in front of which we happen to stand is surrounded by a garden; it is on a street; the street leads to other parts of the city; etc. Every thing is encountered within a perceptual environment or, as Husserl calls it, an "outer horizon" (*Aussenhorizont*) which is not delimited by fixed boundaries but continues indefinitely in both space and time.[43] *This all-encompassing spatiotemporal horizon*—all-encompassing because every thing and event has its place within it—*defines the universal form of the perceptual world, an invariant structure of every life-world or cultural world* whose unity is founded on the unity of space and of time. Deliberately we have spoken of the outer horizon as continuing indefinitely and not infinitely in order to eschew all mathematical connotations. The question of whether the space of the perceptual world is Euclidean or non-Euclidean cannot be meaningfully raised, since it is *perceptual* space and not the idealized, still less the formalized, space of geometry.

Things pertaining to the life-world are subject to changes. However, these changes do not take place haphazardly but with a certain regularity. In particular, changes of a certain kind are concomitant with other events which occur either in the changing thing itself (e.g., a glass falls and breaks) or in its environment (e.g., a piece of ice melts when brought into a warm room). Things have "habits" of regularly behaving in typical ways under typical circumstances. Regularities of the kind in question are also exhibited by the world as a whole, as exemplified by the alternation of day and night, the sequence of the seasons, and the like. Differently expressed, causal connections and regularities of a certain style and type prevail in the behavior of particular things as well as in the behavior of the life-world as a whole.[44] On this account, inductions and predictions are possible whose importance for practical conduct and the orientation in the life-world—any life-world—is too obvious to need further comment. Again, it must be stressed that the regularities of the causal connections in question here are determined merely as to style and type, i.e., they admit of fluctuations and variations within certain limits not precisely defined. They are not relations

43. *Crisis*, §§ 47, 37; *Phänomenologische Psychologie*, §§ 6, 11; the most detailed description and analysis are to be found in *Ideas*, § 27, and *EJ*, § 8, Cf. *FC*, pp. 382 ff. and pp. 85 ff., below.

44. *Crisis*, § 9b; *Phänomenologische Psychologie*, pp. 68 f., 101 f., 133 ff.

of functional dependency capable of being expressed in the form of mathematical equations.

In addition to the invariant structures of every life-world as such, which Husserl has set forth, we may mention the fact that every such world is apprehended and interpreted in some way or other. Though the interpretations vary in content from one sociohistorical group to another and, therefore, are relative to those groups, *all these relative apprehensions are diverse specifications of interpretedness at large,* which itself is not relative but is the invariant ground on which, or the invariant framework within which, all relative specifications arise. By virtue of its being apprehended and interpreted in a certain way, a life-world is a sociocultural world of a given historical group. Schutz has pointed out invariant structures and features of every social world of any description whatever.[45] According to him, these invariant structures of social existence in a cultural world have their roots in the human condition; therefore, their ultimate clarification calls for a philosophical anthropology.

At this point it is possible to formulate the theoretical motivation for the aforementioned abstraction by means of which cultural objects are reduced to mere corporeal things. In the face of the multiplicity and diversity of cultural worlds, the question arises of whether there is not a "world" common to all sociohistorical groups, the same for all of them, a universal human life-world, so to speak. To arrive at it, all acts of apprehension and interpretation are disregarded and their contributions discarded—which means stripping cultural objects of their cultural sense and human significance.[46] What remains is a perceptual world, a world given in—as we have expressed it before—pristinely pure perceptual experience. It is not a mathematized world, it is not conceived from a perspective of its possible mathematization, and it does not have the sense of being amenable to objective scientific explanation of the specific modern variety. Finally, the objects encountered in it are perceptual things retaining what are called their secondary qualities. Still, it is attained by means of an abstraction. It may, therefore, seem advisable to introduce a terminological distinction between the perceptual world and the life-world, though Husserl has not made that distinction, at least not explicitly.

45. "Equality and the Meaning Structure of the Social World," *Collected Papers,* II, 229 ff.
46. *Phänomenologische Psychologie,* p. 121.

In the spatiality of perceptual things, the indefinite spatio-temporal extendedness of the perceptual world, and the specific causality prevailing in it, the invariant *categorial structure or constitution of the perceptual world* becomes manifest. The categories which pertain to the life-world or, as we should prefer to say, to the perceptual world are denoted by the same names as those which underlie the elaboration of the objectively valid scientific universe (*Crisis*, § 35). However, the former categories are not to be understood in the light of subsequent theoretical idealizations, formalizations, and constructions of geometry and physics but, on the contrary, in the sense of typicality and conformity to style as prevailing in the perceptual world. Hence Husserl establishes a distinction between the a priori pertaining to the perceptual world (*lebensweltliches Apriori*) and the logico-objective a priori of the exact sciences. If, as it must be, the former is made the theme of special investigations, there emerges the idea of an "ontology of the life-world," *an a priori science of the universal structures of the perceptual world*, a discipline whose objective is the *systematic description of the categorial constitution* of that world, the explicit articulation of the "notion of the natural world" (*natürlicher Weltbegriff*).[47]

Husserl conceives of a "transcendental aesthetics" in a sense different from that which Kant gave to the term, though not totally unrelated to it. Transcendental aesthetics in Husserl's sense concerns itself with "the eidetic problem of any possible world as a world given in 'pure experience' " and is to provide "the eidetic description of the all-embracing Apriori, without which no Objects could appear unitarily in mere experience . . . and therefore without which the unity of a nature, the unity of a world . . . could not become constituted at all" (*FTL*, p. 292). Its task consists in disengaging the "logos" of the perceptual world, the logicality which prevails in it. Of course, logicality as here meant must not be understood in the sense of fully conceptualized—still less formalized—logic but, rather, in the same sense in which Husserl understands the a priori and the categories of the perceptual world, namely, determinateness as to style and type but absence of exactness. Since the logicality in question proves to be the germ from which logic in the

47. *Crisis*, § 51; *Phänomenologische Psychologie*, § 8; concerning the term "natürlicher Weltbegriff," see *Phänomenologische Psychologie*, pp. 62, 93 f.

proper and formal sense develops, it may be appropriately denoted as "protologic."[48] In fact, the transition from protologic
to logic proper (understood in the widest sense so as to include
all mathematization, algebraization, and formalization) requires
specific idealizing operations which, of course, work on the protological structures as underlying pregiven materials.[49] Future
phenomenological research will have first to complete Husserl's
work in exhaustively setting forth the protological structures and
then to account for the acts and operations of consciousness
which are involved in the transition to the logical level in the
wider sense.

This is not the place to embark on those problems. We wish
only to illustrate the transition in question by one of Husserl's
examples. As a rule, the perceptual process related to a certain
material thing develops harmoniously, that is, later phases of
the process confirm earlier ones, all of them being in agreement
and conformity with one another. Throughout the perceptual
process, the thing perceived proves to be what it had appeared
to be at first. Occasionally the harmonious development of the
perceptual process is broken. Then discrepancies and conflicts
arise, as when what we see in a display window appears to be a
living person and, a few moments later, a clothed dummy.[50]
Such discrepancies have always been resolved in the course of
perceptual experience, whose coherence and inner consistency
have been reestablished by means of revisions and corrections.
Perceptual experience carries with it the horizonal presumption
(Horizont-Präsumtion) that further experience will come into
play by virtue of which all horizons will be explored, all conflicts
reconciled, and the world disclosed as intrinsically concordant
(einstimmig).[51] The idealization of this horizonal presumption,

48. For the term "protologic," the author is indebted to his
student, Lester Embree. We prefer the word to the Husserlian "prepredicative experience," because it indicates the logicality inherent
in "prepredicative experience."

49. Crisis, p. 140: "A certain idealizing performance is what
brings about the higher-level meaning-formation and ontic validity
of the mathematical and every other objective a priori on the basis
of the life-world a priori"; see also the German edition, p. 398,
ll. 36–38.

50. EJ, p. 91. For a criticism of Husserl's theory of underlying
sense data and alternating perceptual apprehensions (Wahrneh-
mungsauffassungen), see FC, pp. 265 ff.

51. Phänomenologische Psychologie, pp. 63 f.

which pertains to the universal style of perceptual experience and the perceptual world, yields the notion of the world as it is in itself, as in its true reality it exists behind and beneath all mere appearances and deceptions. Obviously, this idea of the world as determined in itself is decisive for the objective sciences, especially the natural sciences, in their endeavor to disclose the true constitution of the real world.

Earlier, we pointed out the difference between the scientific universe and the life-world. Now we have come to see that the scientific universe as well as its construction is rooted in the life-world, from which it arises by the mediation of what we have called the perceptual world. In a very important, though perhaps not the only, aspect, *the methodological significance of the notion of the life-world lies in the fact that this notion provides the basis for a phenomenological theory of the sciences, especially the exact sciences.* To that end, a phenomenological account of the constitution of mathematics along the suggested lines is required.[52] Substantially the same question arises with respect to formal logic, both traditional and modern, in the narrower technical sense. Its philosophical foundation and justification, the elucidation of its sense, cannot be given except on the basis of the theory of prepredicative experience (*FTL*, § 86). We can here do no more than refer to *Experience and Judgment*, with its significant subtitle, *Investigations into the Genealogy of Logic*. In that work Husserl attempts to trace the phenomenological origin of the logical categories back to the protological categories of prepredicative experience.

In recent decades the theory of science has not received sufficient attention in phenomenological literature.[53] Thus the impression could arise that phenomenology did not have much

52. Concerning geometry, see *Crisis*, app. VI. This text, initially published by Eugen Fink in *Revue internationale de philosophie*, Vol. I (1939), has been carefully analyzed by Dorion Cairns, *Philosophy and Phenomenological Research*, I (1940), 98 ff.

53. Among the exceptions are Suzanne Bachelard, *Husserl's Logic*, and her *La Conscience de rationalité: étude phénoménologique sur la physique mathématique* (Paris: Presses Universitaires de France, 1958); J. J. Compton, "Understanding Science," *Dialectica*, Vol. XVI (1963), and "Natural Science and the Experience of Nature," in *Phenomenology in America*, ed. James M. Edie (Chicago: Quadrangle Books, 1967); Joseph J. Kockelmans, *Phenomenology and Physical Science* (Pittsburgh: Duquesne University Press, 1966).

to say in that field of research, had withdrawn from it altogether to leave it to those contemporary philosophical trends, such as logical positivism, which call themselves "scientific." Since the necessary preparatory work was done in Husserl's later writings, the time seems to have come for phenomenology to reclaim possession of the field from which it had its departure in Husserl's earliest writings.

CONCLUSION

LET US GLANCE BRIEFLY at the preceding discussion. As far as the role of consciousness is concerned, we have come to the same conclusion as in our earlier discussion of existentialism and philosophical anthropology. As a cultural world, the life-world refers to acts of apprehension and interpretation. The same holds for the perceptual world, which is attained by an abstraction. Mental operations of a specific kind are involved in the elaboration and construction of the scientific universe. The notion of the life-world is of central importance because of its location at the junction of a great many roads. Along each one of them the problem of access is bound to arise, to remind us of the privilege and priority of consciousness.

2 / Husserlian Perspectives on Galilean Physics

HUSSERL'S ANALYSIS OF GALILEAN PHYSICS is contained in his book *Die Krisis der europäischen Wissenschaften und die transzendentale Phänomenologie*. A translation true to the spirit rather than the letter could render the title as "The Crisis of Western Sciences and Transcendental Phenomenology." Husserl did not intend "European" to be taken geographically; rather, he meant it to have a historical sense as referring to the Occidental world, understood as the scene of an unfolding and unified intellectual development. *Crisis* is Husserl's last work.[1] After the first two parts, whose central piece is the analysis of "Galileo's Mathematization of Nature," appeared in 1936, that is, during Husserl's lifetime, he continued to work on the planned subsequent parts until the onset of his final illness in August, 1937. This is mentioned to recall that at the time of his preparatory studies for that book (some of the studies date from the late 1920s; some of the relevant ideas can be found, at least in germinal form, as early as 1913), phenomenological philosophy was already in existence.

The work is subtitled *An Introduction to Phenomenological Philosophy*. Of course, "Introduction" is not to be understood in

This chapter is a synthesis of "Comment on the Paper by H. Marcuse 'On Science and Phenomenology,'" in *Boston Studies in the Philosophy of Science*, Vol. II, ed. Robert S. Cohen and Marx W. Wartofsky (New York: Humanities Press, 1965), and "Galilean Physics in the Light of Husserl's Phenomenology," in *Galileo, Man of Science*, ed. Ernan McMullin (New York: Basic Books, 1967).

1. See "The Last Work of Edmund Husserl," in *SPP*.

the sense of an elementary exposition for beginners. Nor does it mean, in view of what has just been said, that phenomenology is presented here for the first time. Rather, it means opening a new avenue of approach to an already existing body of phenomenological thought. *The novelty of this approach consists in the fact that,* in contradistinction to his earlier writings, *Husserl takes his departure from certain basic problems that beset modern natural science or, more accurately, from the very existence of this science of "modern style" itself.* It is possible and perfectly legitimate to isolate Husserl's analysis of Galilean science and to concentrate on it almost exclusively, provided one does not lose sight of the contextual linkage between that analysis and the later parts of *Crisis,* as well as Husserl's earlier writings, and is prepared to reinsert it into that context at some appropriate point. When read in this light, Husserl's book acquires a significance of the first order for the theory of natural science. It marks a turning point in the development of this discipline and inaugurates a new phase in its history.

GALILEAN PHYSICS

GALILEAN PHYSICS DENOTES THE SCIENCE inaugurated by Galileo. The name is used as a symbol for the historical development of modern science from, roughly speaking, 1600 to 1700, that is, the period of the constitution of classical physics and even beyond. Within the meaning of Husserl's definition, Einsteinian physics and quantum physics are sciences of the Galilean style.

What characterizes this style? Let us describe it in one phrase: *the cleavage between the world as it presents itself in the perceptual experience of everyday life and the world as it is in scientific truth and "in reality."* The world as it appears in direct perceptual experience is the world of common sense, called by Husserl the life-world. Its description would require too lengthy an exposition to be tackled here. Some aspects will be mentioned later. Attention must be called now to a few points, however briefly. The things encountered in the world of common experience exhibit chromatic qualities as properties belonging to them in their own right. Human voices, musical notes, and noises of all kinds are accepted as occurrences being in reality as they are given in auditory experience. Finally, there are observed regularities and causal connections but certainly not of such a nature as to be expressible in the form of functional dependencies in the mathematical sense.

Modern science of the Galilean style starts by refusing to accept the perceptual world at face value. Instead, reality is believed to contain, embody, and conceal a mathematical structure. As to its true and real condition, in contradistinction to its perceptual appearances, the world (to express it in more modern terms) is a mathematical manifold. To pierce through the veil of appearances, to discover the mathematical structure of the universe, and to disclose reality as a mathematical manifold constitute precisely the task of Galilean science. It is the task Galileo set for himself and passed on to his successors. As Husserl points out, Galileo, the founder of physics, was not a physicist himself in the same sense as his successors who, as heirs to a scientific tradition, are already in the possession of the "correct" methods of physics; and here "methods" are not understood in the sense of techniques and technical procedures but rather in the etymological sense of access and way of approach. Being the first to conceive the idea of nature as a mathematical manifold, Galileo had to develop the methods of physics, understood in this sense, to substantiate that idea. This is what justifies the use of his name as a symbol. The point requires some emphasis, because the contention that the world is not in reality as it looks but that its true condition and constitution must be disclosed and discovered by means of mathematical construction is not retrospectively formulated on the basis of results attained. On the contrary, it is the guiding principle of the science of physics still to be developed and institutes its very development.

THREE PHASES IN THE MODERN THEORY OF NATURAL SCIENCE

1. *The Period of Validation*

ROUGHLY SPEAKING, one can distinguish two phases in the theory of natural science prior to the appearance of Husserl's work. The first extends approximately from the middle of the seventeenth century to the middle of the eighteenth century. Descartes's *Meditations on First Philosophy* may be considered as a representative document of this first period. Descartes sets out to provide a foundation for, and a validation of, the new science. It is to rest on and be guided by the thesis which we have already stated: The universe is not as it appears in common experience and its nature and structure do not lay themselves open to perception; on the contrary, they must be uncovered by means of mathematical notions. In reality, then, the universe is not as it seems to be but as it is conceived and constructed by the mathematical physicist.

We children of the twentieth century may find it difficult to realize the boldness of this thesis, because we are heirs to a tradition of science which we have come to take for granted as something definitively possessed rather than as something to be acquired and justified. We hardly see any necessity, therefore, for a justification of the thesis on which modern science rests. In the seventeenth century, the situation was quite different. The men of that day were not heirs but inaugurators, to whom the legitimacy of their endeavor presented a real problem. Descartes's solution to this problem was to call on the divine veracity to guarantee the validity of the principle that whatever is clearly and distinctly perceived is true. It was on the basis of this principle that Descartes considered mathematical knowledge and the geometrical conception of the external world to be justified. Along similar lines, though in some respects differently from Descartes, Malebranche conceived of the intellectual life of man, insofar as he engages himself in genuinely cognitive endeavors, as some kind of participation in the intellectual life of the Deity. In a famous passage Galileo spoke in the same vein.

2. *Science as a Fact*

The second period in the development of the theory of science began in 1748, when Leonhard Euler, the great Swiss mathematician, submitted to the Royal Prussian Academy of Berlin a memoir entitled *Réflexions sur l'espace et le temps*. This memoir, which is concerned with the problems of absolute motion, absolute space, and absolute time, is Euler's contribution to the discussion regarding the nature of space that had been going on for over a century, in which Descartes, Malebranche, the Cambridge Neo-Platonists, Newton and his followers, Leibniz, Berkeley, and others had taken part. Euler grants that philosophy must concern itself with the fundamental concepts of the sciences, especially those of physics. However, the decision as to whether or not a given concept should be admitted among these falls under the competence of physics rather than of philosophy. If it appears that the laws of dynamics, especially the law of inertia, require for their formulation the notions of absolute space and absolute time, then these notions (as well as that of absolute motion which they immediately imply) must be admitted as valid. They derive their right of citizenship from the part they play within the theoretical context of physics. Against such a decision, which is based on the theoretical exigencies of physics, no appeal is possible. Consequently, philosophy must accept this decision and accommodate its constructions and theories accordingly.

Euler's memoir contains in effect a "declaration of independence" by physics with regard to philosophy. Such a claim to autonomy was made possible by the accomplishments of the science of physics during the preceding century and a half, and it expresses a self-confidence rooted in those accomplishments. Euler's memoir opened the second phase of the philosophy of science—a phase in which science is no longer considered as being in need of justification and validation but, on the contrary, as a given fact simply to be accepted. The phrase "science as a fact" is, as a rule, associated with the name of Kant. But what Kant did was to provide an elaborate realization of the program which Euler had not only anticipated but conceived in a rather concrete fashion.

3. *Science as a Problem*

It is the historical significance of Husserl's Galileo analysis to challenge and even to abandon the acceptance of science as an ultimate fact and to see in it a problem. Husserl is far from questioning the technical or, more precisely, intrinsic validity of science, and nothing could have been further from his mind than dismissing that validity in any sense. What is in question is not science itself or any particular scientific theory but, rather, the interpretation of science. Husserl concerns himself with the problem of the very existence and sense of science of the

Galilean style, that is, with the conception of nature as in reality possessing a mathematical structure. Galilean science rests on presuppositions which make it possible, which orient scientific methods and procedures, and which determine the sense of the scientific explanation of the universe in the Galilean style. Partly because the presuppositions in question were not made explicit and partly because they were taken for granted, the sense of science had been obfuscated since the earliest phases of its history. Explication of those presuppositions does not mean their denial or their nullification. It means their elucidation and the clarification of what is built on them, an account of the grounds on which the validity of science rests, and, by that very token, a delimitation of its legitimate validity, that is, a clarification of the sense of its validity and legitimacy.

Husserl's analysis of Galilean science is a critique, but in a sense significantly different from that of Kant's *Critique of Pure Reason*. Kant confined the fundamental concepts and principles of Newtonian physics to the realm of possible experience, and he precluded their application beyond that realm. As to the phenomenal realm, Kant, along the line of Euler's orientation, endeavored to demonstrate the unrestricted validity and necessary applicability of the mentioned concepts and principles. Husserl, on the contrary, in calling attention to the presuppositions of Galilean science, raises the problem of its sense, and of the sense and limits of its validity, precisely with regard to what in Kantian parlance is called the phenomenal world.

Two remarks are worth making at this point. In the first place, this attribution of a problematic status to science must not be mistaken for an expression of an "antiscientific spirit." Awareness of problems which beset the very existence of modern science is something quite different from hostility toward science itself. I feel impelled to apologize for this truism. Yet, judging by what one too often reads, it seems necessary to insist on it. Hostility to science was totally alien to Husserl; his own scholarly career had begun in mathematics. It was, in fact, because of his training in and firsthand acquaintance with modern mathematical science that Husserl was not prepared to listen in an attitude of superstitious awe to slogans about "science" or "scientific method."

Second, Husserl was not a historian of science and never made any claim to be one, even though he presented his views on "science as a problem" in the form of an analysis of Galileo's work. One may doubt whether he ever gave to the study of Galileo's writings that time and attention which a professional historian would devote to them as a matter of course. Cassirer's discussion of Galileo in *Das Erkenntnisproblem in der Philosophie und Wissenschaft der neueren Zeit* may well have been one of Husserl's main sources of information. He remarks himself that he does not distinguish between Galileo's own contributions and those made by his predecessors (or those made by some of his successors, one may add). As a matter of fact, he ascribes some ideas to Galileo with which Descartes or Huygens should have been credited. In the face of such historical inaccuracies of fact, it may not be out of place to recall the judgment of an authority in the history of science, the late Alexandre Koyré, who once remarked to me that, even though Husserl was not a historian by training, by temperament, or by direction of interest, his analysis provides the key for a profound and radical understanding of Galileo's work. He submits his physics to a critique, not (once again be it said) a criticism.

THE PHILOSOPHICAL PROBLEM OF SCIENTIFIC PRAXIS

HUSSERL COMPARES SCIENTIFIC ACTIVITY, as it has developed during the last three centuries, to the functioning of a machine. He has in mind not so much the machines of industry as the "machines" of the logician or mathematician, i.e., the symbolic procedures which have proved of such paramount importance for the development and formalization of mathematics. Algorithmic procedures can be applied in a purely mechanical fashion, since their use demands no more than the observance of formal rules of operation. Methods of science, once invented, tend to become formalized and to undergo a process of "technization" of this sort, in the course of which their application becomes a matter of routine. We possess scientific methods; we operate and manipulate; and we invent new and better—that is, more effective—methods. In this way, results of the highest importance from both the theoretical and the practical points of view are obtained. If by an "understanding" of science no more is meant than the successful application of methodical procedures, there seems to be no difficulty. In fact, the "technician of science"—a term not meant in any pejorative sense but simply as denoting someone whose exclusive interest lies in "practical" achievement (theorizing is, according to Husserl, a praxis of a special sort)—may simply rest his case on the successful operation of the scientific "machine," since it yields results of the kind he wished to obtain.

Not so the philosopher, whose very *raison d'être* is to raise radical questions—"radical" in the etymological sense of going to the roots. The philosopher cannot be satisfied with the actual working of the machine; he must wonder why and how it functions. From the machine as a fact here and now, he will go back to the mechanism which makes it work, to the principles involved in its construction, to the conditions on which this construction depends. To express this less metaphorically, we have to inquire into the presuppositions which underlie the elaboration of science of the Galilean style, presuppositions from which that science derives its sense and which define, in consequence, its limitations. They are well concealed and remain so as long as one adopts what I have called the attitude of the scientific technician. Since they determine the sense of scientific activity, to make them explicit is to elucidate the meaning of science itself. What is in question is not the meaning of particular scientific conceptions and theories, like quantum physics or the theory of relativity, but, rather, the meaning of modern science in its entirety—the meaning, in particular, of that *progressive mathematization of nature* which Galileo first conceived.

A question that must occur to anyone who has to deal with the historical aspect of science is why the mathematization of nature started around 1600 and in Italy. Why did it not start before then, or in another civilization? Why not in Greece, or in Rome, where the engineers were of a remarkably high level of competence? Why did it not start during the Middle Ages? It would obviously be silly to try to explain this in terms of some sort of intellectual inferiority during those periods. To answer the question, one would have to turn to a historically oriented sociology of knowledge. I am raising the question merely for the purpose of emphasizing that the existence of science of the modern style must not be taken for granted. For many centuries, a highly civilized mankind got along without the mathematical conception of nature. To be sure, there were the Pythagoreans and there was Archimedes. But these thinkers left no enduring imprint on the intellectual development that immediately followed them. At all events, what does it mean "to mathematize" nature?

MATHEMATIZATION

AMONG THE PRESUPPOSITIONS of Galilean science and of the historical Galileo himself, we must mention first the conception that the model and standard of knowledge—knowledge in the genuine and emphatic sense denoted by the Greek term *epistēmē*—is mathematical knowledge, which in Galileo's historical situation meant the geometry of Euclid. In that respect Galileo was himself an heir to an existing and accepted tradition. The disclosure of Galileo's presuppositions therefore necessitates going beyond Galileo and inquiring into the origin of Euclid's geometry.[2]

In the life-world where we find ourselves, we encounter things of a circular contour or, to express it more properly, things whose contour presents a circular physiognomy. However, these contours are not circles in the strict sense in which the term is understood in geometry, any more than trees whose shape presents a cylindrical physiognomy are cylinders in the geometrical sense. As the etymology of its name indicates, geometry was originally an art of measurement, especially of measuring the earth—demarcating adjoining fields and the like. Measurement requires a technique and admits of varying degrees of accuracy. The degree of accuracy to be attained in a given case depends on both the available technique and the purpose at hand. Practical exigencies may, and do, require an increasingly higher degree of accuracy, and this may lead not only to a "better" use of the available technique but also to an improvement of the technique itself. All such improvements are, and remain, in the service of practical purposes. The same holds for the practice of the craftsman who, e.g., is working on a wooden plank and tries to make its surface smoother and flatter. Here again, the exigencies of the practical situation may demand perfections of the available technique, like the invention of new tools. As before, all

2. "Origin" is not meant to be understood in historical or psychological terms. Husserl intends it to indicate an origin or genesis of sense (*Sinnesursprung, Sinnesgenese*); see pp. 66 ff., below.

improvements and perfections are motivated and guided by practical ends and purposes.

In the course of such improvements and perfections, notions of *ideal limits* may arise, like that of the plane whose surface is of "absolute" smoothness and cannot be made still smoother, that of the straight line which has no width, that of the circle whose points are equidistant from the center—"absolutely" and no longer more or less so, as in the case of perceptual configurations exhibiting physiognomical circularity. Thus geometrical figures in the strict sense come to be conceived. In the geometry of Euclid, the geometrical notions still have intuitive content; the figures can be visualized, though they cannot be perceived because they cannot be encountered in reality. One can speak of them as ideal limit-poles located at infinity insofar as they indicate a direction for the process of progressive perfection, but they can never actually be reached in the course of this process. In this sense, geometrical notions designate models of perfection. *Geometrical concepts arise on the basis of perceptual and other experience in the life-world by means of idealization.* Once the ideal limit-poles have been conceived, the spatial configurations encountered in perceptual experience—like the trees of cylindrical shape, the lines actually drawn—can be seen in their light and from their perspective, that is, the configurations acquire the sense of approximations, more or less close, to the ideal figures which, because of their ideality, can never be actually realized. Plato compared the relation between the configurations drawn in sand and the geometrical figures which the mathematician has in mind even when looking at those configurations to the relation between the reflections of objects in water and the objects themselves.

Ideal geometrical figures lend themselves to exact and definitive determination, valid once and for all and for everyone. Geometrical determination is independent of the circumstances, conditions, and contingencies of actual observation and measurement. For the same reason, the reference of perceptual configurations to ideal geometrical figures which the former more or less closely approximate is emancipated from all consideration of practical exigency. Of equal importance is the momentous discovery that, on the basis of comparatively few fundamental propositions, the axioms, all possible geometrical figures can be constructed and all properties of these figures demonstrated. Geometrical proofs are conclusive, not a matter of opinion. It can be proved that, in Euclidean geometry, the sum of the interior angles of a plane triangle equals two right angles and that a denial of this proposition entails a contradiction. Assuming the character of a demonstrative science, geometry proves to correspond to and to realize the idea of *epistēmē;* geometry appears as the model and the standard of knowledge worthy of the name.

Idealization is only the first step in the constitution and development of geometry. Soon after Galileo's time the *algebraization of geometry* by means of the analytical geometry of Fermat and Descartes begins; and, later, the differential calculus is invented by Leibniz and Newton. The path is opened for a progressive algebraization and even logicization of geometry, culminating in contemporary axiomatics and the geometry of abstract spaces. This development is not confined to geometry alone. All of modern mathematics develops in the direction of increasing *formalization.* In a formalized discipline—of which common algebra and, incidentally, traditional Aristotelian logic are the oldest and most elementary examples—the terms are divested of all intuitive content and are defined merely by the relations obtaining between them and the operations which can be performed on them. This development culminates in group theory, in which even the relations and operations are left undetermined as to their intuitive meaning and are defined solely by formal properties, such as symmetry and transitivity in the case of relations and commutativity and associativity in that of operations. Formalization is tantamount to the development of *algorithms,* that is, the establishment of systems of symbols and of rules for operations on those symbols. The operations can be performed "blindly" and mechanically; the only requirement is that they conform with the operational rules. Because of their formal nature, algorithmic systems lend themselves to multiple interpretations, so that the results of blind and mechanical operations on symbols can receive the appropriate intuitive meaning, according to their interpretation in a given case.

The entities which arise by means of idealization and formalization acquire a semblance of independence, self-containedness, and self-sufficiency. Once established, geometrical and algorithmic methods can be taught and learned; they can be transmitted from generation to generation. In using and perfecting them, one proceeds from invention to invention, the accomplishments of later generations surpassing those of earlier ones. Such use and perfection of methods, the gradual development of the several mathematical disciplines, the ever increasing growth of mathematical knowledge as manifested in the last three centuries, do not require reference to and explicit disclosure of the foundations on which the edifice of mathematics rests. The presuppositions underlying mathematical thought and construction, namely, the experience of things as encountered in the life-world, on the one hand, and, on the other hand, the processes of idealization and formalization, may and do fall into oblivion. Severed from the sources from which they spring, the products resulting from idealization and formalization—that is, all the formal disciplines, like geometry, the whole of mathematics, and contemporary mathematical logic—come to be considered as autonomous in the sense of seeming to have no presuppositions outside of themselves. This proceeding on the basis of obfuscated and even forgotten presuppositions is what Husserl means by *traditionality*. It is the right of the positive scientist, the logician, the mathematician, and the physicist, to remain within his scentific tradition and to abstain from concerning himself with its origin and institution. It is the duty of the philosopher to raise precisely that question in order to clarify and account for the very sense of modern science.

Let us return to Galileo, who was an heir to Euclid's geometry and stood within its tradition, which includes the unquestioned acceptance of geometry as the standard of knowledge in the true and genuine sense. Consequently, if there is to be an authentic science of nature, it has to be fashioned after the model of geometry. Galileo attempts to mathematize nature and he succeeds: Nature does lend itself to mathematization. The mathematization of nature can be regarded—and has been regarded by Husserl—as a successful venture; its success assumes the form of an historical process, the history of modern physics, physics of the Galilean style, from its beginnings to the present day. That means that the venture has thus far proved successful and may be expected to prove successful in the future.

THE HYPOSTASIS OF MENTAL CREATIONS

BECAUSE OF THE OBFUSCATION of the presuppositions underlying the elaboration of the science of physics and determining its sense, this elaboration is not seen for what it actually is. It is the construction of an exact *universe*, consisting of entities defined and definable exclusively in mathematical terms. This construction is guided by certain principles and is meant to accomplish the specific purpose of providing an ever extending rationalization of observed phenomena and their unitary explanation. Previsions and predictions on a previously unheard-of scale are thus made possible that could not be obtained as long as one relied merely on the regularities as experienced and even as methodically observed in the life-world. Overlooking the processes of idealization, formalization, and whatever other forms of conceptualization may be involved—processes which are mental operations in and through which the entities with which the physicist deals are conceived and constructed—he or the interpreter of physics is wrapped up in the very products to the disregard of the producing activity from which those products spring.

Failure to refer the accomplished products and results to the mental operations from which they derive and whose correlates they are makes one the captive of those products and results, that is, the captive of one's own creations, and that is a further aspect of traditionality. Thus, as Husserl expressed it, a cloak or tissue of ideas (*Ideenkleid*), of mathematical ideas and symbols, is cast on the life-world to conceal it to the point of being substituted for it. What in truth is a method and the result of that method come to be taken for reality. Thus we arrive at the conception of nature (mentioned in the beginning) as possessing a mathematical structure or being a mathematical manifold. This conception is expressed in the famous statement of Galileo: "Whoever wants to read a book, must know the language in which that book is written. Nature is a book and the characters in which it is written are triangles, circles, and squares."

Nature as it really is thus does not reveal itself in direct sense experience; it must be disclosed by means of the specific methods of mathematical physics. Such disclosure is interpreted as the discovery of the true reality behind and beneath the appearances. As to the appearances, i.e., the life-world as it presents itself in perceptual experience, they are relegated to the domain of mere subjectivity. Hence a new science becomes necessary, one whose task is to account for the rise of the perceptual appearances on the basis of the true and real condition of nature as discovered by the science of physics. It is no historical accident—it is deeply rooted in the logic of the historical situation of the incipient physics of the Galilean style and its subsequent development—that *psychology* in the specific modern sense as the science of error has evolved along with that physics and in logico-historical continuity with it.

Let us approach our problem from another angle. At every period of the historical development, the distinction, according to Husserl, must be made between the state of the science of nature at that time, the conception of nature prevailing at that period or nature as it was believed to be at that time, and nature as it really is. "Nature as it really is" can only mean the definitive conception of nature, or nature as it will finally come to be believed to be, when the historical process of the development of science will have reached its end. Nature as it really is denotes a goal which the historical process of the development of science is supposed to pursue, which the successive conceptions of nature are supposed to approximate. In the interpretation under discussion, the goal is anticipated as attained, though not by us, and therefore it is as yet unknown to us. Moreover, the goal—if I may say so—is projected into nature as its true and real condition, waiting to be discovered; in a word, it is hypostatized. Another version, among several, is Leibniz' conception of the omniscient God who, as the supreme logician, is from eternity to eternity in the possession of all the knowledge for which we humans must strive, to the extent that it is accessible to us.

By now the sense of Husserl's Galileo analysis and of his critique of modern science has become clear. "Nature as it really is," the nature of the physicist in contradistinction to nature as it presents itself in common perceptual experience, is a mental accomplishment, more precisely, the Idea of a goal toward which a sequence of mental accomplishments is converging—an Idea, in the Kantian sense. No notice is taken of the mental processes of mathematization, idealization, and formalization from which those accomplishments derive as correlates and results. Finally, sight is lost of the life-world as given in common experience, that on which the mentioned processes operate in reinterpreting it in the light of idealized and formalized entities.

PHYSICS AND THE LIFE-WORLD

THE MATHEMATICAL CONCEPTION OF NATURE is therefore not essential to the human mind. In direct experience, nature does not present itself as a mathematical system. From the beginning, there has been a discrepancy between the *universe* constructed by physical science and the *world* given to us in immediate (mainly perceptual) experience. This latter is the world into which we are born, within which we find ourselves at every moment of our lives, no matter what activities we are engaged in or what goals we are pursuing. Within that world, we encounter our fellow men, to whom we stand in relations of the most diverse kinds. With the ways of this world—the "life-world," as Husserl calls it—we have acquired, both through education and through personal experience, a familiarity of a very special sort. The objects which we encounter in this world have human significance; they present themselves as tools, as utensils to be handled in specific ways so that desired results may be obtained. Moreover, they exhibit certain intrinsic properties of their own. For instance, a blue chair is over there. In the life-world, we take our bearings from perceptual experience and thus unhesitatingly consider the blue color to be a property intrinsic to the chair. Unless we have studied physics or are indirectly influenced by the study of physics, it would not occur to us to regard the color as a subjective phenomenon, a content of our consciousness on the same footing as, say, a feeling of joy, a desire, or the like. There is more at issue here than merely the substitution for the color of processes that are completely describable in mathematical terms, like wave length, frequency, velocity of propagation, and the consequent replacement of qualitative differences by quantitative ones.

Of equal importance is the ever growing alienation of the universe of physics from the world of perceptual experience. The physics of the nineteenth century, even the field theories of Faraday and Maxwell, still made use of models that had intuitive content and lent themselves to visualization. Lines of force were conceived by analogy with rubber bands which stretch and contract. Contemporary physics, however, relies on constructs of a totally abstract nature which have to be treated according to algorithmic rules of operation alone. They no longer have a visualizable content, and no intuitive significance is claimed for them. What in the beginning appeared as a discrepancy has grown into an ever widening gulf.

In an earlier phase of the modern period, the constructions of mathematical physics were not simply regarded as models meant for convenience of systematization, prediction, or even explanation. On the contrary, they were thought to express the true state of affairs, the real nature of the external world. By means of his mathematically expressed theories, the physicist was believed to pierce through the veil of perceptual appearance and thus to describe nature as it really is. This realistic interpretation of physics finds few defenders today, yet so recent and so great a physicist as Max Planck still adhered to it.

We seem somehow to be confronted with two realms. One is the realm of reality, of nature as mathematically conceived and constructed; the other is the world of appearances. Malebranche spoke of "illusions naturelles." They are natural because they are grounded in the real condition of things, on the basis of which they occur in regular fashion. But they are illusions, since they do not correspond to the true state of affairs. Nevertheless, the persistence of these illusions is most remarkable. Despite the rapid development of science, the perceptual world continues to be its familiar self. To the physicist and layman alike, things continue to exhibit chromatic qualities as though they were intrinsic to the things themselves. On a summer evening by the seashore, we still see the sun dipping into the ocean, all our knowledge of astronomy notwithstanding. Such facts point to some sort of priority on the part of the life-world. After all, scientific theories must be verified by means of observations, which, even if reduced to mere pointer readings, are still perceptual experiences.

One may object that this priority holds good only *quoad nos:* To arrive at the universe as it really is, we naturally must take our departure from the world as it appears to us. Even if this point were to be granted, the original point is still strong enough to make it worthwhile to inquire into those general features of the world of common experience which provide the initial motivation for constructing a mathematical conception of nature. Then we shall have to ask further what, in addition to that motivation, is required for the actual elaboration of a mathematical physics.

Fortunately for us, it is not necessary to present a full

analytic description of the general structure of the *Lebenswelt*. This would be a very arduous task indeed, the more so as no complete and exhaustive analysis of it has yet been made, though many authors in recent decades have made valuable additions to Husserl's pioneer work. For our purposes, a few major points from Husserl's analysis will suffice. In the first place, *the world of everyday experience is extended in space and time;* these constitute a comprehensive frame in which all the existents of our experience can be related in spatial and in temporal terms with one another. Moreover, things have spatial shapes, not in a strictly geometrical sense but rather physiognomically, not as a determinate figure but rather as a generic type of spatial configuration—one that within limits not precisely defined allows for variation and deviation. Going beyond Husserl's analysis, we may note that psychologists, especially of the Gestalt school, have long used terms like "circularity" or "rectangularity" in this physiognomic sense, when they speak, for instance, of a circle as "bad" or of one right angle as "better than another." From a strictly geometrical point of view, such phrases are nonsense. They make good sense, however, when applied to the phenomenal aspects of perceptual experience, whch is always affected by some vagueness and indefiniteness; its determinations hold only by and large. (For reasons to be made clear in a moment, I avoid speaking of "approximation.") One may, perhaps, characterize perceptual experience by saying that it is determinate as to type but that there will ordinarily be some latitude about the manner in which the type is particularized.

In the second place, *the life-world exhibits various regularities.* As far back as we can remember, we have been familiar with the alternation of day and night and with the change of the seasons. Living in the northern hemisphere, we have always known that in July it is hotter than in February, and we act accordingly in choosing our clothing. Things, as Husserl expressed it, have their habits of behavior. It is not from science, either Aristotelian or Galilean, that we learn that stones, when lifted and released, fall down. It is a matter of everyday experience in the life-world that water can be boiled and that, when further heated, it evaporates.

Generally speaking, the life-world exhibits universal causality of a certain style. Events hang together with each other; occurrences of one type are regularly followed by occurrences of another type. Familiarity with such regularities, that is, with the "style" of the universal causality, is of paramount importance for our existence and the practical conduct of our lives. It, and it alone, permits anticipations. Because of this familiarity, we know fairly well what to be prepared for in the near future; we can often influence the course of affairs to bring something about. As the late Alfred Schutz has shown in his penetrating analyses, all activities within the life-world are dominated throughout by the pragmatic motive. Since causal connections come to our attention originally because of their pragmatic significance, it is natural that this same significance should determine the degree of accuracy with which these connections will be established and described. In other words, our familiarity with particular causal connections as well as with the universal style of causality in the life-world is affected by the kind of indefiniteness and vagueness already mentioned, which thus appears to be a general feature of perceptual experience.

Finally, things in the life-world present themselves, as Husserl expresses it, in a certain relativity with respect to the experiencing subjects. All of us perceive the same objects in this room, but each one of us sees them from his own point of observation. The same things appear under a variety of changing aspects. The exigencies of social life make adjustment of these differences absolutely necessary. Some are considered to be irrelevant and are therefore ignored; others are handled by what Schutz calls the "interchangeability of the standpoints" or the "reciprocity of perspectives." Intersubjective agreement is effected in a number of different ways, into the details of which we have no space to enter here. All of us find ourselves living, therefore, in one and the same life-world. The pragmatic motive still retains its predominance here, since it is essentially related to the concrete conditions under which a certain social group exists. Hence the intersubjective life-world remains subject to a degree of relativity—no longer, to be sure, with regard to this or that individual but with respect to the social group in question, however small or large.

GALILEAN PHYSICS AND PLATONISM

GALILEO INHERITED NOT ONLY GEOMETRY as a body of technical knowledge but also the Platonic interpretation of geometry as embodying the ideal of true knowledge. Following Cassirer, Koyré, and Crombie, I consider Galileo as a "Platonist" and, going even further, I maintain that the whole of modern physics—the "physics of Galilean style"—is of Platonic inspiration. This involves a broad sense of the term "Platonism," to be sure, but one I consider preferable. Galileo, it is true, did not espouse the mathematical speculations of the *Timaeus*. Platonism, however, need not necessarily be construed in the narrow sense of endorsing all the doctrines found in the writings of Plato. I shall take it to signify the defense of a two-world theory, of a distinction between two realms of unequal ontological status, where one domain is assumed to be subordinated to the other and to lead a merely borrowed existence—a domain that must be explained in terms of the domain of higher order. Galileo's work may be said to make a turning point in the historical development of "Platonism" in this sense of the term; it was thoroughly transformed and renewed by him.

Greek philosophy claimed to discover an opposition between the multifarious appearances involved in perpetual change and an immutable realm of existence, forever persisting in strictest self-identity. This latter was called "Being-as-it-is-in-itself," *ontōs on.* To this distinction there corresponded one between *epistēmē* and *doxa. Doxa* covers our beliefs about appearances and thus is changeable. *Doxa* is necessary (and also sufficient) for the practical conduct of affairs in the realm of appearances. It depends on the situation in which the subject finds himself, on his interests and plans. The Greek term *doxa* thus conveys something of the relativity and indeterminateness that we have seen characterize our relation with the life-world. *Epistēmē,* on the other hand, is knowledge in the genuine and emphatic sense. Since it is concerned with Being-as-it-is-in-itself, it is free from all relativity with regard to subjects, their standpoints, and the vicissitudes of their lives. Because of the persistent self-identity of this Being, genuine knowledge is perpetually true, under all circumstances and for everyone. Whereas the domain of opinion is that of persuasion and plausibility (i.e., of rhetoric in the classical sense of the term), these qualifications have no place in the domain of *epistēmē,* where only cogent argument and conclusive demonstration count. Either a thesis can be fully demonstrated, e.g., by proving that its negation leads to contradictions and absurdities, or it has no right to be advanced at all. If any disagreement appears, it can, at least in principle, be definitely resolved. Otherwise the argument would not have the permanent and universal binding force claimed for it.

Geometrical figures conceived as ideal entities may well pass for beings-in-themselves. Free from every ambiguity, exempt from all change and variation, they persist in self-identity, irrespective of knowing subjects. Whereas measurements in the life-world admit of varying degrees of accuracy, geometrical determinations are made with exactness. Exactness implies the absence both of fluctuation and of any restriction in terms of practical purpose. In Euclid's axiomatization of geometry, a small number of fundamental propositions, as well as some elementary methods of construction, were explicitly specified. From them, various properties of plane figures can be cogently demonstrated. Thus an infinity of exact spatial forms are situated relative to one another by means of a single coherent theory—coherent because deductively developed. Geometry thus perfectly exemplifies the ideal of *epistēmē*. Mastery of the methods of geometrical reasoning allows one to reach results that are permanently and universally valid. All relativity with regard to subjects and their situations is overcome.

Galileo's acceptance of geometry as the model of knowledge is, in Husserl's view, his fundamental presupposition. One may even speak of a "prejudice," since Galileo makes use of a Platonic conception of genuine knowledge and a corresponding conception of true Being, without attempting in any way to justify them, without apparently even noticing that they require justification. The sort of reflection we made above on the origins of geometrical concepts was very far indeed from Galileo's mind. Once geometry has been accepted as the standard of knowledge, it follows that, if a science of nature is to be possible at all, it will somehow have to be conceived after the model of geometry. Galileo's Platonism appears in the distinction between the perceptual appearance of nature and its true, that is, its mathematical, structure. The disclosure of this structure is the task of the new science of physics, which proceeds to a thoroughgoing mathematization of nature. Spatiotemporal occurrences must, in consequence, be idealized, that is, referred to exact mathematical relationships.

If motion be simply considered as change of spatial position in time, an exhaustive mathematical treatment of mechanics becomes possible, though this will require a redefinition of the concepts of velocity and acceleration. This is necessary because these concepts already have roles in describing the life-world, where, however, they denote quantities only roughly estimated. The mathematization of motion leads to the study of the different possible forms of motion, among which uniformly accelerated motion proves to be of special interest. Mathematically expressed hypotheses are developed and tested against observation in order to ascertain which hypothesis applies to a given case, e.g., that of freely falling bodies.

Testing the consequences of such hypotheses against experimental data requires measurement, eventually under laboratory conditions. The accuracy of the measurement once again depends on the available techniques, and improved techniques yield results of increasing accuracy. It seems very like the situation we have already seen regarding measurement in the life-world, independently of geometrical idealization. This idealization bestows, however, a radically new sense on the results of measurement. No longer do the increasingly accurate results obtained by means of improving techniques stand side by side with one another, each fully justified by the practical purpose for which it is intended. By being referred to an ideal limit-pole, the results of measurement come to be interpreted as *approximations,* in the strict sense of forming a sequence which converges toward a true and exact value. Technically speaking, measurement is still carried on under the conditions prevailing in the life-world; its interpretation, however, is placed—as Husserl puts it—under a "horizon of infinity."

For this reason, the perfectibility of measuring techniques now begins to acquire the overtone of an unlimited perfectibility. We have already seen that the art of measurement in the life-world prepared the way for geometrical idealization. Now the relationship is, in a sense, reversed. Geometrical (and, more generally, mathematical) idealization comes to inspire the application of measuring techniques, in that the idea of mathematical exactness yields incentives not only for the obtaining of increasingly closer approximations but also for the contrivance of "better" techniques. Mathematical idealization thus provides a built-in method for improving on itself, as it were, without direct reference to any practical purposes—hence with the sense of a possibly unlimited, i.e., an infinite, progress.

INDIRECT MATHEMATIZATION

THUS FAR, the idealization and mathematization of only space, time, and motion in the life-world have been considered. Things encountered in perceptual experience exhibit, in addition to these aspects, qualitative properties—color, temperature, and so forth—which fill the spatial forms. These properties do not lend themselves to quantification. A certain red may be said to be "brighter" than another, but it is not possible to go beyond rough estimates of this sort and to ask "how much brighter?" and expect an answer in numerical terms. There is only one geometry, and it is related to space, not to qualities. This becomes clear if one notes that any spatial shape can be conceived as a limited portion of the one, unique, all-encompassing space, whereas there is no universal qualitative form into which all qualitative configurations could be inserted in an analogous manner. Hence if a mathematization of qualities is possible at all, it can, at best, be contrived only in an indirect way. It is to this indirect mathematization that we must now turn. Husserl associates it too with Galileo, though it would be historically more correct to mention Descartes and, especially, Huygens. As we have seen, Galileo's name is a symbol for Husserl.

Indirect mathematization of qualities requires that they be correlated with occurrences which, because they are describable in spatiotemporal terms, are capable of direct mathematization. Take, for instance, the Pythagorean discovery of the dependence of the pitch of a musical note on the length of the vibrating cord. This dependence by itself does not warrant the conclusion that the note heard is a mere subjective datum and that all that exists in reality are the vibrations of the cord. Rather, we have here the regular correlation of one occurrence with a different one, an instance of the "universal causality" found in the life-world. As far as our experience of that causality goes, events of one kind are known to depend on events of a different kind; changes in one respect are accompanied by changes in other respects. This, however, gives us no reason to assume that qualitative phenomena are causally dependent on spatiotemporal occurrences in some simple unilateral way.

But this is just what *has* been assumed as physics has continued to progress. It has become more or less taken for granted that qualitative phenomena are produced by processes that interact with our sense organs and are definable in spatiotemporal terms exclusively. Qualitative phenomena and their changes are thought both to reveal and to conceal the true state of affairs. They reveal it because, as effects of quantitative processes, they point to these processes and can be read as their symptoms, at least by the physicist who has learned to decipher the language. They conceal the true state of affairs (so it is said) because of the utter heterogeneity between the symptom itself and that of which it is a symptom. Nature as it *really* is (in contrast with its perceptual appearance) is a mathematical structure, perhaps a plurality of such structures, and it matters little whether the structures are comparatively simple, as in the early phases of modern science, or extremely complex and abstract, as in contemporary physics.

The "Idea" of Mathematical Natural Science

WHAT LOGICAL STATUS SHOULD BE ASSIGNED to the thesis that nature is mathematical throughout? Obviously, it is not a formulation of empirical findings, nor does one arrive at it by generalization from experience. On account of its generality, it cannot pass for a law of nature; in fact, every determinate law of nature is one of its particular specifications. Because of its generality, it cannot be considered as a hypothesis in the usual sense. If, as Husserl does, one calls it a "hypothesis," one must, following him, emphasize its peculiar nature. One may speak of it as the "hypothesis underlying hypotheses," as a "regulative idea" in the sense of Kant, as a methodological norm which directs the formulation of scientific hypotheses and guides all scientific activities, theoretical and experimental alike. A "hypothesis" of this kind cannot be defended by direct argument but can be substantiated only by the continuing success of the methodological norm itself. And this means ongoing, never ending work. The thesis that nature is mathematical throughout can be confirmed only by the entire historical process of the development of science, a steady process in which nature comes to be mathematized progressively. No matter how far the process has advanced, that is, no matter what confirmation the thesis has already received, it still remains a hypothesis in the sense of needing further substantiation. The distinction between nature as it is conceived by science at a moment of its history and nature as it actually is in scientific truth must never be overlooked. This last phrase does not denote a concealed reality lying behind the appearances in the life-world and waiting to be discovered but, rather, a goal to be reached or, more correctly, to be approximated asymptotically.

Instead of stating that nature is mathematical, we should more appropriately say that nature lends itself to mathematization. This is not just a matter of words. The latter formulation brings out the point that mathematization does not necessarily mean the disclosure of a pregiven, though yet hidden, reality. On the contrary, it suggests an accomplishment yet to be achieved, a universe yet to be constructed. Science takes on this task and, under the guidance of its own methodological norms, constructs its universe by means of a complex continuing process of idealization and mathematization. The resulting universe is the product of a methodological procedure, a "tissue of ideas," which must never be mistaken for reality itself. Reality is, and always remains, the life-world, no matter how vast the possibilities of systematization and prediction that have been opened up by the development of natural science of the Galilean style.

This science is certainly one of the greatest accomplishments of the human mind. This phrase is no pious declamation but, rather, suggests a problem for future research. It is at this point that the analysis of Galilean physics flows into the mainstream of phenomenology. As a product of the mind, science of the Galilean style requires phenomenological clarification. Because of the role of the life-world as the presupposition of scientific construction, the problems which (if one is to be systematic) must be attacked first are those related to the life-world itself and the experience through which it presents itself, i.e., perceptual experience. Subsequently, a phenomenological account must be given of the higher intellectual processes which, like idealization, formalization, and so on, are basic to the construction of pure mathematics and the mathematization of nature.

CONCLUSION

THUS FAR, we have confined ourselves to Husserl's Galileo analysis in *Crisis* and to its immediate consequences. Now the perspective must be enlarged. *Crisis* is only one of three literary documents which together express what may be called the late phase of Husserl's thought. The two others are *Formal and Transcendental Logic* and *Experience and Judgment*. Returning to and continuing his earlier work in *Logical Investigations*, Husserl, in these two books, concerns himself with the foundations of formal logic and the genesis of its sense. *Experience and Judgment* has the significant subtitle *Investigations Concerning the Genealogy of Logic*. As in *Crisis*, he is brought before the life-world and led to emphasize the specific mental processes involved in the constitution of logic. The three books form a unitary group and should be seen as related to one another.

These three works show that logic as well as mathematics and physics have to be understood as correlates and products of activities of consciousness and mental life. Correspondingly, the same can be shown with respect to the life-world itself. It is the world in which we find ourselves and pursue all our activities, which in our everyday life we take for granted. It is permanently experienced by and permanently present to us; it is an experienced world and the world as given in direct and immediate experience, prior to all conceptualization, idealization, and formalization. Primarily, the term "life-world" has a sociohistorical meaning. Properly speaking, there is no life-world per se. Every concrete life-world refers to a certain social group at a certain phase of its history, such as the world of the ancient Babylonians, that of the ancient Egyptians, etc., and, of course, our own life-world, the world of the Occidentals in the twentieth century. That is, every life-world is understood, conceived of, and interpreted in a specific way by the social group whose life-world it is. The schemes of interpretation are transmitted from the older to the younger generation and so are the socially accepted or approved modes of conduct and ways of coming to terms with typical situations. Though the life-world refers to a sociohistorical group and accordingly changes from group to group and also for the same group in the course of its history, the question arises of whether there is an invariant structure pertaining to every possible life-world. Of special interest in the present context are spatiality, temporality, and a certain style of typical causality—what may be called the customs of nature, the habits which things have of behaving typically, with greater or lesser regularity, under given circumstances. All processes of idealization take their departure from such invariant structures.

The analysis of the foundations of both logic and physics leads to the discovery or, rather, rehabilitation of the life-world, which can no longer be dismissed as a merely "subjective" phenomenon requiring an explanation on the grounds of nature as it really and truly is. On the contrary, the life-world proves to underlie and to be presupposed by the elaboration of "objective" nature. Still, we have not yet reached the ultimate, but only the penultimate, presupposition and foundation. *The life-world, in its turn, refers to and, in that sense, presupposes mental life, acts of consciousness, especially perceptual consciousness through which it is experienced and presents itself as that which it is,* that is, *as that which we accept.* It is not until we arrive at consciousness as the universal medium of access (in the sense of Descartes's *Second Meditation*) to whatever exists and is valid, including the life-world, that our search for foundations reaches its final destination. As far as the processes of conceptualization, idealization, and formalization are concerned, they now appear in their proper place as acts of consciousness of a higher order insofar as they presuppose the more elementary and more fundamental acts through which the life-world is given or, in Husserl's parlance, they are built on prepredicative experience. This is another expression of our previous conclusion that the universe of physics—objective nature as conceived by physicists—is a product of mental life constructed on the basis of the prepredicative experience of the life-world.

It is a misconception, frequently encountered, that, in reinstating the life-world in its right, Husserl meant it to be the final dwelling place for philosophical thought. On the contrary, in *Crisis* itself he emphasizes again the principle of a universal and thoroughgoing correlation between objects of any description whatever—objects in the broadest and most general sense, so as to include ideal constructs of every kind—on the one hand, and, on the other hand, acts of consciousness and the systematic interconcatenations of such acts through which the former present themselves. In other words, the Galileo analysis is intended to lead us to the threshold of phenomenology.

These have been no more than sketchy hints for a phenomenological theory of the natural sciences. Notwithstanding the voluminous recent literature on the philosophy of science (whose value I do not in the least belittle), we do not yet possess a philosophy or theory of science in a truly radical sense. Husserl's analysis of Galilean physics indicates the direction in which a "radical" (i.e., properly rooted) theory of natural science must develop. I can just begin to see something of its outlines. As always when Husserl's writings are involved, at the end of work accomplished, more work looms on the horizon. The labor will be long and hard but—I am convinced—most rewarding.

3 / Reflections on Mathematics and Logic

IN THE FOLLOWING PAGES, we shall attempt to show how the phenomenological philosopher reflects on the positive sciences of mathematics and logic. The role that these sciences play in the modern natural sciences is obvious. But it is not so obvious how experience of the perceptual world plays a role in the background of those sciences. Let us begin with a problem in the theory of geometry and then consider other themes pertaining to the theory of the formal sciences.

THE PERCEPTUAL FOUNDATION OF GEOMETRICAL SPACE

FROM THE POINT OF VIEW OF MATHEMATICS as a positive science, i.e., as a matter of constructive work, it is perfectly legitimate to restrict oneself to results of this work and to the properly mathematical steps which lead to these results. Philosophical reflection, however, cannot be limited to the manifest content, as it were, of mathematics. On the contrary, it must go beyond that content to the presuppositions of that positive science. The essential function of such a reflection consists in ascertaining *the conditions for the possibility of mathematics.* It is essential that such conditions do not play a role in the science itself, i.e., that they are not included in it as premises,

This text has been extracted from a longer manuscript, ca. 1950, entitled "Le Monde perceptif et l'univers rationalisé." Translated by Lester Embree.

even though they support the entire edifice. Thus the philosopher must explicate what mathematicians pass over in silence because they are interested only in explicitly formulated assertions —either the axioms they accept or the demonstrated theorems they use as points of departure for their subsequent deductions.

In the present reflection we shall *not* discuss the deductive method of geometry through which all ideally possible forms and all the relations between them can be constructed beginning from a limited number of axioms which imply all geometrical truths—these truths are only their consequences (see *LI*, pp. 239–43; *Ideas*, § 72; and *FTL*, pt. I, chap. 3). Nor shall we discuss the methods of formalization so emphatically characteristic of modern geometry according to which the geometrician no longer speaks of "points," "lines," "planes," etc., but only of completely indeterminate entities defined by relations established between them—relations which themselves are defined in the last analysis only by certain entirely formal characteristics. It is, furthermore, a truism that the ideal figures of geometry are not encountered in the perceptual world, for one can transform a perceived shape as much as one wants, actually or in imagination, and all that results are other spatial shapes. In order to reach the "pure" and ideal figures of geometry, we need the specific operation of idealization, which Husserl has distinguished from other categorial activities (*EJ*, § 10; cf. *Ideas*, § 73). However, we are not even interested here in the particular spatial figures. Rather, we ask: *What is the foundation in the aspect and structure of the perceptual world for the idealization of geometrical space?*

In the homogeneous and isotropic nature of geometrical space, no place is privileged in relation to any other and no spatial direction is privileged in relation to any other. A system of coordinates can be set up anywhere and can be oriented in any way. In contrast, with regard to its spatial aspect,[1] the perceptual world is encountered as oriented and organized under the relationships of above and below, of right and left, of before and behind, and, finally, of near and far. The center of reference for this organizational structure is the organism of the perceiving subject. This is particularly clear where the contrast between near and far is concerned. The actual place of the

---

1. On the relation of the spatial to the temporal aspect of the concrete perceptual world, see *FC*, pp. 382–87.

perceiving subject defines an *absolute here* in such a way that every other place is characterized as *there*. Only the perceiving subject's organism is *here;* every other body is *there.*

Taking the orientation of the perceptual world in terms of right and left and before and behind into consideration, one can speak with Merleau-Ponty of the "installation of the primary coordinates." [2] In relation to the *absolute here,* the objects actually perceived as well as those which are perceivable even though not perceived at the moment—in short, all of the objects which play or can play a role in the perceptual world—are separated into those which are near and those which are far. The terms "near" and "far" should be understood as having that lack of precision and exactness which is characteristic of all notions directly formed in perceptual experience.

Now the perceiving subject can and, in fact, does move. We are free to leave the place where we find ourselves at present and to go to another place which is now *there* but which, after we have finished our locomotion, will be *here.* Even if we remain where we are we can readily imagine the aspect under which the world and the things in it would present themselves if we were in a different place. In his analysis of the apprehension of the Other (*CM,* § 53), Husserl refers to the possibility of transforming any there into a here and vice versa. In effect, the Other is grasped as perceiving the world in a perspective different from mine but nevertheless as perceiving it as I would perceive it if, literally, I took his place, if I were where he is. By virtue of the mobility of the perceiving subject, the *absolute here* is infected with a certain relativity. From being the absolute here it becomes the *absolute here of the moment* and a *potential there.* Reciprocally, every *actual there* acquires the sense of a *potential here.* Under certain conditions, the *actual here* can even appear as a *past here* (when I remember having been in the place in question) or a *future here* (when I am in the process of going there).

Thus the way is paved and the foundation is laid for the

2. *Phenomenology of Perception,* trans. Colin Smith (New York: Humanities Press, 1962): "The word 'here' applied to my body does not refer to a determinate position in relation to other positions or to external co-ordinates, but to the laying down of the first co-ordinates [*l'installation des premières coordonnées*], the anchoring of the active body in an object, the situation of the body in the face of its tasks" (p. 100).

geometrical idealization of homogeneous space. Yet actually, the free mobility of the perceiving subject only founds the possibility of installing an exact system of coordinates into which the subject can place himself. The homogeneity of space in the geometrical sense also implies the idea that a coordinate system can be installed anywhere, regardless of whether the perceiving subject actually places himself at the place which he quite freely and arbitrarily chooses as the center of reference. Hence the transition must be made from "any place which is accessible to the subject" to "any place whatever." [3]

Reflecting on his de facto mobility, the perceiving subject can readily imagine being endowed with a greater freedom of movement than he actually enjoys. In other words, the subject can imagine that in principle he can move to any place at all in space, even though technical reasons prevent the exercise of this total freedom of movement. The transition in question can be defined as a generalization from "accessibility in fact" to "accessibility in principle." Let us note, however, that the operation of the imagination involved here differs from the operation by means of which, beginning from morphological shapes, we arrive at ideal figures in the geometrical sense. In the latter case, the operation of the imagination, even though necessary, is insufficient, insofar as the ideal geometric figures belong to an order of existence different from that to which the shapes resulting from the imaginative transformation of perceived shapes belong. Here, on the contrary, it only seems to be a question of extending in imagination our actual freedom of movement. [4]

The establishment of a coordinate system appears linked to

3. The need for this transition seems to have escaped the notice of Oskar Becker, who did clearly see the relationship between the constitution of homogeneous space and intersubjectivity. See "Beiträge zur phänomenologischen Begründung der Geometrie und ihrer physikalischen Anwendungen," *Jahrbuch für Philosophie und phänomenologischen Forschung*, VI (1923), 458–59.

4. Husserl has emphasized the capital and indispensable importance of the imagination and the operations of the imagination, above all, "free variation," for the constitution of "pure general ideas," i.e., ideas in the Platonic sense; for the establishment of eidetic relationships, relations between the ideas in question; and finally, for the formation laws, the a priori laws which are based on eidetic relationships. See *LI*, pp. 440–48; *Ideas*, §§ 4, 70, 149; *CM*, § 34; *EJ*, §§ 87, 89. See also *FC*, pp. 190 ff.

a perceiving subject, to the place of his organism, and finally, to his motoric possibilities. None of this is mentioned in mathematics or even in mathematical physics, where, of course, the geometrical conception of space has a central importance. This is because even the physicists are interested only in the description which can be made of the world by taking up a point of view, i.e., in relation to a certain reference system, for the analytic formulation of the laws of figures defined in terms of relations among spatial elements, in the analytic expression of the movements of bodies (when these movements come under certain laws), and, above all, in the invariant relationships which, because they are valid in every possible coordinate system, do not depend on any one system.

The Ideal Identity of Propositions

Like mathematics, logic can be pursued in the spirit of pure positivity. Conceiving of logic as the science of possible forms of propositions as well as of objects, one begins by defining the most elementary forms and the basic operations. By applying the operations to the given forms, one obtains new forms. Now, all logical operations are dominated by the law of reiteration. A form that results from the application of an operation to a primitive form can in turn be subjected to the same operation again as easily as to a different operation, and a higher-order form is thus derived from it. Thus, after having constructed the hypothetical propositions, "p implies q" ($p \supset q$) and "r implies s" ($r \supset s$) on the basis of the categorical propositions p, q, r, and s, one can make one of these hypothetical propositions the antecedent and the other the consequent in a new and more complex hypothetical proposition, e.g., "if p implies q, then r implies s" ($[p \supset q] \supset [r \supset s]$), or one can construct the alternative proposition, "either p implies q or r implies s" ($[p \supset q] \vee [r \supset s]$). With simple elements one can construct complexes [*ensembles*] which can be compared with one another or which can be used to construct a higher-order complex, a complex of complexes. In this case, the "elements" of the higher-order complex are the complexes which were constructed in the first place.

The reiterated application of operations to forms engendered by the same operations yields ever new and more complicated forms. Every construction contains an existential theorem in the sense of mathematics. The validity, i.e., the mathematical existence, of the most primitive form used in the construction, be it a propositional form or an object form, and the validity of the operation in question give a new form a validity and a mathematical existence which is assured by the constructive procedure itself. Thus one can conceive of an ideal construction of the infinite totality of possible forms beginning from the primitive forms and the basic operations (*FTL*, § 13). If logic is developed in this way, it is an autonomous constructive science. When he wrote the *Logical Investigations*, Husserl did more than anyone else to establish the autonomy of logic.

Instead of confining himself to logic as a calculus, which the technical logician can do and does legitimately, the theoretician of logic must ask about the meaning of the constructive procedure and find its place in the context of knowledge. This endeavor brings him to the presuppositions of logic, which are not explicitly formulated in the elaboration of the calculative technique but are nevertheless in the foundation of any constructive process. Husserl's *Formal and Transcendental Logic* is entirely devoted to bringing these presuppositions to light. Let us consider how this is done.

We are always sure of being able to return to any proposition as identically the same as often as we wish. If a mathematical demonstration terminates in the formulation of a certain theorem, the latter can be taken up again, be it in the reexamination of the demonstration or in a continuation of the mathematical argument where the same theorem which before appeared as a result now serves as point of departure. A proposition which was affirmed can be doubted, submitted to a closer examination, and then reaffirmed with consciousness that it is the same one that was originally affirmed, subsequently doubted, etc. We have seen that, by the application of logical operations to given propositions, new propositions of more complex structure are engendered. The same proposition, p, is affirmed as an independent proposition and then, when a certain operation is performed on it, it enters with the title "element" into a more complex proposition where it has a definite role.[5] The same p and the same q function, the one as antecedent and the other as consequent, in the hypothetical proposition $p \supset q$

5. For the role of context in logic, see *FC*, pp. 325–35.

and appear as alternatives in the alternative proposition $p \lor q$.

Everywhere we are concerned with the ideal identity of propositions and, correlatively, with the possibility of dealing with them repeatedly as identical. The ideal identity of propositions is the more in need of radical clarification, since it is used not only in the thought of the solitary logician but also in intersubjective communication. When we submit our results to other thinkers and examine their results in any sort of discussion or collaboration, in science or in everyday life, it is admitted —or, better, it is tacitly presupposed—that the propositions and the systems of propositions are the same for everyone.

Nowhere is the ideal identity of the proposition mentioned among the premises from which the constructive procedure of logic begins. Yet the logician constantly uses it and cannot abstain from using it. In effect, without the presupposition (which is tacit) that a proposition which the logician considers, which he compares with other propositions, to which he applies operations, etc., is the same every time he comes back to it, the development of a system of logic and the elaboration of a calculative technique are surely not possible. While the constructor-logician can pass over the ideal identity of propositions as "a matter of course which goes without saying," the task of the theoretician of logic is to make such tacit presuppositions explicit, to thematize them, and to see and attempt to solve their problems.

THE HISTORY OF SENSE

JUST AS ONE CAN CONSTRUCT more and more complex forms by means of operations beginning with simpler forms, one can begin with a complex form and go back to the more elementary forms from which a given form was constructed. In proceeding in this way, one retraces the *history* of the form which one takes as point of departure for the regressive movement. By no means is this history a psychological history; it is not a matter of the manner in which the form in question actually originated in a temporal process which, under certain conditions and under the influence of various factors, took place in an actual mental life. Let us recall what we have said about progressive construction: The validity, i.e., the mathematical existence, of the form constructed is drawn from that of the more elementary forms and also from the legitimacy of the operations performed. Consequently, every complex form refers by its very sense to more elementary forms and to operations by means of which it is derived from those elementary forms (*FTL*, §§ 85, 97). These are included in the complex form. They do not form part of its manifest content but are included there as implications and sediments.

The signification which is the complex form to be analyzed, by containing "moments of sense [*Sinnesmomente*]" which pertain to a more elementary and fundamental level, contains them as "hidden" presuppositions, presuppositions which in their tacit efficacy contribute no less essentially to the construction of the complex form in question. If we speak in this connection of analysis, the term should not be understood in the usual way, i.e., as a decomposition of a whole into its real parts. By "analysis" here we mean, on the contrary, an *intentional* analysis, the function of which consists in disengaging the effective sense moments as tacit presuppositions, in order to render them explicit, and finally to fit the sediments back into the process of their formation. It follows from this that the history of forms, which is retraced by the method of intentional regression, reveals itself as a "history of sense [*Sinnesgeschichte*]," just as the production of forms in the course of the process of construction should be understood as "genesis of sense [*Sinnesgenesis*]."

By following regressive analysis to its end, one comes—where the forms of objects are concerned—to individual objects which have still not undergone any logical formation. Where forms of propositions are concerned, one comes to categorical propositions of the form "S is p," propositions in which an "ultimate" predicate, i.e., one which cannot be reduced further, is attributed to a subject which is "ultimate" in the same way, e.g., "this table is brown" (*FTL*, §§ 82–84). Now an individual object devoid of logical formation, an "ultimate substrate," as Husserl calls it, is precisely the object as it presents itself in perceptual experience prior to any logical operation which in the broad sense could be applied to an object, e.g., collection, permutation, relating, etc. On the other hand, an "ultimate proposition," in the sense just defined, necessarily relates to an individual object of perceptual experience; it designates this perceptual object and must be considered as the result of the most elementary logical operation which may be applied to the data of perception.

Finally, *regressive analysis ends at the perceptual experience prior to any logical operation,* or, as Husserl calls it, "prepredicative experience" (*FTL,* § 86). Hence it is from this prepredicative perceptual experience that one must start in the radical clarification and justification of logic. All propositions, whatever their form, have their basis in the ultimate categorical proposition, which only expresses perceptual experience.[6]

The philosophical theory of logic must hence begin with prepredicative experience, it must base itself on a theory of this experience, and then it must interpret the progressive systematic development of logic in terms of construction and reiterated operations. To accomplish its task, the theory of logic must first show how the "ultimate" categorical proposition arises from prepredicative experience. This is one of the main themes of Husserl's posthumous *Experience and Judgment. One of the fundamental presuppositions*—perhaps even the most fundamental of all—*which is sedimented at the bottom of logic and implicitly determines its sense is prepredicative experience and, correlatively, the perceptual world as it appears in that experience.*

Formal Science and Objects

Too often, the advanced state which logic and mathematics have reached in the modern epoch is taken to mean that these sciences are concerned only with the manipulation of symbols devoid of signification. According to this interpretation, the symbols used in mathematical and logical calculations serve only to designate terms which are not related to objects; an operation sign, such as "+," has no signification and, in particular, does not signify a genuine operation, such as addition. Only certain entirely formal rules for the manipulation of symbols are defined, and the whole matter is hence considered as a sort of game. Thus, for example, $a + b = b + a$ means that it is permissible to replace the combination of symbols $a + b$ with the combination $b + a$.

It is correct to say that mathematical as well as logical terms

6. For the author's more recent thoughts in this connection, see chap. 10, below; and "On Thematization," in *Research in Phenomenology,* Vol. IV (1974).

do not relate to *any determinate objects* and thus can play the role of *indeterminate variables*. When, beginning from a concrete proposition, e.g., "This chair is yellow," one goes on to the form of that proposition, "this *S* is *p*," one replaces all the terms of determinate material content with terms of variable signification in such a way that abstraction is made from all material content and, within certain limits, the terms thus formalized relate, or, better put, can relate, to any object, whatever its nature.[7] Also, propositions which, concerning the material content of the objects to which they relate, are as different as "this chair is yellow," "this number is algebraic," "this melody is sad," "this argument is valid," etc., are all examples or particularizations of the same propositional form, namely, "this *S* is *p*." Any one of the mentioned propositions can serve to illustrate the propositional form involved because, beginning from any one of them, one can go in the indicated way to the same form.

Analogously, and without yet speaking of algebra, any number at all, e.g., the number "5," can be related to any group of five items or units, whatever their nature and material content. It does not matter whether the items in question are "ultimate," i.e., individual, objects or groups of such objects; it equally does not matter whether in the latter case all of the groups consist of the same number of individual objects or if this number varies from one group to the next. All that matters is that each group counts as a unit in the group of five. If the number concepts— ordinal as well as cardinal—are formal, it is because of this complete indifference concerning the nature and the qualitative and material content of the items or objects to which a determinate number may be related. Here the items or objects are considered only in the formal relationships of "how many [*combien*]" and "which place [*quantième*]," in such a way that, from the point of view of the particularization of the number 5, any group of five objects whatever can be substituted for any other group of five different objects.

In this sense, the notions which are central to the formal sciences, notions such as "object," "property," "relationship," "relation," "plurality," "number," "quantity," "whole," "part," etc.,

7. *FTL*, §§ 12, 23a, 87; see also *LI*, pp. 450–53, 457–62, on the limits beyond which the variation in question cannot go. Reflection on these limits leads to the idea of a philosophical or "pure logical grammar."

are qualified by Husserl as pure varieties of the concept "anything whatever [*Etwas überhaupt*]" (*LI*, p. 455; *FTL*, § 24). In the formation of these notions, notice is not taken of the nature of the objects which only function as materials subject to certain relations, e.g., counting, enumerating, comparing, relating, etc. Every time the same operation is applied to objects the qualitative and material nature of which is left indeterminate, the corresponding correlatives of the operation in question cannot but have the same form (*FTL*, § 27a).

Formalization can be taken further, as when one passes from arithmetic to algebra. Algebraic terms have still more indeterminate significations in that each of them relates indifferently to any number at all. Thus algebra includes the formalization of notions which in turn have already undergone formalization. Carrying formalization to the limit, one reaches the idea of the theory of multiplicity (*Mannigfaltigkeitslehre*) (see *LI*, pp. 241 ff.; *FTL*, pt. I, chap. 3). There, the terms function as indeterminate variables in relation to objects without regard to their material and qualitative natures; moreover, even the significations of the operation symbols which, in algebra, signify specific operations like, for example, addition, are left completely indeterminate except for utterly formal characteristics, such as those expressed by the laws of association, commutation, and distribution.

Now, *to maintain that symbols have indeterminate and indefinite significations* even in the case of extreme formalization *is surely something different from considering them to be devoid of signification.* Also, as to the manner in which, from the standpoint of *Mannigfaltigkeitslehre*, the formula $a + b = b + a$ is to be understood, Husserl offers this interpretation: " 'There shall obtain among the *objects* belonging to the multiplicity (conceived at first as only empty Somethings, "Objects of thinking") a certain *combination*-form with the *law*-form $a + b = b + a$' " (*FTL*, p. 100). It follows that the theory of multiplicities, i.e., mathematics at the state of complete formalization, still refers to objects which are, it is true, indeterminate and indefinite in every respect, except that the relations among these objects—themselves also indeterminate—have certain formal characteristics which themselves alone are well defined.

This applicability of purely formal and purely analytical mathematics must not be considered as accidental and extrinsic to mathematics. On the contrary, this applicability to objects, determinate only as to the formal characteristics of the relations which hold between them, belongs to the intrinsic sense of analytical mathematics by the very nature of the significations of the formalized symbols and, thereby, by the very nature of the theorems (*FTL*, § 40). To be sure, from the positive point of view in mathematics, such possible or potential application is of no interest at all. The actual development of mathematics goes on, and the question of the existence of objects to which it may be applied neither intervenes nor needs to intervene (*FTL*, §§ 51, 52). For philosophical reflection, however, the potential relationship of formal and analytical mathematics to possible objects is of the greatest importance, because the applicability of mathematics betrays the provenience of mathematics in the experience of a world which cannot be other than the perceptual world.

Now, this provenience is not only—and above all, it is not in the first place—a simple fact of history. If it is a matter of historicity at all, it is not one of *factual historicity* but of *intentional historicity*. The origin of mathematics in the experience of the world and its development through progressive formalizations are written into the very sense of this discipline and define it as the science bearing on the formal structure of the world— not only, and even not necessarily, the actual world, but *any* possible world. From its "genesis of sense," analytical mathematics is the most general science of the form of any world as such.

EXPERIENCE AND THE PRINCIPLES OF LOGIC

WHAT ROLE does the experience of the world play for logic—more precisely, for the sense of the principles of logic, logic of pure consequence as well as logic of truth? Pure consequence-logic raises the question of the compatibility or compossibility of propositions by virtue of their form alone and thus without any concern for truth or falsehood in the sense of conformity between a proposition and the state of affairs it is about. Inasmuch as the compossibility of propositions is a condition for truth, however, the pure logic of consequence becomes part of the formal logic of truth where, instead of considering propositions as such, one takes them in relation to states of affairs and raises the question of their conformity with them (see *FTL*, §§ 14–15, 18–20, app. III).

The principle of excluded middle may be interpreted in subjective terms[8] and formulated as follows: "When confronted with the state of affairs to which it relates, every proposition is either confirmed or disconfirmed" (*FTL*, § 77). Thus formulated, the principle of excluded middle affirms that, for every proposition, the alternative of confirmation or disconfirmation is exhaustive; it also implies that every proposition can in principle be verified, i.e., confronted with a state of affairs. This possibility subsists for every proposition, whether the confrontation has been made, whether it is feasible, or whether for technical reasons it cannot be performed.

Abstracting from the idealization which is included in the affirmation implied in the principle of excluded middle, we see clearly that the possibility does not hold for the type of proposition which is represented by the assertion, "The sum of the angles of a triangle is equal to the color red." Obviously, while grammatically correct, this sentence does not make sense. Yet it is not senseless from the point of view of pure logical grammar (*FTL*, §§ 12, 23a, 87), or because it contains a contradiction. In the purely and strictly formal perspective—the only perspective of the algebraizing and formalizing logician—the sentence must be considered as the expression of a genuine and possible proposition. If it lacks sense and is thus impossible, it is because the terms—or, as Husserl says, the "material cores"—pertaining to it have no relationship with one another.[9] They have nothing

8. On the possibility and even the necessity of two-sided analyses —subjective as well as objective—in logic, see *FTL*, §§ 8–10, and pt. II, chap. 1.

9. It is apparent that the opposition between sense and senselessness cannot be established in an absolute fashion, or once and for all. Husserl (*LI*, pp. 457–58, 518–26) distinguishes between nonsense (*Unsinn*)—e.g., "king but or similar is" (the laws of "pure logical grammar" are violated)—and counter-sense (*Widersinn*) which pertains either to a formal analytic contradiction (e.g., "this red book is not red") or to a contradiction in terms (synthetic or material counter-sense), e.g., "this square figure is round." The case of senselessness in the text above reflects a total absence of relationship among the terms. As Gaston Berger has pointed out, the opposition between sense and senselessness is repeated at different levels; on each level it assumes a specific signification which pertains to that level. See *Recherches sur les conditions de la connaissance* (Paris: Presses Universitaires de France, 1941), pp. 106–8.

to do with one another because the things to which the terms relate are not encountered in a coherent and concordant unity of possible experience. Consequently, there is not and in principle there cannot be a state of affairs with which the proposition in question can be confronted. Hence the question of truth, in the sense of conformity with a state of affairs, does not and cannot arise. Here the middle is not excluded in that the proposition in question, since it is devoid of sense, is, so to speak, below or, better, beyond, the opposition between the true and the false (*FTL,* § 90). In other words, the presupposition implicit in the principle of excluded middle, namely, that every proposition can be confronted with the state of affairs it is about, holds only for propositions in which the component terms relate to one another. Only propositions which meet that condition are considered by logic. Yet, because of the substitution of symbols for the material terms whose signification remains indeterminate in the sense we have outlined, the importance of this condition can easily be overlooked.

One need not think that a proposition like "the sum of the angles of a triangle is equal to the color red" is impossible only from the point of view of the logic of truth, for it is also impossible from the point of view of the logic of consequence or purely analytical logic. The proposition which is the theme of analytical logic is the proposition given in the "evidence of distinctness [*Evidenz der Deutlichkeit*]" (*FTL,* §§ 16–17). A proposition is given in evidence of this sort when it arises or can arise from a spontaneous synthetic activity of thought by which the component partial significations are united into an articulated significational unity which is the propositional signification itself as such. To express it in a less atomistic way, one can say that, by the spontaneous activity of the mind, partial significations are grasped each in its place and in its contributive function within the articulated unity of the total signification. The evidence of distinctness is the original conscious apprehension of the proposition, which means the conscious apprehension in which the proposition presents itself in itself ("Selbstgegebenheit"), in "flesh and blood" (*CM,* § 4). It is a conscious apprehension which is to the proposition what perception is to the material thing. Still, let us add that what makes a "personal appearance" in the evidence of distinctness is *the proposition as such,* not the state of affairs it is about, and not the agreement or conformity between the proposition and the actual or possible state of affairs. The latter is called by Husserl "evidence of clarity [*Evidenz der Klarheit*]" (*FTL*, § 16b).

As for the proposition which we are using as an example, it goes without saying that it cannot be given in evidence of distinctness. Since evidence of distinctness is the conscious apprehension by which the proposition is grasped in its ideal existence, i.e., in that specific mode of existence which properly pertains to a signification, it follows that the proposition in question does not have ideal existence, does not exist qua signification (*FTL*, § 89). Each of the words in this sentence has its own signification, but these partial significations are not united into an embracing articulated signification. When the logic of consequence considers propositions, they are grasped with evidence as having ideal existence. Despite the formalization of the symbols, it is implicitly and tacitly granted that the symbols designate terms which are in a relationship with one another. This relationship among the terms refers us back to the experience of a coherent world in the heart of which objects of all sorts have to do with one another and are linked with one another by the most various relations—the relation of agreement as well as the relation of disagreement.

The intentional origin of the proposition in the experience of the world imposes a limit on the free and arbitrary variability of the terms which can be substituted for the formalized symbols. The intentional history or genesis of the proposition is thus inscribed in the conditions under which terms can function in a proposition, conditions which are always tacitly admitted as met but are hardly ever expressly formulated. The conditions need not be rendered explicit insofar as analytical logic is constructively developed in the spirit of positivity. Since every proposition refers to a coherent world for its very existence, the presupposition of the world enters in an implicit and even dissimulated way into the logic of pure consequence, even though this logic considers only propositions as such and studies them only from the point of view of their strictly formal compatibility and incompatibility, without being at all concerned with questions of conformity between a proposition and a corresponding state of affairs.

Formal Science and Consciousness

Looking more closely at the presuppositions of logic and mathematics which we have surveyed, we recognize immediately that we are not concerned here with premises that we simply have forgotten to formulate and can establish later. What our reflections have briefly—perhaps too briefly—attempted to show is that the whole structure of mathematics and logic, i.e., the formal sciences, is founded on the experience of the world. The presupposition of the world is not a premise, nor is it an axiom which holds a well-determined place within a deductive system and leads to certain consequences. If logic and mathematics presuppose the world, it is as the source from which they spring or, better, as the nutritive matrix into which they plunge their roots, since the entities and the forms which are constructed and studied in these sciences depend for their very existence on the relation to the world.

Also, the presupposition of the world in no way functions in the manifest theoretical content of logic, even though it underlies the entire formal edifice. It is the nature of such presuppositions —which are not presuppositions in the technical sense but rather conditions of possibility, hence presuppositions in the philosophical sense—to be everywhere effective and at the same time to pass unnoticed. It is just because it is everywhere effective and that the existence and the possibility of logic depend on it that the presupposition of the world does not function as one premise among others and that no determinate place within the system of logic is assigned to it. If the presupposition of the world is everywhere effective, it is in a form hidden and qua implication enclosed in every valid and existent form, i.e., in every form in which logic is interested.

Now, the presupposition of the world is not the sole or even the most fundamental presupposition of the sort we are attempting to reflect on here. According to Husserl's analyses, the world reveals itself as the intentional correlate of acts of consciousness, above all, perceptual acts, which are organized in groups and systems with well-determined structures (*Ideas*, §§ 42, 47–51, 55, 135). In this sense, the world presents itself as relative to conscious life and, above all, to perceptual life. Hence, if logic presupposes the world, it also presupposes the constitutive consciousness of the world as intentional correlate. For this reason, the world is presupposed by logic in an equally tacit and implicit way.

But logic even presupposes consciousness in a more direct way. In effect, all operations by which numbers, sets, propositions, etc., are formed, all those by which new forms are engendered in growing complexity beginning from more elementary forms, all formalizing operations, etc., are steps in thinking. Consciousness is thus implicated everywhere. Numbers, sets, classes, propositions, etc.—in short, all of the entities of concern in logic and mathematics—reveal themselves as intentional correlates or even as products of acts of consciousness and systematically interconnected groups of acts. We have seen that every proposition—and it is also true for a number, a set, etc.—is an identical ideal object for a multiplicity of acts which relate to it, i.e., by which the ideal object is grasped as identically the same. Whether we consider a proposition statically, i.e., take it as such, or whether we study it in relation to its intentional history, i.e., from the point of view of its genesis and its origin from other propositions, we are led to specific acts of consciousness which, in view of what we have shown about the presupposition of the world by logic, must be reinserted into the totality of conscious life or transcendental subjectivity.

Just as the ultimate sense of the world can be drawn only from conscious life, one must follow a bilateral orientation and turn to logical and mathematical consciousness for a radical elucidation of the ideal entities dealt with in logic and mathematics (*FTL,* § 100). Also, these philosophical reflections on logic and mathematics can lead one—and, in fact, did lead Husserl—to the principle of phenomenological idealism, according to which all that exists and is valid exists and is valid because of certain acts and groups of acts and can derive its radical clarification and radical justification only from the analysis of the conscious life in which it is given its existence and validity (*FTL,* § 94).

4 / Edmund Husserl's Conception of Phenomenological Psychology

HUSSERL'S FREIBURG LECTURES of the summer of 1925 and selected parts of his courses of the winter of 1926–27 and the summer of 1928 are contained in *Phänomenologische Psychologie*. It may be considered a companion for both *Ideas II*[1] and *Crisis*, for it has in common with the former work a certain number of problems, themes, and theoretical conceptions which are further developed ten years afterward in *Crisis*.[2] Apart from the difference concerning the maturation of Husserl's thought and apart from preparing or anticipating *Crisis*, *Phänomenologische Psychologie* has an importance in its own right.

Crisis is subtitled *An Introduction to Phenomenological Philosophy*. Taking his departure from modern physical science, the science of Galilean style, and inquiring into its presuppositions, Husserl is gradually led through an extended analysis toward and into the dimension of transcendental phenomenology. In the lectures of 1925, on the contrary, he abides by the "natural attitude" throughout. Transcendental problems are not raised;

This was originally a critical study, under the same title, published in *Review of Metaphysics*, Vol. XIX (1966), of Husserl's *Phänomenologische Psychologie*, ed. Walter Biemel, *Husserliana* IX (The Hague: Martinus Nijhoff, 1962).

1. *Husserliana* IV (The Hague: Martinus Nijhoff, 1952). See the reports by Alfred Schutz, in *Philosophy and Phenomenological Research*, Vol. XIII (1953); and by Paul Ricoeur, in *Husserl: An Analysis of His Phenomenology* (Evanston, Ill.: Northwestern University Press, 1966).

2. See our report, "The Last Work of Edmund Husserl," in *SPP*; and chap. 2, above.

indeed, they are deliberately avoided.[3] Husserl could proceed in *Crisis* as he did because the intrinsic scientific validity of modern physics as a positive science is, of course, not questioned. The problem there concerns rather the philosophical interpretation of physics, the delimitation of its sense and meaning as determined by its various presuppositions. For its philosophical elucidation and ultimate justification, modern physics, accepted as an established positive science, motivates and even requires resort to the dimension of transcendental subjectivity.

The situation is entirely different as far as modern psychology is concerned, both in Husserl's time and, to a large measure, in our own. Without altogether dismissing experimental and physiological psychology and psychophysics, Husserl still does not accept these disciplines of recent origin as forming an established positive science even remotely comparable with physics. As the science of the mind, psychology has to account for mental accomplishments such as science, art, religion, the facts of political life, etc., in short, for culture and its history. Hence it is the task of psychology to provide the theoretical foundations for the human sciences. Insofar as mental activities and operations are involved in the phenomena dealt with by ethics, aesthetics, logic, and epistemology, philosophy has important relations with psychology. An account of the laws of correct reasoning and of scientific thought, for example, must have reference to the psychic processes involved. Modern psychology, developing in the course of the late nineteenth century, started its career with aspirations of this kind. Yet it has not fulfilled its hopes and promise, not even in incipient form. Moreover, as Husserl sees it, modern psychology is, in principle, not able to realize those aspirations, not able to become a genuine science of consciousness and mental life. What dooms it to failure is its blindness with regard to intentionality, the essential characteristic of the mind and all its activities and operations. This blindness has prevented modern psychology from taking possession of a vast domain of research to which it has a rightful claim. Intentionality, therefore, must be made the central theme of all psychological theory.

3. Husserl does attempt the transition from phenomenological psychology to transcendental phenomenology in the *Encyclopaedia Britannica* article and in the Amsterdam lectures, which are not part of but addenda to *Phänomenologische Psychologie*.

Therefore, rather than submitting an existing science, i.e., physics, to a philosophical critique, as in *Crisis, Husserl has first to found and establish the science of psychology as a positive discipline.* This he sets out to do in *Phänomenologische Psychologie,* and for this reason he remains within the natural attitude. On numerous occasions Husserl has spoken of the radical reform of psychology implied in his phenomenology. *Phänomenologische Psychologie* gives a concrete idea of that reformed psychology. Its foundation and establishment require extended methodological considerations. "Method" is to be understood here not as a technique of research but in the etymological sense, as a means of access to a field of research, that is, these considerations belong to the theory of science. First, it is necessary to demarcate the place which the subject matter of psychology holds within the total realm of reality. Then it is possible to delineate the type of problems which arise for the science of psychology and to define, or at least to pretrace, the theoretical orientation of that science. In addition, there are considerations involving the prerequisites of theoretical explanation as such— prerequisites which, because of their generality, have validity for psychology no less than for any other science. Rather than presenting the reformed psychology in a straightforward manner, as would be done in a manual, Husserl devotes a considerable part of his effort to laying its foundations through considerations which are philosophical in nature, though they remain on "this side" of the transcendental dimension.

As we have mentioned, *Phänomenologische Psychologie* contains the text of university lectures. This explains the frequent repetitions and also what seem to be digressions. Probably, Husserl desired in those lectures to communicate as much of phenomenology as he could, while abiding by the natural attitude. He has entered into very detailed expositions and developments of special phenomenological problems and theories, with the result that the general trend of the presentation is at times in danger of obfuscation. In what follows we shall attempt to present Husserl's ideas in a more centralized way than he has done himself. This will compel us to mention only very briefly, or even to omit mentioning altogether, some topics which are of great importance in themselves but which cannot adequately be treated except within a context of their own. For the same reason, we shall abstain from developing the transition from phenomenological psychology to transcendental phenomenology.

EIDETIC PSYCHOLOGY

PART OF THE MENTIONED CRITICISM of the psychology of the late nineteenth century was formulated by Dilthey in his *Ideen über eine beschreibende und zergliedernde Psychologie* of 1894.[4] Contemporary psychology emulates the example of the exact natural sciences, especially atomistic physics. It dissects or decomposes psychic and mental life into well-defined last elements and, by means of hypotheses and inferences, endeavors to establish causal connections between them and to construct a thoroughgoing causal context which transcends what is given in immediate experience. According to Dilthey, such a procedure is fully justified and even necessary in the natural sciences, because the facts of nature as encountered in external experience are given as *partes extra partes* in spatial disconnectedness and separation, so that the connection between them—precisely because it is not directly experienced—must be established in a constructive way. This procedure, however, is utterly inadequate where psychology and the human sciences are concerned. In inner experience, mental life is directly and immediately given as a thoroughgoing context (*Zusammenhang*).

Over and against the "dissecting" psychology, not so much to replace but rather to supplement it, Dilthey advocates a descriptive psychology, whose central theme is the very context of personal mental life. No idea, feeling, mood, hope, desire, etc., is ever given as an isolated fact. On the contrary, they arise within a psychological milieu, out of an all-encompassing context, as motivated by other mental states and in turn motivating still further ones. Moreover, descriptive psychology, in Dilthey's sense, is concerned with the establishment of typologies—a typology of particular mental states, of the connections between them, and finally of total contexts of mental life, that is, of personalities. This kind of psychology may well provide a basis for the human sciences, insofar as it permits us to refer the decision of a statesman, the creation of a poet or other artist, the conception of a philosophical system or a scientific theory, and the like, to the person concerned in his totality, and to show how those events

4. *Gesammelte Schriften,* Vol. V (Leipzig and Berlin: Teubner, 1924).

emerge by necessity from a total context of personal mental life.

Husserl not only endorses Dilthey's criticism of contemporary psychology but furthermore expresses deep appreciation for his insights and intuitions. Yet Dilthey's ideas seem to be beset by a paradoxical difficulty. Dilthey speaks of necessity with respect to individual personal contexts. By its very sense, necessity presupposes universal laws referring to general forms and their concatenations, that is, to pure possibilities as such. The individual can partake of necessity insofar, but only insofar, as it proves to be one possible case among others, hence, insofar as it is seen with reference to the realm of possibilities. To partake of necessity, the individual case must appear as a specification of a general structure standing under universal laws. Dilthey's typology, on the contrary, can yield no more than an empirical comparative psychology, of a rather old style, which sets forth diverse types of persons, characters, temperaments, and the like. It may lead to a morphology or "natural history" of mental life in its various forms. However, here as everywhere, a morphology or natural history, no matter how significant it undoubtedly is, must be supplemented by and grounded on rational nomothetic explanation. For psychology to be founded and established as an explanatory science, i.e., a theoretical discipline, principles of theoretical explanation are required that can be derived only from a conceptual system. It is precisely the latter which Husserl finds lacking in Dilthey.

Therefore, the very first task is the disclosure of the essential nature of consciousness and mental life or, as Husserl says, its *eidos*. This Platonic term must, of course, be stripped of all speculative connotations and must not be understood in the terms of any metaphysical hypostasis. It is meant to denote a set of characters or structural elements which belong to consciousness insofar as it is possible, either quite in general or as consciousness of a certain sort, such as perception, memory, mathematical thinking, etc. For numbers, sets, mathematical propositions, or theories to be apprehended, the apprehending subjective acts must exhibit a well-defined invariant structure, and the same holds for the correlative objects of every type and category. Throughout, a strict correlation obtains between the essential nature of objects of a certain category and the essential structure of acts of consciousness, if these acts are to be apprehensions of those objects. It does not matter whether the subjects experiencing the acts in question are real human beings or deities, demons, or whatever other conscious beings may be imagined. In other words, it does not matter whether or not those acts are even experienced at all, because eidetic truths are not about actual occurrences but concern only that which is possible and what essentially and necessarily belongs to the possible. Eidetic truths express, if one may say so, that without which the possible would not be possible. Thus no conclusion as to actual occurrence can be derived from an eidetic truth. On the other hand, if acts do actually occur, they must conform to eidetic structures both universal and specific, since whatever is actual must fulfill the eidetic conditions of its possibility. If individual occurrences partake of necessity, it is on account of their conformity to *eidē* and eidetic structures.

In this sense Husserl speaks of an a priori with respect to consciousness and mental life. Accordingly, he advocates an a priori psychology as a whole. The meaning of the a priori is defined by its independence with regard to acts actually experienced, whereas the latter are dependent on the a priori for their qualification and structure but not for the actuality of their occurrence. The central ascertainment of a priori or eidetic psychology is the intentionality of consciousness in all its ramifications, the conception of the essence of every act of consciousness as a consciousness of something, as directed to an object. Intentionality is the essence or *eidos* of mental life and consciousness. And intentionality undergoes corresponding specification correlative to the various types of objects encountered, while retaining throughout the general character of directedness. To Dilthey, however, the notion of intentionality remained unknown.[5] Therefore, his respect and admiration notwithstanding, Husserl does not take his departure from Dilthey's work. Instead, he refers to his own beginnings in the *Logical Investigations*.[6]

5. This is not the place to enter into a discussion of Brentano's contribution toward the theory of intentionality or of Husserl's advance beyond Brentano. See Ludwig Landgrebe, "Husserl's Phänomenologie und die Motive zu ihrer Umbildung," *Revue internationale de philosophie*, Vol. I (1939); and Herbert Spiegelberg, *The Phenomenological Movement* (The Hague: Martinus Nijhoff, 1960), Vol. I, 17 and III C 2c. As to the development of the theory of intentionality in four of Husserl's major writings which appeared in his lifetime, see Quentin Lauer, *Phénoménologie de Husserl* (Paris: Presses Universitaires de France, 1955).

6. According to Biemel (p. xxi), only a few self-interpretations of the kind offered here are found in Husserl's manuscripts. This

To be sure, the *Logical Investigations* are not concerned with psychological questions but with the philosophical clarification of formal logic and formal mathematics from the subjective point of view, that is, the point of view of the acts and operations of consciousness involved in those formal domains and the essential structure of those acts. The results obtained, however, prove amenable to translation into psychological terms. If properly generalized and consistently developed, they lead to the very idea of eidetic psychology.

That idea is basic for the radical reform Husserl proposes for psychology. In the volume under discussion, he is concerned with laying the foundations for the eidetic part of psychology, not with its several empirical disciplines. Empirical psychology is by no means ruled out. Eidetic laws grounded in eidetic structures constitute no more than a framework within which there is room for contingent varieties. Empirical research concerning such varieties, especially the regularities and laws of actual occurrences, is perfectly legitimate from the perspective of eidetic psychology and is even called for by it. However, it must be stressed that, in all empirical work, one has to rely on and explicitly avail oneself of the results attained in eidetic or a priori psychology. To express it differently, in every scientific account of matters of fact, allowance must be made for the essential conditions of the possibility of those very matters of fact.

Psychology is not the only science to require an eidetic discipline as its foundation. Husserl refers to the development in modern times of the empirical physical sciences, a development contingent on and made possible by the simultaneous elaboration of rational sciences like pure mathematics, geometry, kinematics, and abstract physics. These eidetic or a priori sciences are not concerned with actual events in nature but, rather, with what essentially and necessarily pertains to any possible nature as such. They are concerned with nature under the aspect of its mere possibility. Nature is here understood in the specific sense of modern science as a spatiotemporal manifold or system. Because the mentioned rational or eidetic sciences concern themselves with possibilities and essential necessities, thus laying bare and formulating the a priori of corporeal, i.e., spatiotemporally

---

self-interpretation, as well as the one in *FTL*, § 27, illuminates not only the *Logical Investigations* but also the remarkable continuity in the development of Husserl's thought.

extended, nature, their results have universal validity and apply to actual facts and events to be studied empirically (as in, e.g., astronomy). The rational sciences of nature provide the empirical physical sciences with the indispensable explanatory principles, thereby making the latter rational themselves. Eidetic psychology is to have significance of a similar kind for the empirical branches of psychology.

There is an analogy between mathematics and eidetic psychology, but that analogy must not be overstressed. To be sure, mathematics must not be narrowly construed as a science of quantities and magnitudes only. Rather, it must be understood as dealing with form and order of any kind. If mathematics is applicable to nature, it is not because facts and events in nature are subject to possible quantification, but because nature requires for its very possibility a formal framework and a system of laws (however specified and varying from one possible nature to another). This formal aspect of nature is the subject matter of the mathematical natural sciences. In an analogous way, eidetic psychology is concerned with the ideally possible forms pertaining to the mental domain; it discloses formal structures which, by necessity, are exhibited by concrete mental events and actual psychological occurrences.

Still, there is a considerable difference between eidetic psychology and the mathematical disciplines. The latter proceed in a deductive way, deriving all their theorems from a small number of axioms. Deductive inferences, if they play any role at all in eidetic psychology, are certainly neither its principal nor its characteristic procedure. Moreover, eidetic psychology does not form its concepts by way of construction, but, on the contrary, from descriptive analysis. Its concepts retain an intuitive and descriptive character and lay themselves open to "viewing." [7] For that reason, Husserl is reluctant to characterize eidetic psychology as the "mathematics of the mind," a characterization which could suggest an emulation of the mathematical sciences. Perhaps justice is done to the several aspects of the situation by saying that *eidetic psychology* is the *logic of the mind and of empirical psychology,* as the mentioned mathematical sciences

7. Husserl uses the expressions "anschaulich" and "intuitif." The latter term and its English equivalent must be stripped of all "intuitionistic" and kindred connotations. The term "viewing" must, in turn, be properly generalized so as not to be understood in the optical sense only.

are the logic of nature (understood in the specific sense of modern science) and of the empirical physical sciences. At any event, eidetic psychology in Husserl's sense must not be misconstrued as a revival of the "rational psychology" of the eighteenth century, which Kant uprooted. The latter proceeded in a constructive and deductive way and had a speculative-metaphysical orientation.

We come to the highly original, and at first perhaps surprising, result that concepts have both a priori status and a descriptive and intuitive content. This view of Husserl is not confined to the concepts of eidetic psychology but has quite general significance. Concepts of such a nature are arrived at by the method of ideation or free variation. To obtain the *eidos* of red, color in general, corporeal and material thing, act of consciousness at large, or act of consciousness of a special kind, e.g., perception, and the like, one starts from any arbitrarily chosen case and submits it to free variation. Varieties are thus generated which may be merely imaginary. Even if the initial case is an actual one, it is considered merely as an example, as one possible variety among others equally possible; its actuality is entirely irrelevant. The purpose of this method is to ascertain the limits which the variation must not transgress, in other words, to disclose a structure or set of structures, invariant throughout the process of variation, which must be exhibited by every variety, actual or freely imagined, for that variety to partake of, or fall under, the *eidos* in question. Such an invariant structure defines an *eidos*. Concepts resulting in this manner are universal and a priori, since they refer to mere possibilities. Because of the manner in which they are formed, they are at the same time of a descriptive and of an intuitive nature. In the present context we cannot go beyond these few sketchy and superficial hints; we may refer to the more detailed exposition of the method of free variation in imagination which we have given elsewhere.[8]

The World of Primordial Experience

MENTAL AND PSYCHOLOGICAL LIFE in all its multifarious forms is encountered in connection with particular beings which,

8. *FC*, pp. 190 ff.; for the application of that method to the phenomenology of perception, see *ibid.*, pp. 204 ff.

whatever else they may be, have corporeality and are mundane existents. That is, they appear in and belong to the real world, the world as given in perceptual experience, or, as Husserl calls it in *Crisis* and also occasionally in the present volume, the life-world. Psychology relates itself to the real world, although it deals only with special mundane existents and, moreover, concerns itself merely with certain of their aspects.

In the perceptual world, the mental and the corporeal are not given in clear separation from one another. They are intertwined and interwoven, as appears from the fact that mental life pertains to spatially extended beings. Far from being a matter of pure experience, the demarcation between the mental and the corporeal is the result of theoretical work in the service and under the guidance of specific theoretical interests. Such a demarcation is brought about by certain methodological procedures which presuppose the perceptual world because they operate on it. The perceptual world as given in pretheoretical experience—the everyday world in which we live and pursue all our activities of whatever kind and, correlatively, the pretheoretical experience of that world—underlies all sciences dealing with reality as a presupposition, necessary though not sufficient, because of the mentioned specific methodological procedures involved in the constitution of the several sciences. For the philosophical clarification and foundation of all sciences, including psychology, one must go back to the perceptual world of everyday life and start by a descriptive analysis of that world, perhaps not a complete analysis but one which discloses at least some of its most general outlines.

Husserl's expressions, "the world of pretheoretical experience" or of "pure experience," indicate that the world in question must not be mistaken for nature in the sense of modern science, since nature in that sense is itself the result of a special method. Purity, as here understood, implies even more, namely, the exclusion from the description to be undertaken of all products and accomplishments of the specific activities of thought, especially logical thought. Activities, such as conceptualization, formation of multiplicities and sets by means of explicit colligation, predicative judging, and so on, presuppose materials on which they operate and which, therefore, must be given through a kind of experience which precedes those activities—an experience which, for that reason, is called primordial, prepredicative, or merely receptive. For example, gold is given in primordial experience and so is the color yellow. But the logical state of affairs formulated in the proposition "gold is yellow," in which "gold" functions as subject and "yellow" as predicate, is not a matter of primordial experience but the product of predicative thinking. In operating on materials provided by primordial experience, predicative thinking gives rise to or constitutes special correlates of its own which pertain to an order higher than that yielded by primordial experience. Because they presuppose the data of primordial experience in operating on them, the specific activities of logical thought can be accounted for only with reference to primordial experience and its yieldings.[9] From the pretranscendental point of view, by which we here abide, primordial experience and the objects given in it prove the ultimate foundation and presupposition of all logical thought, all theoretical elaborations, hence all sciences.

Primordial experience is basically perceptual experience and, of course, also comprises the derivative modes of perception, namely, memory (the object of which has the sense of having been given in earlier perceptual experience) and expectancy (anticipation of future presentation in perceptual experience). Perceptual experience may, therefore, be understood in a broad sense as synonymous with primordial experience.

In that experience, particular things are given—houses, dogs, human beings, and the like, and whatever properties, attributes, and qualities they exhibit. However, none of those things is given in isolation. The house is surrounded by a garden, it lies in a street, in short, it is perceptually given in a certain environment. Not all parts of the latter are actually perceived (the street extends further than we can see), nor are all of them completely determined by the memory of previous actual perceptual experience (we do not know what we shall encounter when we go along the street which we never went along before). However, we feel free to go along the street to become acquainted with it. Quite in general, we are aware of our freedom to explore wider and ever wider surroundings of the house by proceeding in any direction. Yet, however far we proceed, our exploration never comes to an end. At every phase we are confronted with some particular thing in its environment. Because of the continuity of

9. This account is the topic of *Experience and Judgment*, which has the significant subtitle, "Investigations into the Genealogy of Logic" (translation altered).

the process of exploration, all those environments hang together both with one another and with the environment of the house from which we started.

The house is not only perceived within its environment in the narrower sense, its perceptual field. To the perceptual experience of the house also belong references to and awareness of ever widening surroundings or, as Husserl calls it, an *indefinitely continuing open horizon* which is nothing other than the *world of primordial experience*. Because that horizon encompasses all special environments of all particular things, there is only *one world* to which all particular things belong and from whose perspective they are, all of them, experienced. Because of its horizonal character, the awareness of the world is attached to the perceptual experience of some particular thing. In other words, the world is not experienced except from the vantage point of some mundane existent. On the other hand, the latter always presents itself under the all-encompassing world-horizon, and this determines the sense of its mundanity.

As a rule, perceptual experience develops unbrokenly and harmoniously. Things continue to present themselves as they have done thus far. Earlier phases of the perceptual process are confirmed by later ones. This also holds for intersubjective communication. On the grounds of their perceptual experience, others confirm our findings and vice versa. *The world of primordial experience is one and the same for everyone,* at least for everyone who belongs to a certain sociohistorical group. *It is the world as it presents itself in intrinsically coherent, consistent, and congruous perceptual experience, both subjective and intersubjective.* Occasionally the harmony is broken, conflicts and discrepancies arise. What had been taken as veridical perceptual experience turns out to be an illusion. Things prove to be different from what they have thus far appeared to be. The findings of our perceptual experience, though coherent in themselves, are contested by others—and we disregard here additional complications which arise as a consequence of the distinction between normality and anomalies such as deafness, blindness, color blindness, and the like. Occurrences of this sort, however, concern only particular things, never the world as a whole. It may become doubtful whether a certain thing is truly and really what it appears, and has for a long time appeared, to be. However, the world itself never becomes doubtful, but is throughout all perceptual experience silently—i.e., inexplicitly and unformulatedly

—taken for granted as a matter of course. This silent and unquestioned acceptance of the world defines what Husserl means by the natural attitude.

In the course of perceptual experience, discrepancies and conflicts of the mentioned kind have always been resolved. The perceptual process has necessitated more or less far-reaching and radical revisions, as a consequence of which its unity, coherence, and congruity with itself have been restored. On the basis of our past experience as a whole, we anticipate—Husserl speaks of a horizonal presumption (*Horizont-Präsumtion*)—that all horizons may be opened up and actually explored, that all indeterminacies may be determined in progressive perceptual exploration, that all discrepancies may be resolved, that the necessary corrections will not be infinite in number but will prove to be ways along which the perceptual process tends toward its definitive form, when it would no longer require further revisions. By idealization, this universal anticipation, which is a matter of primordial experience, is transformed into the presumption, underlying all sciences as one of their presuppositions, of one objective world which has its true being behind and beneath all deceptive appearances and is accessible to knowledge—one whose true condition can be disclosed by theoretical determination and experiments, by way of progressive, though perhaps only asymptotic, approximation. This may serve as an illustration of the fundamental and necessary rootedness and motivation of the presuppositions of science in the primordial experience of the world of everyday life, though they transcend that experience because of the idealizations involved.

The world of primordial experience exhibits throughout a universal typical style, not merely as a matter of contingent fact but by eidetic necessity. Applying the method of free variation in imagination, we disclose a set of structures and forms which delineate what necessarily belongs to every possible world of possible primordial experience, in other words, the a priori invariant structure of every possible world as such. Among those forms, space and time must be mentioned first. We may not know what kind of things we will encounter when we proceed into an as yet unexplored region of the all-encompassing horizon; we are free to contrive fantastic things pertaining to fictitious "worlds." Still, whatever those creations of our fancy may be, however those things thus far unknown may look, insofar as they are imagined real things they will present *some* spatial shape and stand in *some* spatial relations to other real things whether actual or creations of our fancy. It is literally true that by no stretch of the imagination can the world be stripped of its spatiality. The same applies to temporality.

What has been said before concerning the appearance of every perceptual thing under the all-encompassing world-horizon as well as concerning the oneness and, therefore, unity of the world holds a priori and with eidetic necessity. By allowing for space and time, the unity of the world, initially introduced in a rather general and unspecified manner, undergoes a first specification. A further specification concerns causality. Things have typical ways of regularly behaving under certain conditions, especially conditions of change in their circumstances. Such typical ways of behavior are expressed by the properties attributed to things—mechanical properties (elasticity), thermal properties (good or poor conductivity), magnetic, electric, and other properties. Taken together, those properties define the causal style of a thing, and its unity and identity throughout all changes it may undergo depend on this style. By the same token, the dependence of a thing on what happens in its circumstances appears as an eidetic or a priori necessity. The circumstantial horizon thus proves a causal horizon. Of course, the specific behavior or the law of such behavior in a concrete case or type of concrete cases can be discovered only through empirical observation. Eidetic necessity reaches no further than the general principle that things regularly display a typical behavior concomitantly with changes in their circumstances. By virtue of that principle, the unity of the world is further specified as a contextual unity which is more than the unity of an aggregate—which it would be on the basis of spatiotemporality alone.

Particular existents are possible only insofar as they conform to eidetic necessities. Where there are mundane existents, they must conform in general to the invariant structures pertaining to all possible worlds as well as to the specific invariants of the special world to which they belong, e.g., the actual world. In the latter, things pertaining to several types are encountered. The actual world is subdivided or articulated into certain regions, such as those of inanimate things, living beings, beings endowed with psychic life, and so on. Each such region exhibits a specific typicality of its own; to each belongs a regional *eidos* or system of regional *eidē*, likewise to be disclosed by the method of free variation. All those more specific *eidē*, however, stand under the general ones which delineate the necessary structure either of a world at large or of the special world in question. That is, every thing, object, or entity of any region whatever must fit into that world and reflect the system of invariant structures essential to it. Conversely, in order to disclose the universal invariant of the world, we start, as we must, from some example which pertains to a certain region; the appropriate variation of that example will yield the universal form of the world. In this connection, the question arises as to whether any region may find a place within every possible world or whether the essential structure of a certain world implies principles of compatibility and incompatibility as far as special regions are concerned.

The disclosure of the invariant structure of the given world as well as of any possible world of primordial experience is the subject matter of a specific discipline, namely, a universal descriptive science of the world at large. Its task is to establish and explicate the "natural concept of a world" (*natürlicher Weltbegriff*), to lay bare the a priori of the life-world, to develop an ontology of the life-world.[10] The universal science of the world has precedence over all the special sciences related to the several mundane regions; the special sciences rely on the universal both for their differentiation and for their integration into a systematic context. Within the theoretical framework established by the universal science of the world, the thematics of each of the special sciences is defined and delineated—i.e., the kind of problems it has to deal with and the theoretical orientation it has to take. This also holds for the science of psychology, whose foundations can be laid only with reference to the world of primordial experience and its invariant structure.

As formal invariants of the world, space and time are among the necessary existential conditions of all mundane beings. The latter can exist only as enduring in time, extended in space, and having their places within a framework of spatiotemporal relations. This also holds in a special way for psychic occurrences and mental phenomena of every kind, insofar as they are encountered in the world and belong to it. Intrinsically, however, the psychic and mental are altogether devoid of spatiality.

10. This terminology is used in *Crisis*, §§ 37, 51. In § 36, Husserl distinguishes the a priori related to the life-world (*lebensweltliches Apriori*) from the objective logico-mathematical a priori. The latter presupposes the former and arises from it by means of the specific operation of idealization.

Consequently, they can partake of spatiality only in an indirect or secondary way. Yet, if they are to belong to the world, they must in some way partake of spatiality. Accordingly, mental and psychic facts cannot be encountered in the world and cannot have the sense of mundanity unless they are connected with or attached and annexed to corporeal things.

Corporeality, therefore, has a certain privilege or priority with regard to the mental and the psychic. All mundane beings are also corporeal things, but not all corporeal things are animated beings. The latter undergo, and are even anticipated as destined someday to undergo, the transformation into inorganic matter. From the mundane point of view, death does not mean the separation of the soul from the body, with the soul's assuming some other form of existence as a real entity within the world. Death as a real mundane event means the annihilation of the soul as a soul within the world. If the doctrine of the immortality of the soul is not to be at variance with the universal experience of the world, it must have a meaning other than a mundane meaning.

CULTURAL OBJECTS

ANY CULTURAL OBJECT indicates the presence of the mental within the world, i.e., as attached to a corporeal thing. Houses, fields, gardens, pieces of furniture, tools and instruments of every kind, paintings, sculptures, other products of artistic creation, and the like are cultural objects. Literary documents of religious, philosophical, scientific, etc., content also belong here. Such objects are, on one hand, inanimate corporeal things, existing in space and time and possessing all the properties characteristic of things made of one or another kind of material. On the other hand, these objects are meant to serve specific purposes; they are to be handled in well-defined ways so as to yield results desired in certain situations. In the case of literary documents, a meaning is conveyed by the corporeal thing. Quite in general, corporeal things become cultural objects owing to the meaning or sense (*Sinn*) bestowed upon them. The cultural sense is not merely superadded to, or superimposed upon, the corporeal thing. Husserl speaks of the sense as impressed (*eingedrückt*). That is, the corporeal thing is permeated, imbued, and impregnated with sense. Consequently, an abstractive process is required for distinguishing the two strata, the corporeal thing as carrier of sense and the sense itself as carried by it.

Obviously, cultural objects refer to the subjective activities in which they originate. They refer to subjects who have certain intentions, pursue certain purposes, and realize their intentions by shaping corporeal things to fit their purposes. Differently expressed, those intentions and purposes are incarnated in corporeal things which are thereby transformed into cultural objects. The reference is not only to the makers but also to the users of cultural objects, that is, to those who understand and endorse the purposes to be served and who, in using them in the appropriate manner, avail themselves of the tools, instruments, etc., produced by others. These persons are not referred to as isolated individuals, however, but as members of a society which considers the purposes in question as vital or, at least, approves of them, and which assigns well-defined functions and roles to the makers and users of the several cultural objects. By its very sense, every cultural object refers to a particular society, the circumstances and conditions under which that society lives, and a system of purposes recognized by it.

It would be erroneous to conclude, from the essential reference of cultural objects to subjective activities, that the sense impressed on a cultural object as such is itself a psychic fact or event—in other words, to identify the sense with the psychic activity in which it originates. Every such activity belongs to an individual person and to him alone; while, on the contrary, the sense, once it has been impressed on a corporeal thing, acquires an independence and objectivity of its own. Fixed in a corporeal thing, the sense becomes a character properly belonging to the cultural object thus constituted. The latter is generally accessible. It can be grasped and understood in a variety of modes by everyone; at first by everyone who belongs to a certain society. The objectivity in question here is intersubjective objectivity in a special sense, namely, objectivity with respect to and for the given society. Even after that society has ceased to exist, archaeologists and historians may reconstruct the sense the cultural objects had for it. In one way, the situation may be compared to the case of a mathematical theorem which, after it has been discovered and expressed, is, so to speak, emancipated from the psychic processes of its discoverer and becomes "public property," i.e., accessible to everyone. Both the meaning of a mathematical theorem (or, generally, any proposition whatever) and the sense of a cultural object denote an "irreal" or ideal entity related to a real corporeal thing. Because of that attachment, the ideal entity may have effects in the real world by motivating and stimulating cultural activities of several kinds, as when instruments are improved, scientific discoveries further developed, and the like.

We are thus led to the distinction between the psychic (*Seelisches*), which is subjective in a preeminent sense, and the mental (*Geistiges*), which is objective with regard to the psychic.[11] Distinction in no way purports separation or severance. One of Husserl's most significant contributions, consequential also for the reform of psychology, consists precisely in establishing the distinction between the psychic and the mental and, at the same time, setting forth the essential connection between them.

The philosophical foundation of the human sciences, especially the historical sciences, must take its departure from the theory of cultural objects. Husserl's phenomenological psychology thus provides the theoretical means for realizing Dilthey's intentions.

Embodied Psychic Life

Next we have to consider phenomena of a different kind which also indicate the presence of the psychic within the world of primordial experience. We have in view our encountering fellow men as beings like ourselves and our encountering animals as living creatures, in other words, our experience of extended objects located in space as animated or organismic.[12]

Each of us has originary experience only of his own somatic body. The body of the other is not encountered as animate in the immediate sense; rather, it is originarily grasped as mere body and only subsequently constituted as animated. The organismic body is, for each of us, the center of his perceptual

11. On p. 114, Husserl uses the expression "objektivierte Geistigkeit."

12. There are no English equivalents corresponding to the German distinction between *Körper* and *Leib*. We render *Leib* by the expressions "organism," "organismic body," and "somatic body."

environment in a double sense. First, for each of us it is with respect to his own organism that the world is oriented in terms of the distinctions between right and left, near and far, before and behind, etc. Second, it is by means of his sensory organs that each of us perceives mundane objects of every kind, including animals and fellow human beings. Our experience of our own somatic body is originary insofar as we not only see a hand moving in space, i.e., describing a trajectory as any inanimate thing can, but also are proprioceptively and kinesthetically aware that we are moving our hand, availing ourselves of and living in our own somatic body, of having some of its organs at our disposal, at least to some degree. Such originary experience is for everyone confined to his own organism. The apperception of bodies other than one's own as somatic, i.e., as organisms of other persons or animals, requires an appresentative transfer by analogy from our own somatic experience to what is at first given only as a corporeal thing.[13]

Data of somatic experience are psychic facts of a lower order, as are sense data of all kinds, including sensuous feelings. Psychic facts of a lower order are characterized by passivity and anonymity, i.e., absence of participation and involvement on the part of the ego. In contrast, psychic facts of a higher order, which are psychic in the proper and preeminent sense, are conceived by Husserl as centered in and emanating from the ego. Such acts as those of perceiving, paying attention, comparing, distinguishing, generalizing, theorizing, explicitly valuing, deliberately willing, and the like are thus contrasted to mere sensing, liking, or striving. Here also belong all those activities in which cultural objects originate and, furthermore, the processes involved in ideation or free variation. Ideation has been presented as a methodological procedure for the disclosure of invariant structures and forms essentially belonging to the world and for the foundation of eidetic psychology. It can—and must —also be made the subject matter of psychological study, for it is a subjective activity.

Whereas the facts of somatic experience relate directly to corporeal things or parts of them and can therefore be said to be

13. The theory of appresentative transfer by analogy, briefly referred to here, has been developed by Husserl in the Fifth Cartesian Meditation; see the detailed criticism of that theory by Alfred Schutz in *Collected Papers* (The Hague: Martinus Nijhoff, 1962–66), Vol. III (1966).

located in space, the case of psychic facts of the higher order is different. They cannot be located in any part of an organismic body or in such a body as a whole, which is to say that they have no direct relationship to corporeality or spatiality. Still, they are ascribed to living beings possessing somatic bodies, living beings like ourselves, our fellow men, and, perhaps, animals, because they are performed by them. Psychic acts of a higher order, therefore, partake of corporeality and spatiality only indirectly and secondarily. More precisely, their partaking is by way of mediation; the mediating role is played by the somatic body. The situation can be clarified by distinguishing two senses of the term "animation" (*Beseelung*). In one sense, "animation" denotes somatic experiences owing to which the corporeal body is an organism. In the other sense, the organism itself is said to be animated by psychic acts of the higher order which specifically pertain to the ego or person.

By partaking of spatiality, either directly or by way of mediation, the whole psychic domain acquires the sense of mundanity. All psychic acts are events or occurrences in the real world of primordial experience. Mundanity means not only spatiality and situation within a spatiotemporal network but also context by causality, which is defined as the typical and regular concomitance of certain events and changes with other occurrences. Causality is inductive and empirical; that is, on the basis of previous experiences, we expect certain events to occur because certain others are occurring or have occurred. Such expectancies are, of course, always in need of being confirmed by further actual experience. As a principle essentially pertaining to mundanity, causality cannot be confined to inanimate things. Rather, it must apply to the whole world of primordial experience and to all mundane, i.e., directly or indirectly spatialized, existents comprised by this world. Hence the principle of causality extends to the psychic domain as well. Psychic acts are, in fact, observed to occur, with typical regularity, concomitantly with somatic and other events. For such connections to be possible, the psychic domain itself must exhibit typical regularities of inductive character like those which obtain within the somatic and, generally, the corporeal domains.

Here we are at the foundation of traditional modern psychology whose somaticopsychological orientation proves to be motivated by findings of primordial experience. It is perfectly legitimate to investigate inductive regularities within the psychological domain as well as to establish empirical laws concerning causal connections and relations between somatic occurrences and psychological acts. Whatever the legitimacy of those investigations, their results do not prejudice the questions of whether the soul, i.e., the person, has unity only by inductive causality or whether it also has unity of a different kind, of which the unity by inductive causality is but a secondary and, so to speak, external manifestation. Another question is whether, besides inductive causality, there is not a specifically psychological causality, namely, motivation. Finally, we should ask whether psychological acts have not an essential nature of their own, for which allowance must also be made in investigations along psychosomatic lines. None of these questions has ever been raised by traditional modern psychology. Because of the prejudice that modern physics represents the prototype and model of all science, it has been taken for granted that the psychic domain is of the same structure and constitution as the corporeal one—the latter being taken as conceived of in modern physics. That prejudice on which it has based itself since its very beginning, and the ensuing consequences, are the reasons for the failure of traditional modern psychology.

PERCEPTUAL INTENTIONALITY

THUS FAR PSYCHIC AND MENTAL LIFE has been considered under the aspect of its mundanity. However, since the world itself and all that it comprises are given to us through psychic and mental life, psychology must also do justice to that life as the medium of access to the world and mundane existents and, quite generally, to objects of every kind. Psychology must account for objects of every description presenting themselves and being experienced through acts of consciousness and, conversely, for the presentational and objectivating function of those acts. A paradoxical situation arises here, insofar as the acts of consciousness through which we have access to the world themselves belong to that world as experienced by persons, i.e., as mundane existents in the sense explained before. That paradox motivates the transition to transcendental phenomenology, a transition which begins with the transcendental phenomenological reduction.

Abiding in the natural attitude, we are endeavoring to lay the foundations of psychology as the universal science of mundane conscious life. In order to disclose this subjective life in all its purity and under all of its aspects, including its presentational and objectivating functions, we are required to perform *the psychological phenomenological reduction*—which is to be distinguished from the transcendental phenomenological reduction. As a rule, we normally find ourselves confronted with the world and mundane objects as simply there. We are interested in becoming acquainted with their several qualities, properties, and attributes. The existence of those objects and of the world at large is taken for granted and simply, i.e., without formulation and inexplicitly, accepted as a matter of course. The phenomenological reduction consists in inhibiting that acceptance, in putting out of action the unquestioned belief in the existence of the world. In no way does this mean negating the existence of the world, doubting it, or holding it as probable only. Rather than being modalized in any sense, that belief is neutralized and no use is made of it. We no longer proceed on the basis of the world as simply accepted. Our interests shift from the world and mundane objects to the experiencing consciousness which, as long as it is investigated from the psychological point of view, retains the sense of mundanity. Our exclusive theme under the phenomenological reduction is conscious life itself and whatever pertains to it in any sense. Under the latter heading fall the objects perceived and experienced but, of course, only to the extent to which, and such as, they present themselves. Under the phenomenological reduction, our concern is not with objects per se, with objects as they really are in themselves, but rather with objects as meant and intended; they must be taken into consideration exactly and only as they are meant and intended.[14] Accordingly, phenomenological psychology proceeds along strictly descriptive lines. No feature actually pertaining to an act of consciousness can be disregarded; conversely, nothing must be imputed to or foisted on an act that the latter does not actually exhibit.

Approaching perceptual consciousness under the phenomenological reduction, we begin by observing that every real thing perceived may, and does, appear in a variety of manners of

14. The terms "meaning" and "intending" must be construed broadly enough to include perceptual modes.

presentation. As we move with respect to the thing, or have it move, or do both, the thing presents itself from different sides, under changing aspects and perspectives, in varying orientations as to the right, the left, near, far, and so on. Such variation of the manner of presentation and appearance concerns not only the shape of the thing but also all of its qualities, e.g., the chromatic ones. Every particular appearance of a real thing is one-sided and partial insofar as the thing presents itself under a certain aspect rather than another under which it could appear as well, and also because the thing possesses properties and attributes which are not given in direct sense experience through the perception in question but may be given in that way through further perceptions. To the thing perceived is related a perceptual process in the course of which various appearances succeed one another; all of them are appearances of the same thing, differences between them notwithstanding. The perceptual process also exhibits a specific unity of its own. All presentations and appearances which it comprises enter into a synthesis with one another, by virtue of which they acquire the sense of appearances of the same thing. To be possible, such a synthesis requires the appearances in question to fit with one another. A mere accumulation of appearances, arbitrarily chosen and combined, does not yield the unity of a thing for a sustained perceptual process.

The distinction between that which is given and the variety of ways in which it is given extends beyond perceptual consciousness of merely corporeal things. My fellow man, e.g., experiences his somatic body in a different manner than that in which it is given to me, though both of us have in view and are concerned with the same thing, namely, his somatic body. Correspondingly, the same holds for psychic states, such as moods like anger and joy, and also for cultural objects which (e.g., literary documents) may lend themselves to different and sometimes incompatible and, therefore, competing interpretations. The distinction between one identical "object" and its multiple "appearances"—both terms construed broadly enough so as not to be confined to perceptual experience in the strict and narrow sense alone—proves to have general significance. So likewise does that between veridical and deceptive appearances; the former stand the test of congruity and conformity with an ever widening context of further appearances.

With regard to perceptual experience in the strict sense,

Husserl always insisted upon the distinction between hyletic data and apperceptive characters (*Auffassungscharaktere*), also denoted as functional characters or intentional characters. Hyletic data are the data of the several senses—chromatic, tonal, tactile, olfactory, etc.—and merely sensuous feelings, such as pleasure, pain, titillation, etc., also belong here. Among hyletic data pertaining to the same compartment of sensibility there obtains sensory or hyletic unity; all visual data lie within one visual field, all tactile data within one tactile field. However, on the hyletic level, the several sensuous fields remain separated from one another; there is no sensory hyletic unity between the visual, the tactile, and other fields. That is, on that level, perceptual space does not yet obtain. Furthermore, by themselves hyletic data are not perspectival perceptual appearances of things; taken in themselves, they have no presentational function. That function is bestowed on them by the apperceptive characters which synthesize hyletic data of different compartments of sensibility and transform them into perceptual appearances of things. As a result of such synthesis, there arises the consciousness of one intersensorial object which, as identically the same, can be perceived under its visual, tactile, and other aspects, and also the consciousness of perceptual space which, as numerically identical, can be both seen and touched.

Intentionality, by which we mean the presentational and objectivating function of consciousness—more precisely, the fact that the same object appears in a variety of manners of presentation—is entirely due to apperceptive characters. Husserl conceives of them as operating functions which require materials on which to operate, namely, hyletic data. The latter, however, are independent of apperceptive characters. They need not assume any presentational or adumbrational role, but they may be experienced purely in themselves and considered as they are in themselves, disregarding whatever accrues to them from apperceptive characters. On the other hand, no perception is possible unless hyletic data are operated on. The independence of the hyletic data becomes manifest in cases of perceptual doubt and ambiguity, as when the same hyletic data undergo different competing apperceptions. Whatever the apperceptive characters bestow or confer on hyletic data does not change or modify the latter in their proper nature, but merely supervenes upon them.

Both hyletic data and apperceptive characters, which together make up the act of perception as a psychic event, are inherent, real (*reell*) parts, elements, or ingredients of that act and partake of its temporality. They endure as long, and only as long, as the act endures; and they are involved in the temporal flux of the act in its duration and the succession of phases in which that duration consists. By contrast, the object perceived, taken exactly as it presents itself through a given act of perception, i.e., as appearing under a certain aspect and perspective—in other words, the perceptual *noema,* as Husserl calls it in other writings—is identically the same throughout the duration of the act and is in no way affected by the act's temporal duration. It is also the same with regard to a plurality of acts, separated by temporal intervals from one another. Consequently, the perceptual noema is not a real element or part of the act of perception. Still, it pertains to the act, though it is not contained in it as a real ingredient. Rather, it pertains to it as an irreal or ideal correlate, as its intentional correlate, as its sense, that is, that which is meant and intended through the act, taken exactly as it is meant and intended, and which in strict identity can be meant and intended through a plurality of acts. More precisely, according to Husserl, the perceptual noema is the intentional correlate of apperceptive functions operating on hyletic data.

Husserl considers both the act of perception and its intentional correlate to be immanent; the term "immanence" is defined by adequacy of perception which, in the case under discussion here, is reflective apprehension. In fact, an act of consciousness, with all its really inherent ingredients and constituents, as well as the intentional correlate of that act, are exactly as they are experienced and grasped through reflection. With respect to neither does it make sense to raise the question of their manner of appearance under varying conditions, from different points of view. There is no identical entity appearing in various manners of presentation here. On the contrary, the thing which is perceived, in contradistinction to the thing as it is perceived through a particular act, does by necessity present itself under varying aspects and perspectives. Since every particular perception of the thing is partial and one-sided, the thing is not exhausted by any one of them, but it is always more than what is yielded by any particular perceptual appearance. In that sense, the thing is transcendent with regard to any particular perception, even with regard to any finite segment of the perceptual process. The very existence of the thing and its continuing to be in truth and reality what it has thus far appeared to be are contingent upon the harmonious and unbroken development of the perceptual process into the future, with all its phases in intrinsic consistency and congruity with one another.

In this connection, Husserl speaks of the object as an ideal-pole. More particularly, he distinguishes the substratum-pole from property-poles. The latter are related to the several objective properties of the thing which, like the chromatic properties, are given in various manners of perceptual presentation. The property-poles have no independence but refer to the substratum-pole in the manner in which, in general, properties inhere in their substratum. To the substratum belong not only the attributes, properties, and qualities of the thing which are directly given through the actual perception and those which have thus been given in the past and have become part and parcel of our acquired perceptual acquaintance with the thing but also properties still unknown which are merely anticipated with greater or lesser determinateness. In other words, to the substratum-pole belongs a more or less empty horizon—whose emptiness and indeterminateness, however, are never complete or total, insofar as the horizon must fit with both the present perceptual appearance of the thing and the perceptual acquaintance acquired in the past.[15] On the other hand, the ideal substratum-pole must not be conceived as an element in addition to the properties, any more than the thing which is perceived is something apart from or supervenient to its various manners of perceptual presentation. Rather, the substratum-pole has an organizing and centralizing function with respect to the properties. In the course of the perceptual process, the substratum-pole undergoes progressive determination, as the empty horizon receives fulfillment. However, this fulfillment is always only partial, and along with it new and more or less empty horizons are continually springing up.

Perceptual experience has here, as in most of Husserl's writings, paradigmatic significance. As far as the notion of intentionality is concerned, the results of the analysis of perception easily admit of generalization. Intentionality denotes the consciousness of a certain identical item with respect to a multiplicity of acts; the identical item is a sense or meaning, that is, something meant and intended. A comparatively simple form of

15. See the detailed analysis of the fittingness here under discussion in FC, pp. 208 ff., 216 ff., 234 ff.

intentionality is exemplified by the "repetition" of a mathematical demonstration or by an inference of any sort. Multiple acts of consciousness are experienced, through all of them the same demonstration or the same inference is grasped, and their identity lends itself to explicit disclosure by means of reflection. Perceptual intentionality exhibits a more complex structure, because a synthesis of multiple perceptual presentations and appearances comes into play. Here the multiplicity involves not only acts of consciousness but also their intentional correlates, namely, the various appearances and presentations of the same thing. Each one of these appearances is a perceptual sense or meaning. Since all of these appearances refer to one another, each perceptual sense can be said to include or contain in itself a multiplicity, even an infinity, of further perceptual senses. From another point of view, Husserl defines intentionality as bestowal of sense, be it on hyletic data by apperceptive characters, be it on corporeal things (which are thus transformed into cultural objects)—to mention only two examples. The essential nature of consciousness as defined by intentionality consists in performing objectivating operations and being aware of itself as existing in a world objectivated by those very operations.

THE EGO

TO COMPLETE THE ACCOUNT of perceptual experience, we must make allowance for the perceiving ego under both its somatic and psychic aspects.

In all perceptions of external things, not only are the sense organs (such as the eyes in seeing, the ears in hearing) involved but the succession on one another of the various perceptual presentations and appearances of the thing perceived is also closely related to, and even depends on, motions on the part of the perceiving ego, motions of his eyes, his head, his hands, walking motions in going around the thing so as to perceive it from a variety of standpoints, and the like. By means of our bodily organs we act on things, pushing them, pulling them, and interfering in multifarious ways with the course of nature. Our several dealings with the world of primordial experience involve an interplay between systems of two kinds. One kind is the result of the aforementioned synthesis, that is, organized groups of perceptual appearances related to the several things perceived. The other is our somatic body. Differently, and perhaps more correctly, expressed, intentional acts of perception referring to external things are continually combined and interwoven with other intentional acts, namely, specific somatic experiences. Hence the task arises of analyzing descriptively the latter experiences as subjective modes of appearance of the somatic body and of accounting for the ways in which those experiences are organized with one another so that through them the somatic body originarily presents itself as a unified system. Husserl does not go beyond formulating that task. It must be stressed that when he speaks of the intentionality *of* the somatic body, the *genetivus* must be construed as a *genetivus objectivus*. In other words, the somatic body is an intentional correlate. It is studied under the phenomenological reduction, which is to say that it must be taken as it is meant and intended in and through our very experience of the somatic body. Husserl explicitly denotes the somatic body as a perceptive meaning (*perzeptive Meinung*).[16]

As to the psychic aspect of the ego, the first thing to be mentioned is the temporality of conscious life. It is best exemplified by the experience of a musical note enduring in time. As long as the note is given as enduring in actual experience, there is a present phase in the strict sense, a phase of momentary presence. Whereas the note endures in time, the phase of momentary presence does not; it does not remain fixed and unchanged. Rather, it undergoes a transformation into a phase which no longer is, but has just been, present and is still retained as having just been present. Given in retention, the phase in question essentially belongs to the present in a wider sense. Otherwise, momentary notes would succeed upon one another.

16. In speaking of the intentionality of the somatic body, Merleau-Ponty, on the other hand, takes the *genetivus* as a *genetivus subjectivus*. Departing from Husserl in a significant and consequential way, he ascribes intentionality to the somatic body, considering it "the subject of perception" and "the general instrument of my comprehension" (*Phenomenology of Perception*, trans. Colin Smith [New York: Humanities Press, 1962], pp. 206, 232 ff., 302 ff., 325 ff., *passim*). For a very clear and thorough presentation and critical discussion of Merleau-Ponty's theory, see Richard M. Zaner, *The Problem of Embodiment* (The Hague: Martinus Nijhoff, 1964), pt. III, especially chap. 2, § 1, chap. 3, § 2.

At every moment, an actually experienced momentary note would be accompanied by memories of notes which had previously been experienced as momentary. But there could be no continuous experience of one note as enduring in time, that is, no consciousness of the note which as identically the same is sounding now, was sounding a moment ago and even for some time, and is anticipated to continue sounding.

What may be considered as the present in the wider sense, that sense in which the perception of a note is said to be a present perception, exhibits a somewhat complex structure: A nuclear phase of momentary presence is surrounded by the horizons of both pastness (retentions of different degrees according to the remoteness of the phases in question from that of momentary presence) and futurity (protentions, anticipations of phases to come, i.e., to assume the temporal form of momentary presence). Furthermore, this temporal structure is in incessant flux. Along with the phase of momentary presence being transformed into a phase retained, every retention of any degree becomes a retention of a higher degree, that is, the phase in question sinks into a more remote past. Correspondingly, the same holds for the protentions. Phases anticipated to become those of momentary presence assume that form or come close to assuming it.

Perception exhibits the mentioned temporal structure and is a mode of consciousness through which the object perceived originally presents itself (*ursprüngliche Gegenwärtigung*), as in the case of the note that is actually experienced as sounding. The note may cease to resound, we may turn away from the object we have been perceiving. That does not mean that the object vanishes from consciousness altogether. The note which sounded, the object which we perceived some time ago, may be explicitly remembered or recalled. If they are recalled, they are recalled as having been perceived. Correspondingly, an event may be expected to occur, i.e., to be perceived at some future time. In contradistinction to perception, recall and expectancy have the sense of representation (*Vergegenwärtigung*). At once their difference from retention and protention becomes clear. Whereas both retention and protention belong to the present in the wider sense—to the present perception in its presentational function—recall refers to the past and expectancy to the future. Both recall and expectancy are variations or modalizations of perception; the former represents its object as having been present, the latter represents it as to be present in the future.

Owing to recall and expectancy, whatever knowledge concerning the world we have acquired becomes a permanent possession at our disposal. We can freely avail ourselves of it and we can rely on it.

Perception is susceptible to variation in a different dimension which yields representation in the sense of fantasy. Perception, recall, and expectancy are positional modes of consciousness involving an existential belief, namely, belief in the object as having being, as having had being, or as to have being. In the case of fantasy or imagination, that belief is modified and transformed into quasi belief, a belief "as if." While the positional modes of consciousness give us access to the real world, fantasy permits us to contrive possibilities, e.g., to imagine that a certain state of affairs may possibly be different from what it actually is. Imagination proves to be the necessary condition of every attempt to bring about changes in the real world.[17]

Besides the temporality of consciousness, Husserl emphasizes its polarization toward the ego, a polarization analogous in some respects to that of the perceptual presentations of a thing toward the substratum-pole. Explicitly referring to Kant's notion of the transcendental ego and his theory of the synthesis of transcendental apperception, Husserl advocates an egological conception of consciousness. All mental states and all experiences, or at least those of a higher order as well as their intentional correlates, have reference to and are centralized in the ego. Because the ego is the identical subject with respect to those experiences, he can himself be neither a special experience among others nor a really inherent element or ingredient of an experience. He is nothing other than the subject-pole in which all experiences are centralized.

The reference of experiences to the ego can assume two forms. In the first place, the ego can be solicited by objects passively constituted, that is, constituted through intentional experiences in which the ego does not partake. Second, the ego can yield to such solicitation and turn to passively constituted objects, attend to and deal with them. In that case, the ego is active; directing itself to the intentional correlate, the ego lives in the corresponding act which thereby acquires the character

17. We have already mentioned the roles of imaginative variation and possibilities in connection with ideation in the first section of this chapter.

of an *actus* emerging and emanating from the ego. The activity of the ego, however, is not confined to explicitly concerning itself with whatever object has solicited that activity. Objects attended to may be compared with and related to one another. By means of specific activities of the ego, states of affairs and relations of all kinds are generated that Husserl considers as objects of a second order, insofar as their generation takes place on the basis of objects of first order, namely, those which are simply perceived and attended to. Finally, egological activities are involved in the bestowal of sense on corporeal things which are thus transformed into cultural objects. All cultural activity is related to some ego or, as Husserl likewise expresses it, to persons and personal life. The ego proves the source (*Quellpunkt*) of all accomplishments, generations, and creations. But his activities are contingent on—because they presuppose— passive affections and solicitations, that is, intentional experiences in the mode of passivity.

No experience in which the activity of the ego manifests itself and which springs from such activity is merely a passing event. On the contrary, it leaves a permanent effect in the ego, who thus acquires habits (*Habitualitäten*) and convictions, and makes decisions by which he abides, at least as long as he is not motivated to revise or to abandon them. Like the substratum-pole, which remains the same while in the course of the perceptual process undergoing progressive determination and re-determination, the ego is the pole with respect not only to actual egological activities but also to acquired habits and convictions. It is the source of egological activities crystallizing into habits which by their very genesis refer to the active ego-pole. Such acquisitions define the history of the ego, a history marked by vicissitudes, since all revisions of decisions and convictions purport genuine changes in the ego. The total system of acquired habits, convictions, and decisions defines the ego in its individuality and personal style. The unity of the person depends on the temporality of consciousness, that is, on all acts' and experiences' being inserted into one phenomenal time; that unity manifests itself in the personal style.

DIRECTIONS OF THEORETICAL INTEREST
AND THE ORIGIN OF THE SCIENCES

ALL SCIENCE PRESUPPOSES the world of primordial experience as the basis on which it arises. Whatever unity or systematic connection exists between the sciences is due to their origin in that common source. On the other hand, the differentiation between them follows the directions of the several possible theoretical interests, which also are motivated by the general structure of the world of primordial experience. According to the theoretical interest in question, specific methods are elaborated by means of which certain aspects of the world of primordial experience are articulated, thematized, even isolated, and submitted to theoretical interpretation. Every science is the product of a specific method—a product, however, which has its roots in the world of primordial experience. In other words, though every science is motivated in its possibility by aspects and structures of the world of primordial experience, the actualization of that possibility requires specific intellectual operations beyond, but on the basis of, primordial experience.

Abstractive reduction leads from the world of primordial experience to "nature." Properly speaking, two abstractive reductions and, accordingly, two concepts of "nature" must be distinguished. The first abstraction bears on those properties of corporeal things owing to which they have the sense of cultural objects. Disregarding these properties, one retains the corporeal things with all the qualities and attributes which they possess in their own right, that is, which are not conferred on them by human actions with regard to human intentions and purposes. Furthermore, there remain the animated beings in both their somatic and psychic aspects. "Nature" as resulting from this abstraction comprises whatever is not man-made in the world of primordial experience. To nature in this sense also belongs human mental and psychic life in every form and on all levels. One abstracts from the yieldings and products of mental and psychic activities only insofar as they are impressed on and incarnated in corporeal things. As far as psychology is concerned, we arrive here at its interpretation as a "natural science," that is, the study of psychic and mental life within a somatic framework.

By means of a second abstraction, the psychic and mental are disregarded altogether. As a result of this abstraction, the world of primordial experience undergoes the reduction to a merely corporeal world which consists of spatially extended things. This means that the things have to be accounted for exclusively in terms of their spatial properties and that they are taken into consideration only insofar as they can thus be accounted for. Spatial properties also include the spatial relations in which the things stand to one another, relations which may and do change in the course of time. In other words, the second abstraction yields "nature" in the specific sense of modern physics, namely, conceived of as a causal context of things and events describable merely in spatiotemporal terms.[18] This conception of "nature" defines the sense of objectivity. Whatever is to be abstracted from as not pertaining to "nature" comes to be considered as subjective. Among such merely subjective facts and data must be counted the various manners in which things present themselves in perceptual experience as well as the several conceptions and interpretations of the world entertained in different sociohistorical groups—varying from group to group, varying also within one and the same group in the course of its historical development. The goal of objective science is to disclose nature as it is in itself, independent of and beyond all subjective appearances and interpretations, stripped of all subjective admixture, severed from all reference and relatedness to persons and personal groups.

Persons and communities of persons, on the contrary, are in the center of thematic interest in the human sciences. They are, however, not considered in a "natural" setting, that is, as psychosomatic entities, because the abstraction which underlies that "natural" orientation is not performed. Rather, the human beings are considered only and exclusively under their personal aspects—as to their function within their society, the multifarious forms of their coexistence and cooperation, both positive and negative; furthermore, as to their dealings with cultural objects of all kinds in producing them, modifying them, making use of them, and like. Even things which are not man-made are not considered in the human sciences as they are from the

18. It is worth noting that mathematization, i.e., reference of spatial configurations to the ideal notions and entities of geometry, which plays such an important role in *Crisis* (§§ 8 ff.) is not mentioned at all in *Phänomenologische Psychologie*.

standpoint of natural science, namely, as merely corporeal objects. Such things must be taken as they are experienced, conceived, and interpreted by the members of the sociohistorical group in question; as intentional correlates of the personal life of those members, in their relatedness to those members as persons. It is not as though the things under discussion were, to begin with, corporeal things in the sense of natural science and were, subsequently, referred to persons and their personal life. Here Husserl is emphatic. In the absence of the mentioned abstractions, the concept of "nature" in the scientific sense has no place within the human sciences except as a subject matter of study, that is, as a cultural and historical phenomenon, the intentional correlate, product, and result of intellectual operations and elaborations by a certain group of persons, namely, the natural scientists whose activities are engaged along a specific line of interest. As used in the human sciences, the term "world" has a "personal," not a "natural," meaning. It denotes the personal environment (*personale Umwelt*) of a certain sociohistorical group, to be taken as conceived and interpreted by that group.

The world of primordial experience is given to us through acts of consciousness, especially perceptual consciousness; there is no other way of access to it and whatever it comprises. Ordinarily and normally we are engrossed in the things perceived and dealt with by us in some way or other rather than in the acts of consciousness and the multiple manners in which the things present themselves to us. Still, for the things in question to be given to us, the acts of perceptual consciousness must be experienced; through these acts the things perceived must present themselves in various manners; between the presentations and appearances syntheses must take place. For conscious life and whatever pertains to it to be experienced, however, does not mean its being reflected on and made an explicit topic or theme. What holds for the nontheoretical dealings with the world of primordial experience can be generalized. In the human sciences we concern ourselves with cultural objects, with legal, political, and other institutions, with persons and sociohistorical groups, and not with the specific acts of consciousness through which the topics of our special interest are given to us and without which we would have no access to the subject matter of our studies. The physicist abstracts from whatever is "subjective," including his own conscious life. Still, in and for his work he depends on his perceptual consciousness and whatever other intellectual functions, among them the mentioned abstractions, are required for and involved in his scientific activity. However, his conscious life is not of thematic interest to the physicist, any more than the mathematician explicitly concerns himself with his mathematizing consciousness, although it is only through acts of such specific consciousness that the mathematical entities with which he deals are conceived by him. Conscious life can be, and usually is, experienced without being reflected on and thematized. However, it lends itself to thematization, which is the gateway to phenomenological psychology.

Conclusion

We have deliberately confined ourselves merely to presenting a report on *Phänomenologische Psychologie* and have abstained from entering into a critical discussion of any particular theory advanced by Husserl. Such a discussion would have overextended this essay, long as it already is. A critical discussion, it seems to us, must find its proper place within the context of systematic phenomenological work on specific problems and can be carried on in a fruitful way only within that context.

Still, in concluding, we wish to indicate some of the doctrines defended by Husserl that seem to us to require revision or, at least, reexamination. Among those doctrines is Husserl's dualistic theory of perception as it manifests itself in his distinction between hyletic data and apperceptive or functional characters. We have advocated that the notion of hyletic data be relinquished altogether.[19] Its relinquishment would entail a revision of the theory of intentionality. Intentionality can no longer be generally defined as bestowal of sense, for, in the last analysis, such a definition implies that, at the basis of the structural hierarchy of intentional functions and accomplishments, there is a bestowal of sense on hyletic data which in themselves are devoid of it.[20] A further theory in point is Husserl's egological

19. See "Phenomenology of Thematics and of the Pure Ego," in *SPP*, pp. 253 ff.; and *FC*, pp. 265 ff.
20. We have presented a sketchy outline of a reformulated theory of intentionality in "On the Intentionality of Consciousness,"

conception of consciousness.[21] Finally, we mention Husserl's conception of the object as substratum-pole and the centralizing function of the latter.[22] The problems involved here concern organization of a kind which Husserl has not treated, and they require further phenomenological work.

Allowance for certain trends in contemporary psychology, especially Gestalt theory, has led us to the discussed reexaminations, revisions, and even departures. Husserl's radical reflections on psychology, its rootedness in the world of primordial experience, its place within the system of sciences (especially its autonomy in several respects with regard to physics), and, finally, his insistence on the notion of intentionality, however redefined, indeed imply a thoroughgoing reform of psychology which would transform it into a genuine universal science of the mind. For that reason, it appears highly desirable to effect a confrontation between phenomenological psychology and such trends in contemporary psychology as have some affinity with it because of their general theoretical orientation. As far as particular theories and the treatment of specific topics are concerned, phenomenological psychology and even transcendental phenomenology may derive considerable profit from the suggested confrontation. Needless to say, such a fertilization would be mutual and phenomenology not its sole beneficiary.

---

in *SPP;* see our "Towards a Theory of Intentionality," *Philosophy and Phenomenological Research,* Vol. XXX (1970); and chap. 9, below.

21. See Jean-Paul Sartre, *The Transcendence of the Ego,* trans. Forrest Williams and Robert Kirkpatrick (New York: Noonday Press, 1957); and Aron Gurwitsch, "Phenomenology of Thematics and the Pure Ego," chap. 4, and "A Non-Egological Conception of Consciousness," both reprinted in *SPP.*

22. See chap. 10, below.

5 / The Common-Sense World as Social Reality and the Theory of Social Science

In these pages, I propose to concentrate on a certain group of problems that were not only of primary importance for Alfred Schutz but also hold a central position in contemporary philosophical thought, especially in the work of Edmund Husserl and later authors who belong to the phenomenological movement. These problems concern the world of common sense, the world of daily life, or the life-world, as Husserl calls it, and our experience of that world. Schutz's contributions to such discussions prepare the way for a phenomenological theory of the social and human sciences.

The World of the Natural Attitude

Let us begin by recalling briefly Husserl's first descriptive characterization of what he later called the "world of the natural attitude" (*Ideas*, §§ 27 ff.). By this he means the world in which we find ourselves at every moment of our life, taken exactly as it presents itself to us in our everyday experience. This world is indefinitely extended in space and time; it comprises both physical things and cultural objects; we encounter in it animal creatures, as well as fellow human beings, with whom we stand in manifold relations. It is in this world that we have

Originally published as "The Common-Sense World as Social Reality—A Discourse on Alfred Schutz," in *Social Research*, Vol. XXIX (1962), reprinted as Introduction to Alfred Schutz, *Collected Papers* (The Hague: Martinus Nijhoff, 1962–66), Vol. III (1966).

our existence, carry on our activities, pursue our goals. We always take our bearings on this world of our daily experience and have a certain familiarity with what we encounter in it.

This familiarity, it must be stressed, is of an entirely different kind and style from scientific knowledge, especially in the modern sense, and in no way depends on or is derived from that knowledge. In fact, when Husserl in his last works came to denote the "world of the natural attitude" as "life-world," he did so in order explicitly to contrast this world as it is given to our immediate experience, independent of and previous to scientific knowledge, with the universe as constructed and elaborated by science, especially modern physical science (*Crisis*, §§ 9 ff., 33 ff.; and *EJ*, § 10). Obviously, the social scientist takes as his point of departure, not the idealized and mathematized constructs of the physical sciences, but rather the world of common sense as the scene of all social relationships and actions.

A primary characteristic of our experience of and attitude toward the life-world is the fact, on which both Husserl and Schutz insist, that this world is taken for granted. Its existence is never doubted or questioned, and this holds for its natural as well as its sociocultural aspects. To be sure, doubts may and do arise, and as often as not are resolved in the course of experience; it may and does happen that things turn out to be different from what they were believed to be at first. Such questions, doubts, and corrections, however, always concern details within the world, particular mundane existents, and never the world as a whole. Whatever activity we engage in, whether practical, theoretical, or other, is pursued within the life-world, whose simple acceptance proves an essential precondition of every activity. It is through its role as general background or horizon with regard to all our mental activities that the life-world appears and discloses itself as accepted and taken for granted. To express it differently, let us say that the belief in the existence of the life-world—a belief that as a rule is not even formulated—accompanies, pervades, and permeates all our mental life, since this life takes place within the world of common experience and is always concerned with certain particular mundane existents (*Ideas*, § 30; and *EJ*, § 7). This also holds in the case of doubting and questioning. Since doubt concerns only particular things and particular events in the life-world, it cannot occur except on the basis of the general belief, silently and implicitly accepted as a matter of course, in the existence of that world. The unquestioned and unchallenged certainty concerning the world at large underlies, supports, and enters into every particular mental activity.

Each one of us does not experience the life-world as a private world; on the contrary, we take it for a public world, common to all of us, that is, for an intersubjective world (*Ideas*, § 29; *FTL*, §§ 95 ff.; *CM*, § 43; and *Crisis*, § 47). Not only do we encounter our fellow men within the life-world as this world is given to us; we also take it for granted that they are confronted with the same world as we are. Every one of us perceives the world and the things within the world from the particular point of view at which he happens to be at the moment, and hence under aspects and from perspectives that vary in dependence on, and in accordance with, that point of view. But notwithstanding such differences as to manner of appearance and presentation, we regard the life-world, as a matter of course, as identical for us and for our fellow men and, quite in general, for everyone. Finally, we take it for granted that our fellow men take the world for granted in substantially the same way we do. Because of this thorough-going reciprocity, we can act and work with our fellow men in the multiple forms that such cooperation can assume. We orient our actions with regard to what we anticipate theirs to be, and we expect them to do the same.

To complete this necessarily sketchy survey of Husserl's theories used by Schutz as points of both reference and departure, we should mention the "horizonal structure of experience," especially perceptual consciousness. Here I have in view mainly what Husserl calls the "inner horizon" (*Ideas*, § 44; *CM*, §§ 19 ff.; and *EJ*, § 8). Every particular perception yields more than merely what it offers in genuine sense experience. Through every perception the object perceived appears, according to the point of view from which it is observed, under a certain aspect, from a certain side, in a certain orientation. Yet its unilateral appearance includes references to other appearances, to aspects under which the object will present itself when it is seen from a different point of view, to phenomena that will be observed under certain conditions not realized at the present moment, and so on.

By virtue of the horizonal structure of experience, every object, even a novel one, appears under the horizon of a certain preacquaintanceship, however schematic and inarticulate, a certain familiarity, however dim and vague. That is, it presents itself in the light of a certain typicality and with a sense determined by that typicality (*EJ*, §§ 80, 83a). Apart from those beings (rather few in number) that have for us the character and value of uniqueness, the objects we encounter and with which we deal do not present themselves as individual and singular things but, rather, as things and creatures of some sort and kind. What we perceive are houses, trees, animals, and the like. We expect of them a more or less well-defined type of behavior—for example, a typical mode of locomotion—even though, e.g., the animal perceived displays no such behavior at the present moment.

Typification as a general feature of perceptual experience denotes a very important and fundamental problem of general phenomenology, for typification is certainly at the origin of conceptual consciousness, if it is not itself conceptualization in an incipient or at least germinal form.[1] Seen from this general perspective, the phenomenon of typification calls for further analysis and elucidation along the lines of constitutive phenomenology in Husserl's sense. Schutz, however, does not orient his work in this direction, though he is, of course, fully aware of it as a possible line of research. Instead, he intentionally abides by what Husserl called the "natural attitude," that is, he deliberately abstains from raising questions of transcendental constitution and pursues his phenomenological analyses within the framework of the "natural attitude."[2]

THE COMMON-SENSE WORLD ACCORDING TO ALFRED SCHUTZ[3]

THE PHENOMENON OF TYPIFICATION may now serve as point of departure for a presentation of Schutz's conception of the common-sense world as social reality. Rather than dealing in

1. See "On the Conceptual Consciousness," in *SPP.*
2. Schutz, *The Phenomenology of the Social World*, trans. George Walsh and Frederick Lehnert (Evanston, Ill.: Northwestern University Press, 1967), p. 44.
3. This account is based mainly on the following essays by Schutz: "Phenomenology and the Social Sciences," "On Multiple Realities," "Choosing among Projects of Action," "Common-Sense and Scientific Interpretation of Human Action," "Language, Language Disturbances, and the Texture of Consciousness," "Concept and Theory Formation in the Social Sciences," "Symbol, Reality, and Society," and "Husserl's Importance for the Social Sciences." These are all in his *Collected Papers*, Vol. I (1962).

general terms with typification as such, Schutz concerns himself with its specification, especially with the variation of specified typification. Encountering an animal, I perceive it one time as a quadruped, another time as a dog, still another time as a dog of a special sort. In every case the animal is perceived as typified; it appears with the sense of a certain typicality. According to the type in question, certain aspects, features, and characteristics of the animal acquire emphasis and prominence, while others pass almost unnoticed. My present interests and the system of relevances corresponding to them determine which form of typification will prevail at a given moment. Every shift in my interest is accompanied by and entails a change in typification.

Of still greater importance is that specification of typification which differs from society to society and, within the same society, varies in the course of its history. This is best illustrated by cultural objects like tools, instruments, and utensils of all sorts, which serve and refer to specific human activities and needs, the latter also being of a typical nature. To a stranger not familiar with our society and civilization, the things and utensils we use, whose typical use and typical meaning are a matter of course to us, will appear in a light highly different from that in which we perceive them. Conversely, if we come to a strange society or discover the material remainders of a civilization of the past, we are more often than not at a loss to "understand" its utensils, since we do not know, at the outset, their typical purposes or, consequently, their typical uses.

Hereby we are brought before the social nature and origin of the world in which we find ourselves, and which is an interpreted world throughout as to both its natural and cultural aspects. Obviously, this interpretation is not of our own making. On the contrary, it has been handed down to us by our elders and has been silently accepted by us as a matter of course. We have been told and shown by our teachers and parents what the things mean, how they are to be used—that is, how they are interpreted and typified in our society. Not only were we born into our sociocultural world, we have also grown into it. Growing into our world and into our society, we have acquired a certain language that embodies the interpretations and typifications in question and is their vehicle as well as their medium of expression. Our lifelong intercourse with our elders and contemporaries appears in a certain sense as one continuous process of acquisition of, and practice in, the typifying interpretations that prevail in our society and come to be accepted by us as patterns to be followed unquestioningly.

Along with the language spoken in our society, we acquire a great number of recipes of all sorts—rules for handling things, modes of conduct and behavior in typical situations. We learn that we have to apply typical means in order to obtain typical results. Such knowledge is continuously confirmed in the course of our experience, in circumstances both trivial and important. Riding on a train, we display a certain typical behavior which we know is expected from a railway passenger. Whoever desires to enter a career or a vocation knows that he has to comply with certain prerequisites, to fulfill certain conditions, to pursue a typical course of action, if he is to satisfy his desire.

Two features are characteristic of all these acquisitions, recipes, rules, or modes of conduct and behavior. First, they are socially approved. This does not necessarily mean that they are sanctioned by laws or in some other formal way, or that they are enforced by special agencies. The overwhelming majority of the rules and recipes are complied with as a matter of course and are hardly ever explicitly formulated, still less reflected on. They define the modes of procedure and conduct regarded as correct, good, and natural by the society in question; they are the ways in which "one" does things.[4] Their social approval, in the form of inexplicit and silent acceptance and compliance, is but another expression and aspect of their social derivation. Second, these recipes are followed and observed because, and only because, of their usefulness. According to Schutz, the pragmatic motive dominates our daily life in the common-sense world. Hence, as long as the recipes permit us to obtain desired typical results, they are unquestioningly applied and complied with; they are not put into question or doubt unless such results fail to materialize.

All the acquisitions under discussion—langauge, the multiple typifications embodied in language, the recipes of all sorts, the rules for handling and manipulating things, the modes of conduct, behavior, and action in typical situations—constitute together what Schutz calls the "stock of knowledge at hand." This is the sediment of the whole history of my life; it comprises what

4. It would be interesting to compare Schutz's analysis of conduct in everyday life—socially determined because socially derived—with Heidegger's interpretation of the anonymity of "das Man" in *Being and Time*, trans. John Macquarrie and Edward Robinson (London: SCM Press, 1962), § 27.

was passed on to me by those whose teachings I accepted on the strength of their authority, as well as what I acquired through intercourse with my associates. Hence my "stock of knowledge" is never completed; on the contrary, it grows as long as my life goes on.

Only a very small part of my stock of knowledge has originated in my personal experience; the bulk of it is socially derived —handed down to me and accepted by me. In fact, going beyond Schutz's explicit formulations but staying in line with the trend and spirit of his theory, we may say that all my personal acquisitions presuppose some socially derived "stock of knowledge at hand," inasmuch as they are inserted into and have to find their place within this socially derived setting. No personal acquisition is ever isolated. Whatever new acquisition I make in the course of my experience must fit into my "stock of knowledge at hand," must be in continuity, even in some conformity, with what at the moment in question I know about the world; and what I know includes both my previous personal acquisitions and what I have been taught and told by others in the course of my growing into the sociocultural world in which I live. The "stock of knowledge at hand" forms the frame of reference, interpretation, and orientation for my life in the world of daily experience, for my dealing with things, coping with situations, coming to terms with fellow human beings.

With his concept of "stock of knowledge at hand," Schutz, I submit, made an important contribution toward further elucidating our specific familiarity with the world of daily experience, a familiarity that Husserl distinguished from scientific knowledge, especially in the modern sense. That the world of common sense is taken for granted—not only its existence but also the way in which it is interpreted—is a consequence and another expression of the unquestioned acceptance of the "stock of knowledge at hand." Just as only details within the common-sense world, only particular mundane existents, may become doubtful—and never the world as a whole—so does the "stock of knowledge" in its entirety never become questionable, but only certain elements pertaining to it. This happens when we are confronted with a situation in which the conventional rules fail us in the furtherance and pursuit of our practical goals and interests.

As mentioned before, we take it for granted that fellow men exist and that they are human beings like ourselves. This implies that we "assume" others to have "stocks of knowledge at hand" of substantially the same kind as ours. It must be stressed that this "assumption" is not explicitly, still less deliberately, made, as though we were free to choose a different assumption. Nor is it an assumption in the sense of a hypothesis that we expect to be confirmed by future experience but for whose invalidation we must be equally prepared. The term "assumption" must not be understood in the proper sense; it carries no theoretical connotations. Like the acceptance of the life-world itself, it is an unquestioned belief and certainty on which we act and proceed, but it is not made a topic for reflection and is not even rendered explicit unless we engage in philosophical inquiries. In fact, the task of philosophy may be defined as the disclosure and scrutiny of "assumptions" that are taken for granted and even pass unnoticed.

To return to this "assumption" concerning my fellow men—it has its roots in the fact that I encounter them in the same world in which I find myself. They were born and have grown into the same world. Their "stocks of knowledge at hand" derive from the same social source as mine. But the "assumption" that their "stocks of knowledge at hand" are substantially the same as mine calls for some qualifications. First, a stock of knowledge admits of degrees of clarity, distinctness, and precision; therefore even when I know the same things as one of my fellow men, I may and do know them differently. In the second place, I am an expert only in a very small field of which I have had genuine experience and have acquired firsthand knowledge; in all other fields I am a layman. Thus I know different things from those known by my fellow men. I know, however, that there are experts in those fields in which I am a layman, and that, if circumstances demand it, I can resort to the advice of the several experts—the doctor, the lawyer, the architect, and so on. Especially in a society like ours, in which division of labor and specialization prevail, the available knowledge is not in its entirety in the possession of every member but is rather distributed among professional groups. Awareness of this social distribution also belongs to the "stock of knowledge at hand."

Living in the world of daily experience, I am normally not a disinterested observer, still less a theoretician, but rather an actor who pursues certain aims and goals and tries to accomplish his objectives. The world in which I find myself is not given to me, at least not primarily, as a field of observation that I survey in an attitude of neutrality. On the contrary, in my very pursuing my goals and objectives I am involved in whatever interests I have to further. Because of this involvement, I do not simply belong to society at large, I occupy a certain place and position within it as a member of the profession I have chosen, of the subgroup into which I was born, and so forth. The vantage point of my position within society is the result of the whole history of my life. It is due to the circumstances, partly imposed on me, partly chosen by me, which in the course of my personal history have contributed toward making me become what I am. In Schutz's terminology, I live in a "biographically determined situation" which is the sediment of my personal past and continues to change as long as I live, developing in continuity with my past. My "biographical situation" is given to me and to me alone; I do not share it with anyone.

My "because motives," sharply distinguished by Schutz from "in-order-to motives," have their roots in my past, which determines my present "biographical situation." Questions about why someone acts as he does, pursues certain goals rather than others, has conceived this life-plan for himself and not a different one, refer to "because motives" and cannot be answered except in terms of the life-history of the person concerned. As an actor, however, I know hardly anything about my "because motives," since I am involved in my actions and live in them. To become aware of my "because motives," I have to suspend the ongoing action, turn back to my past, and refer to it the goals I am pursuing. I am free to do so, but then I transform myself into an observer of myself and am no longer an actor. In contradistinction to my "because motives," my "in-order-to motives" are always given to me in my very acting. In fact, I act in order to bring about a certain state of affairs, and I endeavor to find and apply the means that will permit me to reach that goal. Hence I am always aware of my "in-order-to motives" as the centralizing factor of my conduct.

All my goals and objectives form a hierarchical order and originate in my "biographically determined situation," which is also the source of my systems of relevancy—both my permanent ones and those that are transient, shifting with my "purpose at hand." The system of relevancy that prevails at a given moment depends on the goals I am pursuing and also, as mentioned before, determines my typifications. My actions as well as my projects are oriented toward my goals and purposes and are organized in terms of my systems of relevancy. Schutz defines planning as acting in imagination, more precisely, as rehearsing in imagination a course of action that I endeavor to lay out for myself. In all my acting as well as my planning, I am guided by my "stock of knowledge at hand," faulty and deficient as it may be. Circumstances beyond my control may occur that I had no means of anticipating. It may also happen that I misjudge circumstances, act without sufficiently complete knowledge of them, fail to allow for future developments I could have foreseen, and the like. Whatever criticism I may later express with regard to any of my actions, they are always oriented and directed by the knowledge at my disposal. That is, my actions and plans have a certain meaning for me. They have that meaning with respect to the goals, more or less ultimate, that I am pursuing, i.e., my goals in their hierarchical order and in the light of my "stock of knowledge at hand." This notion of the meaning that an action has for the actor himself is what Max Weber has in mind in speaking of *subjektiver* or *gemeinter Sinn*.[5] It will be encountered again presently within the context of my understanding of my fellow men, but we must point out that the notion arises even when I consider my own action and planning.

It is taken for granted by me that my fellow men perceive the world and act within it at their places and positions as I do at mine and that, like me, each of them has his own "biographically determined situation" given to him and to him alone. Yet we all live in one and the same world. My fellow men see the same things I see, though they see them differently, from different perspectives. While I see a thing from "here," that is, from the place where I happen to be now, the Other sees it from his standpoint, which is different from mine and for me is "there." Accordingly, certain objects are now "within my reach"—of hearing, seeing, grasping, for example—or within my manipulatory sphere, but outside his, and vice versa. Furthermore, our goals and systems of relevancy cannot be the same, since the "biographically determined situations" in which they originate must of necessity differ among different persons.

Two idealizations, together termed by Schutz the "general thesis of the reciprocity of perspectives," come into play here. The first is the "interchangeability of standpoints." I take it for

5. Max Weber, *Gesammelte Aufsätze zur Wissenschaftslehre* (Tübingen: Mohr, 1922), pp. 405 ff., 503 ff., 508 ff.; see also pp. 334, 336.

granted that I can put myself at the place now occupied by a fellow man, so as to see things from his point of view and his perspective, and that he can place himself at my actual point of observation; by the same token, I assume that objects beyond my actual reach but within the reach of my fellow man can be brought within my reach and still, under certain conditions, remain within his as well. The other idealization leads us to the congruency of different systems of relevancy. We take it for granted—and we "assume" our fellow men do the same—that differences in perspective originating in differences of "biographically determined situation" can be eliminated or considered immaterial, and that therefore different systems of relevancy can be harmonized. Thus we arrive at a common world comprising identical qualities and properties, identically interpreted by all of us—"identical" to the extent to which such identity is required for practical purposes of cooperation and collaboration.

With his notion of "stock of knowledge at hand," his theory of the social origin of that knowledge, and his "general thesis of the reciprocity of perspectives," Schutz makes a most important contribution toward the analysis of the phenomenon of intersubjectivity. To see this, one has only to consider these conceptions in conjunction. The world of our common-sense experience and daily life is an interpreted world, having sense and meaning for us; and as thus interpreted, it is taken for granted. Its interpretation is socially derived, and this holds not only for the bulk of the content and detail of the interpretation but also, and chiefly, for its style, that is, the general lines along which the world as a whole as well as particular mundane existents are conceived and understood. Knowledge socially derived—which, it may be added, is to be communicated and passed on to others —is by its very nature socialized knowledge throughout. Socialized knowledge obviously stands under the condition of the "reciprocity of perspectives."

Intersubjectivity denotes, in the first place, the character of the life-world as a public world. Herein is implied the possibility of my understanding of things and events; my planning and acting are "tuned in" with those of my fellow men. This, in turn, means that my acts and activities contain references to fellow human beings—both to my contemporaries, who may be said within the limits of the aforementioned qualification to share with me a "stock of knowledge at hand," and to my elders, from whom I derived that "stock of knowledge." Such references, however, are not to determined particular individuals but to "whomever it may concern," that is, to anyone and everyone who lives in our sociocultural world and is a member of our group, and whose systems of relevancy are not only compatible but also congruent and conformable with those that prevail in our society, because they are approved in it. The references are to fellow men of a certain specific kind but, within the limits of this specification, to anonymous ones. By the same token, the world of daily experience appears as social reality, as a world common to all of us, and hence as objective; the sense of its objectivity is essentially determined by its anonymity.[6] This anonymity manifests itself most clearly in the case of cultural objects. A utensil, for example, refers both to an anonymous producer and to anonymous users—to anyone who avails himself of it in a typical way in order to accomplish a specific typical purpose.

SOCIAL REALITY

BOTH INTERSUBJECTIVITY and, closely connected if not identical with it, the social character of the world of common experience can be disclosed and brought out by analysis of the planning and acting of a single individual considered in solitude, i.e., by abstracting from actual social relationships in the proper sense. This possibility seems to suggest that the life-world's character as a social world is not acquired through additional features being superimposed on it, as though it had not initially exhibited such features. Rather, one of Schutz's original contributions consists in his contention that the social character belongs to the life-world essentially and intrinsically. That world is a social and intersubjective world from the outset and throughout; it does not become so subsequently, as was maintained in a certain sense by Husserl.

Turning to social relationships in the proper sense, we must distinguish, according to Schutz, what he calls the "face-to-face

6. It goes without saying that anonymity is constitutive of the notion of objectivity on every level, but the connection between these two concepts cannot be pursued here, since we have to confine ourselves to that form of objectivity which prevails on the level of common sense.

relationship" between "consociates" from all other relationships. The face-to-face relationship is defined as actual copresence of consociates who share a community of space during a certain length of time, be it even for only a short moment. Of such a nature is the meeting of old friends exchanging ideas or planning some common action; but in a fugitive and superficial form, the face-to-face relationship also obtains in the casual conversation between strangers who have never seen each other before and do not expect to meet again—for example, passengers who happen to be seated side by side in a railway car. Whatever degree of intimacy or fugacity the relationship may have in a given instance, consociates share a "vivid present." By means of the words they exchange and by their immediate observation of gestures and other physiognomical expressions, consociates grasp one another's thoughts, plans, hopes, and fears, though only partially and fragmentarily. As long as the face-to-face relationship lasts, the consociates partake in one another's lives; their biographies intertwine; as Schutz used to formulate it, "consociates grow older together." Here, and here alone, do the partners grasp one another in their unique individuality; the selves of consociates mutually reveal themselves more or less superficially, fragmentarily, and fugitively, according to the lesser or greater degree of intimacy in their relationship.

No other social relationship exhibits those distinctive features by virtue of which the face-to-face relationship acquires the quality of a meeting of persons as unique individuals. In all other forms of social relationship, we must resort to typification. We must typify the personality of our partner, his motives, his attitudes, his general behavior, and the like—even if in the past we have had a great many intimate face-to-face interactions with him. When I write a letter to my absent friend and submit a proposal to him, I must typify what I know about him and form some idea of his likely reaction, in order to formulate my proposal in terms acceptable to him. These typifications admit of varying degrees of anonymity. When anonymity becomes complete, the typified individuals appear as interchangeable, as is illustrated by an example to which Schutz repeatedly refers. Putting a letter in a mailbox, I expect that people whom I never met—and in all likelihood shall never meet—will behave in a certain typical way (called "handling the mail"), so that my letter will arrive at its destination and be read by the addressee, whom perhaps I also do not know or expect ever to meet, and the final result will be that within some "reasonable" time I shall receive the commodity I ordered.

In all our activities within the social world we have to rely on our fellow men's conducting themselves in typical ways in typical situations. Except in the face-to-face relationship, we do not deal with consociates, that is, individuals as such, but rather with typified individuals to whom a certain typical role or function (socially approved) is assigned. And, according to the degree of anonymity of the typification, these individuals appear more or less exclusively in the light of the functions they are expected to perform in typical ways (also socially approved if not institutionalized or explicitly sanctioned by the legal order). But in typifying partners, I must also typify myself—assume a typical role, see myself in it, and perform it. While riding in a train, for instance, I have to conduct myself in the way I know the typical railway employee expects the typical passenger to behave.

Such typification and self-typification permit me to tune in and interlock my typical behavior with what I may reasonably expect to be the behavior of my typified partners. All social interaction is based on the unformulated assumption that I stand a chance of attaining my objectives provided I act in a typical and socially approved way—an assumption implying the equally unformulated expectancy that my more or less anonymous partners will also conduct themselves in accordance with the requirements of the roles assigned to them. With increasing typification, and corresponding standardization of the ways in which the functions are performed, the chance is obviously enhanced.

This brings us to the phenomenon of "understanding" our fellow men. What is here in question is not understanding in a theoretical sense, or the kind that a detached and disinterested observer might have, but rather the form of understanding prevailing in the actual practice of social life, without which no cooperation or social interaction would be possible. To refer to the example of my writing to an addressee unknown to me, I expect him not only to read my letter but also to act on it; that is, I expect him to appropriate and to assume my motives in a certain sense. I write him that letter *in order to* obtain the commodity in question, and I expect him to ship it to me *because of* my desire as expressed in my letter. In other words, typifying my partner, in whom I see a seller of the commodity, I rely on an expectancy that my "in-order-to motive" will become his "because motive" (this "reciprocity of motives," as Schutz calls it, depends on the aforementioned "general thesis of the reciprocity of perspectives").

"Understanding" as here meant has the sense of anticipating my partner's likely actions and reactions. Such an anticipation, which is always based on typification, proves of utmost importance whenever, for the attainment of my goal or the realization of some project, I depend on the cooperation of others. My prospective partner may pursue interests that not only differ from mine but even conflict with them. To obtain his cooperation, or to bring about some sort of compromise or agreement, I must form some idea of what my project may possibly mean to him. Unless I have such an idea, it will be impossible for me to come to terms with him, to interlock my course of action with what I may expect his to be; there will be nothing to orient and to guide me in the negotiations on which I am about to enter.

Obviously, my project cannot have the same meaning to my prospective partner that it has to me, since even in the absence of a conflict of interests his "biographical situation" differs from mine. To conceive of the meaning my project may have for my partner, I must impute to him typical goals, interests, motives, attitudes, and so on. I must construct the image of a certain type of person who pursues typical interests—those that the position of the type in question requires him to pursue, or at least those that are congruent with his position. To this construct I must refer my project, in order to see it in the light and from the perspective of my partner's goals, motives, and interests, as typified by me. And I must impute to my partner some knowledge of the meaning the project has to me, a knowledge that I suppose him to attain in substantially the same way I form my knowledge of my project's meaning to him. A reciprocity of this sort prevails in all social interactions.

Again we arrive at the notion of *subjektiver* or *gemeinter Sinn*. Previously we were confronted with the meaning that an action or project of action has for the actor himself. Now we are dealing with the meaning of that action or project of action as imputed by the actor to his actual or prospective partner, that is, to another actor (for the sake of simplicity, I ignore here the meaning for the disinterested observer, whom Schutz still distinguishes from the social scientist as a theoretician). At once it is clear that, as Schutz repeatedly emphasizes, the notion of *subjektiver* or *gemeinter Sinn* must not be mistaken for a particularity of Max Weber's sociology or for a specific methodological device peculiar to the social sciences. On the contrary, the "subjective interpretation of meaning" proves to be a common practice of social life in the world of everyday experience. Therefore, as we shall see presently, this notion must be allowed for within the context of social theory. Schutz's analysis provides a definitive clarification and justification of the concept of *subjektiver Sinn,* for this concept is referred to, and shown to arise from, the total contexture of our experience of social reality and our life within it.

Needless to say, the "subjective interpretation of meaning" has nothing to do with introspection: Indeed, how could introspection ever lead me to grasp the meaning my action or project of action has for someone else? Nor should it be misinterpreted as my identifying myself with my prospective partner, who may in fact pursue interests at variance with mine. When, for the realization of my project, I depend on his cooperation, I must foresee his likely reaction and even endeavor to influence it. But in trying to come to terms with him, I am far from relinquishing my interests and appropriating his. Throughout my negotiations and whatever other dealings I have with him, my project retains the meaning it has for me in the light of my "biographical situation," even though for the sake of its furtherance I must have some knowledge of its meaning for my partner, a knowledge at which I cannot arrive except by referring it to the described typifications.

TOWARD A THEORY OF THE SOCIAL SCIENCES

I HAVE SKETCHED SCHUTZ'S CONCEPTION of the common-sense world as social reality in only its broadest outlines. On the basis of Schutz's conception and in continuity with it, a theory of the social sciences could be established. Schutz has not developed such a theory in a fully elaborated and coherent form, although he has given a great many most valuable hints about it that should be gathered and systematized. Here I shall discuss only one, which is centrally important in Schutz's thinking. The problem, which is closely connected with the notion of *subjektiver Sinn,* concerns the difference between the natural and the social or human sciences—the latter understood in so broad a sense as to include all sciences dealing with man.

Guided by the scientific knowledge available in his special field (the corpus of his science), following and applying the rules of procedure and method generally accepted in his science, the scientist—the social as well as the natural—selects and interprets the phenomena he sets out to explain. Both, in their scientific activity, proceed along the lines of their specific interests, which depend on their scientific situation, that is, the state of the science in question at this particular phase of its historical development. The natural scientist, however, does not have to take into consideration any preinterpretation of the facts and events on whose study he embarks. Whatever interpretation his objects are subject to derives from him and from him alone. His objects are not expected to interpret themselves or the environment or field in which they are located and move. Schutz characterizes the theoretical constructs pertaining to the natural sciences as "constructs of the first degree," a term deliberately meant to express the absence of precedent or underlying constructs.

In this respect, the position of the social scientist differs from that of the natural scientist. The objects of the social scientist are actors in the social world, human beings involved and engaged in all kinds of social relationships. These actors have "biographical situations" and "stocks of knowledge at hand"; they pursue interests, have goals, motives, and the like; they have a certain conception of the world they live in, and of themselves as living in that world; in some way or other they interpret whatever they encounter in their world; their actions as well as those of their fellow actors have meaning to them. Among the data, facts, and events with which the social scientist has to deal as the subject matter of his studies belong all such preinterpretations and preconceptions. They must be taken into account in the elaboration of an organized knowledge of social reality in its full concreteness, that is, as experienced by the social actors themselves in their daily lives.

Like the natural scientist, the social scientist contrives theoretical constructs, but his are, as Schutz expresses it, "of the second degree," for allowance must be made in conceiving them for the interpretations that the social actors have of themselves, of one another, of their world. These constructs are homunculi, or puppets endowed with consciousness, which the social scientist creates at his discretion, in accordance with the scientific problem he sets himself. A model of the social world is thus created by means of homunculi—"ideal types," in Max Weber's phrase. The construction of ideal types is subject to the condition (among others) that understandable relations obtain between what is attributed to the homunculus and the actual conduct of the corresponding actor on the scene of social reality. That is, the actor must recognize himself in the homunculus and see in it an idealization of himself. The construction of homunculi is, I submit, an idealization of those typifications and self-typifications that are continually practiced in everyday life.

Since about the turn of the century, the problems related to the philosophical foundations of the social or human sciences—both their difference from the natural sciences and their proper nature—have been much discussed by thinkers like Windelband, Rickert, Max Weber, Simmel, and Dilthey. Dilthey in particular—himself a most eminent historian of philosophy and of ideas (*Geistesgeschichte*)—perceived with increasing clearness the urgency of laying the philosophical foundations of historical knowledge and understanding. He believed that the great German historians of the nineteenth century successfully attempted to reconstruct the sociohistorical and intellectual life of the past, but that they were not able to give an account in conceptual terms of what they were actually doing. Dilthey concerned himself through almost all his life with the justification of the science of history and the philosophical account for the very possibility of such a science.[7]

He was well aware that, for the advancement of his problems, specific concepts were required, concepts related to the interpretation and self-interpretation of life in the intellectual and cultural, not the biological, sense. Such concepts could not be provided by the philosophical trends prevailing in Dilthey's time, since these trends were almost exclusively oriented toward the mathematical science of nature. Nor could they be provided by the new experimental psychology that had begun to develop after the end of the nineteenth century. Hence Dilthey came to conceive the idea of a "descriptive" (*beschreibende*) in contradistinction to an "analyzing" (*zergliedernde*) psychology; he

7. One of the best presentations of Dilthey's problems and ideas is to be found in Ludwig Landgrebe, "Wilhelm Diltheys Theorie der Geisteswissenschaften," *Jahrbuch für Philosophie und phänomenologischen Forschung*, Vol. IX (1928).

seems to have been the first to advocate a psychology of a new style, one that would not simply emulate the procedures of physical science.[8] This also explains Dilthey's interest in the beginning of Husserl's phenomenology, for Dilthey believed he discerned intentions akin to his own in Husserl's *Logical Investigations*. He regarded this newly rising trend of philosophical thinking as a possible source from which those concepts could be derived that he needed for the advancement of his problems.[9]

Schutz is related to the later and even the latest phase of Husserl's thought, rather than to the beginnings. Bringing the methods, points of view, and general theoretical orientation of Husserl's phenomenology in its latest form to bear on the analysis and description of the life-world and of common experience, Schutz laid down a series of notions. Their relatedness to and relevance for the problem of interpretation and self-interpretation of life (in Dilthey's sense) are so obvious as to need little elaboration. I therefore venture the opinion that Dilthey's expectations may find fulfillment in the original development that Schutz gave to Husserl's phenomenology, at least to some of its parts. To be sure, it is the problem of history and historical knowledge that occupies the focus of Dilthey's thinking, whereas that problem does not play a role of primary importance for Schutz, who concerned himself rather with the relations between contemporaries living in the same world. Yet there is, I believe, a possible continuous transition from the problem of intersubjectivity and the understanding of contemporaries to the problem of reconstructing the past. Clarification of the foundations of the social sciences (in a more restricted sense of the term) prepares for and contributes to the clarification of the foundations of the historical sciences. For this reason, I suggest as a desirable and promising enterprise a study of Schutz's concepts and theories from the point of view of their significance for the work inaugurated by Dilthey and continued by some of his successors.

8. "Ideen über eine beschreibende und zergleidernde Psychologie," in Dilthey, *Gesammelte Schriften*, Vol. V (Leipzig: Teubner, 1924).

9. On the relations between Dilthey and Husserl, see Georg Misch, *Lebensphilosophie und Phänomenologie*, 2d ed. (Leipzig and Berlin: Teubner, 1931).

6 / On the Systematic Unity of the Sciences

MODERN THEORY OF SCIENCE, like modern philosophy in general, has developed under the impact of the growing prestige of the natural sciences, especially physics. This prestige is not based exclusively or even originally on the technical advances which modern science has made possible, for the connection between science and technology, i.e., the technological utilization of scientific discoveries and results, did not begin until the later part of the nineteenth century, along with the development of the electrical and chemical industries. Rather, the prestige which has accrued to the natural sciences is due to their undeniable theoretical accomplishments, their success in rationalizing and systematizing a wide range of most diverse and heterogeneous phenomena. As one of the most striking examples of such a unifying systematization, we may mention the theory of radiant energy developed in nineteenth-century physics by Heinrich Hertz.

Because of the theoretical prestige of the physical sciences, the general method employed in them has come to be considered as the paradigm of all scientific method, as *the* scientific method itself, that is, as the only method legitimately to be admitted in all scientific and, in general, in all cognitive endeavors. This view is advocated by a trend in contemporary philosophy of science which has very appropriately called itself the "unity of science movement." What is considered as *the* scientific method

This essay originally appeared under the same title in *Phänomenologie Heute: Festschrift für Ludwig Landgrebe*, ed. Walter Biemel, *Phaenomenologica* LI (The Hague: Martinus Nijhoff, 1972).

is to be applied beyond the realm of the physical sciences—to biology, psychology, and the social or human sciences as well. Furthermore, following the example of physics, the members of this movement perceive the aim of scientific activities as making predictions which are to be verified by ascertaining facts, events, and occurrences which are said to be public, that is, accessible to any observer at all. In other words, the only kind of verification admitted as legitimate is by means of mere sense perception.[1]

If the method in question is applied to the psychological and social sciences, only overt behavior may be taken into consideration. Accordingly, those sciences are nowadays often designated as behavioral sciences. Moreover, since only such facts and events which are public in the aforementioned sense are considered to be the legitimate subject matter of scientific investigation, whatever sense and meaning those facts and events have for the actors involved is to be left out of account. What is of decisive and crucial importance is not whether the existence of consciousness is conceded or denied but rather that, even if its existence is conceded, consciousness and whatever pertains to it are considered as "private" and thus not on principle subject to scientific investigation. Thus, the methods to be used in the psychological and human sciences do not derive from the specific nature of the reality to be investigated. Instead, a special method—which has come to be regarded as *the scientific method* on account of the theoretical successes it has yielded in the circumscribed field of the natural sciences—has decided which aspects of the psychological and human realities may legitimately lend themselves to scientific treatment.

TRADITIONAL SYSTEMATIZATIONS OF THE SCIENCES

ON THE GROUNDS THUS FAR DISCUSSED, the unity of the sciences rests on the unity or, more correctly, the unicity of the method. There is no question of a hierarchical or systematic order among the sciences. Still, the idea of a hierarchical organization

1. Peter Schwarzburg has critically discussed this view of verification in "On Meaning and Relevance in Primordial Experience" (Ph.D. diss., Graduate Faculty of Political and Social Science, New School for Social Research, 1971), which, it is to be hoped, will be published in the not too distant future.

of the sciences, with some being founded on others, is also advocated in some trends of contemporary theory of science. As far as we can see, Comte was the first to formulate that idea. In the present context, we are concerned with the general tendency and outline of his classification of the sciences rather than with the specific features of the positivism by which his classification is colored.[2]

According to Comte, there are six sciences. The most fundamental is mathematics, dealing with quantity at large, regardless of the specific nature of what is quantified. Next in order is astronomy, the study of masses as subject to central forces (Newton's law of universal gravitation), a discipline which would more properly be designated as mechanics. Since electric and magnetic phenomena and also heat and light are, according to Comte, not reducible to gravitation, they are the subject matter of a special science which he calls physics. Chemistry, in turn, concerns itself with qualitative differences in matter, while biology, next, deals with organized matter. Finally, the new science of sociology is conceived as a study of the cohesive forces and factors of society that do not depend on the biological organization of its members.

If one reads that enumeration of the sciences in the reverse order, one proceeds in the direction of increasing generality and decreasing specificity. Reading it in the ascending order, one moves in the direction of increasing complexity. That is, with regard to a given science, the factors which play a role in the preceding ones remain in play and a new factor, specific to the science in question, is superadded to the former. This scheme suggests reductionistic tendencies, i.e., the attempt at conceiving phenomena pertaining to a "higher" science as resulting from the combination and interplay of "simpler" phenomena. Comte has rejected such reductionistic tendencies, e.g., the explanation of chemical affinity in terms of electrical forces, such that chemistry would become part of physics, because chemical phenomena would then appear merely as especially complex physical phenomena. Comte rejects reductionism and explanation as implying or, at least bordering on, metaphysics. It is his strictly legalistic, in contradistinction to explanatory, conception of the task of science that has led him to leave intact the specific nature of

2. For a succinct exposition of the ideas of Comte, see E. Bréhier, *Histoire de la philosophie*, Vol. II (Paris: Presses Universitaires de France, 1962).

the factors involved in the phenomena which are the subject matter of the several sciences.

Since the time of Comte the situation has changed drastically. Not only have all sciences relinquished Comte's phenomenalistic-legalistic orientation and begun admitting explanatory hypotheses. Reductionism has also come to be accepted and advocated both as a methodological principle guiding concrete scientific research and explanation and as a postulate in contemporary theory of science. In the former respect, the first step to be taken consists in ascertaining the "simplest" phenomena which occur in a given field of research, e.g., the reflex in biology. All other facts are to be reduced to those simple phenomena, i.e., they are to be explained by the interaction of the latter which may reinforce as well as inhibit and counteract one another. "Reducing to" has the sense of "resolving into." Any fact which is not a simple phenomenon itself is considered as satisfactorily explained if it can be presented as the resultant of elementary phenomena. In the final analysis, the fact to be explained proves to be nothing other than the sum total of simple or elementary phenomena which enter as components into the fact under consideration and bring it about by interacting with one another in multifarious ways.[3]

Whereas, for Comte, increasing complexity means the super-addition of specific factors and forces, each of which has a nature of its own and is therefore irreducible to any other, in contemporary reductionism increasing complexity has the sense of

3. The application of this methodological procedure in psychology has been rejected by William James (*The Principles of Psychology* [New York: Henry Holt & Co., 1890], chap. 6), who emphatically denies that mental states are capable of "self-compounding." Its application to biological phenomena has been thoroughly criticized by Kurt Goldstein, *Der Aufbau des Organismus* (The Hague: Martinus Nijhoff, 1934), chaps. 2, 5. See also our two reports on that work: "Le Fonctionnement de l'organisme d'après K. Goldstein," *Journal de psychologie normale et pathologique*, Vol. XXXVI (1939); and "La Science biologique d'après K. Goldstein," *Revue philosophique de la France et de l'étranger*, Vol. CXXIX (1940) (English trans., "Goldstein's Conception of Biological Sciences," in *SPP*). For a discussion of the methodological procedure in question as applied to economics, see A. Lowe, *On Economic Knowledge* (New York: Harper & Row, 1965), pt. II, § 4, and "Towards a Science of Political Economics," in *Economic Means and Social Ends*, ed. R. L. Heilbroner (Englewood Cliffs, N.J.: Prentice-Hall, 1969); and "Social Science and Natural Science," *ibid.*

an increasing number of facts and phenomena coming into play all of which, however, are on principle of the same specific nature. In other words, increasing complexity means, strictly speaking, increasing complication. For this reason, reductionism can be generalized from a methodological principle of concrete research into a universal postulate for all scientific explanation. According to that postulate, all phenomena, at least of nature, including biological and psychological ones (the latter because of their relation to physiological processes in the nervous system), are to be reduced to, i.e., resolved into, facts and occurrences investigated in the science of physics—the latter, of course, being understood in the generally accepted modern sense, not in Comte's.

Obviously, this postulate does not present the actual state of scientific knowledge concerning nature. Rather, it defines a direction for scientific research, a goal to be reached in progressive approximation. By this very token, the postulate implies an ontological view of nature: All natural phenomena are on principle conceived to be vast complications of physical phenomena combining and interacting with one another. Accordingly, the task of scientific research consists in the specification of that general conception, a specification both of the physical facts involved in a particular case and of the laws of their combination and interaction. On these grounds, the systematic unity of the sciences purports not only unicity of method but, as far as nature is concerned, the mentioned ontological view as well. Physics passes for the fundamental and even the only science, the latter in the sense that all other natural sciences are resolvable into it.

For the sake of completeness, let us also mention Jean Piaget's conception of the system of the sciences, which significantly departs from Comte's.[4] Within Piaget's system, there is a place for the science of psychology which Comte excluded. Moreover, it is to psychology that Piaget assigns the task of accounting for the formal sciences, logic and mathematics. Because of their use of the axiomatic method, the formal sciences at first give the appearance of autonomy, of standing on their own feet, and of having no presuppositions outside themselves.

4. J. Piaget, *Introduction à l'épistémologie génétique* (Paris: Presses Universitaires de France, 1950), Vol. I, Introduction, § 6. See *The Origins of Intelligence in Children*, trans. Margaret Cook (New York: International Universities Press, 1956), Introduction.

According to Piaget, however, axioms are the results of axiomatization. They are conceptual expressions and fixations of intellectual operations which themselves are subject matters of psychology. Since Piaget gives a genetic turn to psychology, he refers psychological operations to biological processes, conceiving of mental assimilation and accommodation, the functional invariants of all intellectual operations, as continuing biological assimilation and accommodation. Biological processes must be explained in terms of physics and chemistry, sciences which make use of and rely on mathematics, so that we are brought back to psychology as the study of the mind and its laws.

Comte's linear arrangement is here replaced by a circular one. Because of the role which Piaget assigns to psychology with regard to the formal disciplines, and, more generally, because he sees, in all of the sciences, mental elaborations and constructions owing to intellectual operations, both his genetic epistemology and his developmental psychology lend themselves to a reinterpretation in terms of Husserlian phenomenology and can be fruitfully utilized for the advancement of some phenomenological problems. On the other hand, Piaget conceives of the approach to and the study of the mind, i.e., psychology, within a naturalistic setting—a conception which expresses an irreducible difference between his orientation and that of Husserlian phenomenology.

Rootedness of the Sciences in the Life-World

Throughout all of his writings, Husserl endeavored to extricate the study of the mind from a naturalistic setting and expressed doubts concerning the monopolistic claim to universal validity and applicability of the methods successfully employed in the natural sciences.[5] At the end of his life, he explicitly challenged the theoretical prestige of modern physics that has caused it to be considered as the paradigm, in the several senses we have mentioned, for all scientific endeavor. Most closely related hereto is Husserl's refusal to endorse the view that

5. See Husserl's casual, ironic remark: "the pious belief in the omnipotence of the inductive method" (*Ideas,* p. 275; translation modified).

mathematics provides the ideal and the norm of genuine knowledge in the sense of *epistēmē* as opposed to *doxa*.

To avoid misunderstandings, we must emphasize that Husserl's analysis is not to be misconstrued as an expression of hostility to modern science. While in no way challenging the legitimacy of scientific pursuits or the intrinsic validity and fruitfulness of the results already obtained and to be expected in the future, Husserl raises questions about the very sense of those pursuits, about the goals in whose service scientific activities are carried on—goals to be reached or, perhaps, only to be approximated asymptotically. Differently expressed, all sciences rest on presuppositions by which their sense is essentially determined. Those presuppositions tend to be overlooked and, in the course of the development of modern science and under the impact of its theoretical (and also technological) successes, they have fallen into oblivion (*Crisis,* § 9). Thus the very sense of the sciences—more correctly, the sense of scientific activity as such and at large (rather than of particular results and theories, e.g., the theory of relativity)—has become obfuscated. For a philosophical understanding of the sciences, as distinguished from the consistent and correct application of methodological procedures and also the invention of new methods—in other words, for their radical understanding—it is imperative to disclose the sense foundations in which the sciences are rooted, that is, to uncover and to make explicit the presuppositions on which they rest and by which they are made possible.

In all scientific elaboration and interpretation, intellectual operations—more precisely, conceptualizations—are involved. This holds for both the natural sciences and the sciences of the mind, the psychological, historical, and social—briefly, the human sciences. As far as the sciences of nature are concerned, it holds for modern science of the Galilean style as well as for pre-Galilean science of Aristotelian provenance. For those reasons, we must leave open, at least to begin with, whether conceptualization is always of the same kind or admits of differentiation. At any event, the mental processes of conceptualization require materials on which to operate, and those materials must, in turn, be of such a nature as to lend themselves to being conceptualized. The materials in question are none other than the things, beings, events, occurrences, and so on in what Husserl calls the life-world or the world of prescientific, pretheoretical, or prepredicative encounter (*"vorwissenschaftliche Erfahrungs- welt"*).[6]

All sciences, without exception, originate in the life-world on the basis of the findings encountered in it. Furthermore, except those sciences which, like mathematics and logic, concern themselves thematically with pure idealities, the sciences find the subject matter of their study in the life-world; their purpose and sense are to provide a theoretical account of the life-world. More correctly expressed, each of the several sciences singles out and focuses on a certain segment or aspect of the life-world. However, those segments or aspects are not given beforehand in neat demarcation from one another. Rather, their delimitation and, along with it, the very constitution of the several sciences, are the outcome of theoretical work guided by theoretical interests.[7] *The first presupposition of the sciences proves to be the life- world itself, our paramount and even sole reality. Whatever unity obtains among the sciences derives from their common rooted- ness in the life-world,* from which all of them originate and to which most of them explicitly relate as their theme.

As here understood, the life-world (and whatever it contains) must be taken as it presents itself in primordial, pretheoretical, and prepredicative encounter, that is, as not yet seen from the perspective of or with reference to an ideal order, e.g., from the perspective of possible mathematization or even affected by conceptualization of any kind. On the other hand, the life-world does lend itself to conceptualization, idealization, and mathematization; it is of such a nature as to motivate theoretical interests and, along with them, the demarcation of the fields of study of the several sciences. In other words, in its very pretheoretical and preconceptual appearance, the life-world exhibits a certain specific logicality of its own, a logicality—it must be stressed— which is not the logos in its fully developed form but merely the germ from which the logos is made to grow by means of specific mental operations. With reference to modern mathematical physics, but in a way admitting of generalization, Husserl

6. Following the suggestion of Robert Sokolowski, *The Formation of Husserl's Concept of Constitution* (The Hague: Martinus Nijhoff, 1964), pp. 4 f., we render *Erfahrung* by "encounter," while "experience" denotes *Erlebnis*.

7. Husserl, *Phänomenologische Psychologie*, ed. Walter Biemel, *Husserliana* IX (The Hague: Martinus Nijhoff, 1962), § 6.

(*Crisis,* § 25) makes the distinction between "lebensweltliches Apriori" and the mathematical or any other "objektives Apriori" and speaks of a certain idealizing operation ("Leistung") which leads from the former to the latter. It, therefore, seems most appropriate to call the specific logicality prevailing in the life-world "protologic." [8]

That protologic manifests itself most strikingly in the typicality pervading and permeating all encounter in the life-world. Whatever is encountered presents itself as somehow familiar, that is, it appears in the light of a certain preacquaintanceship, of knowledge previously acquired which is brought to bear on the present encounter (*EJ,* § 8). Reference may be made to Schutz's notion of the "stock of knowledge at hand" which is available to the actor and guides him in his interpretation of the situations he encounters and in his actions.[9] Obviously, the knowledge here in question is familiarity with a type: What is at present encountered appears to be of a familiar kind. According to circumstances, the type may be more or less vague and unspecified, delineated merely along highly schematic lines, but even in the case of a maximum of vagueness it is never completely devoid of all determinateness (*FC,* pp. 234–47). Two questions arise in this connection. (1) How is the impact of acquired knowledge upon future encounter to be accounted for? (2) In which way is typification as a pervasive feature of conscious life rooted in the very nature of consciousness? While we have endeavored elsewhere to provide an answer to the first question (*FC,* pp. 48–52, 98–101), the second can only be mentioned here. Without inquiring into the grounds of typification, let us confine ourselves to accepting it as a fundamental fact of conscious life and proceed to illustrate it with a few examples.

In the life-world, we encounter fellow human beings, i.e., beings of the same type as ourselves. A first differentiation according to type is that among men, women, and children. Moreover, we encounter our fellow men in a further differentiation—as strangers in the street, fellow passengers on a train or airplane, postmen and policemen (recognizable by their uniforms), business associates, students, teachers, physicians, patients, and so on. Our fellow men appear to us as typified in terms of their

8. The term "protologic" was coined by Lester Embree in one of our seminars.

9. Alfred Schutz, "Some Structures of the Life-World," *Collected Papers* (The Hague: Martinus Nijhoff, 1962–66), Vol. III (1966).

social role and function. Following Husserl, Schutz has brought out and emphasized typicality and typification as—far from being confined to the social realm—pervading all encounter in the life-world.[10] In fact, we encounter, as we may say, another dog, another tree, another car, another residential building, and the like, that is, beings and objects of a certain kind rather than individuals whose properties are given in complete determinateness.

Thus corporeal things exhibit spatial shapes which have to be distinguished from geometrical forms and figures in the proper sense (*Crisis*, § 9a). Dinner plates, for example, have circular shapes. "Circular" is here not to be understood as denoting an ideal geometrical figure in the strict sense or even as an approximation to one. To conceive of spatial shapes as approximations requires their being referred to ideal geometrical entities and, consequently, presupposes the latter entities as already constituted. This constitution, although originating within the life-world and on the basis of occurrences encountered in it, leads beyond the life-world to an ideal realm which may be called "transcendent" with regard to the life-world. Terms like "cubiform," "circular," "pyramidal," "cylindrical," and the like, when applied to objects as encountered in the life-world, rather denote physiognomic types admitting of a latitude for variations and vacillations; the latter are confined within certain more or less vaguely circumscribed limits which are determined by the special type in question. The same holds for the regularity of the changes observed in the life-world. Things—as Husserl expresses it— have their "habits" of behaving in typically similar ways under typically similar circumstances (*Crisis*, § 9b). They undergo certain typical changes along with those occurring in other things and, generally speaking, in their environment. The regularities here in question must also be understood as typicalities which admit of vacillations and not as mathematically expressible functional dependencies; but the typical regularities underlie the functional dependencies which arise on their basis by means of idealizing operations.

In general, the life-world as a whole exhibits an invariant typical total style whereby inductions and predictions, again in

10. Schutz has dealt with the topic in a great many of his writings, so that we may refer to the entries under the headings "type," "typicality," "typification," and "self-typification" in the indexes to the three volumes of his *Collected Papers*.

the sense of a more or less vague typicality, are made possible. The typical total style of the life-world is such that, although the harmonious development and coherence of encountering it is occasionally broken by the occurrence of discrepancies, conflicts, and incompatibilities, such discrepancies have thus far been resolved in the course of perceptual processes—later encounters, i.e., encounters under more "favorable" conditions, correct the yieldings of previous encounters. Idealizing extrapolation leads to the idea or—as Husserl puts it—the presumption of the world as it is in itself, that is, the true condition of the world which may be discovered in the course of a perhaps infinite process of encounter and exploration. At the ideally conceived end of this process, no further corrections or revisions will be necessitated.[11]

In one of his last writings, Schutz has called attention to Husserl's using the notion of typicality in at least two different senses.[12] In *Experience and Judgment*, typicality is defined in terms of indeterminacies affecting the "inner horizon" and the "open possibilities" contained in it, whereas in *Crisis* the emphasis is on the margin of latitude for variations and vacillations. We cannot enter into a discussion of the question of whether or not the two senses of typicality exhibit sufficient kinship for them to be subsumed under a common notion—the mentioned difference between them notwithstanding—in the present context.

PRELIMINARY IDEAS TOWARD A PHENOMENOLOGICAL THEORY OF THE SCIENCES

FROM THE POINT OF VIEW of Husserlian phenomenology, the elaboration of the theory of science proves to be tantamount to accounting for the transition from protologic, i.e., the specific logicality which pertains to the life-world and manifests itself in the typicality prevailing in the latter, to the conceptual and logical realm in the strict and proper sense. In other words, *the first task of a phenomenological theory of the sciences is to develop a phenomenological theory of conceptualization*, that is, *a phenomenological account of the transition from type to a concept and eidos.*

11. Husserl, *Phänomenologische Psychologie*, § 19.
12. Schutz, "Type and Eidos in Husserl's Late Philosophy," *Collected Papers*, Vol. III, §§ 1, 4.

Conceptualization is possible along two different lines of direction which Husserl has distinguished from one another under the headings "generalization" and "formalization." [13] In the present context, we must confine ourselves to pointing out that the theory of conceptualization, generalization, formalization, and algebraization is one of the most urgent tasks with which phenomenological research finds itself confronted at the present stage of its development. To be sure, especially in *Experience and Judgment*, whose subtitle is "Investigations into the Genealogy of Logic," Husserl has tackled the problem of conceptualization, among others, from a genetic point of view, "genetic" understood in the specifically phenomenological sense (*EJ*, Pt. III, chaps. 1, 2). Still, the problem is far from being exhausted. Not only is there ample room for further investigation, but some of Husserl's results—we submit—require revisions and modifications. Even a superficial consideration of those matters would lead us beyond the scope of this discussion.

If all sciences originate in the life-world and arise on the basis of encounters within it, is there a systematic, i.e., logical, order concerning their constitution? We have argued in Chapter 1 that the life-world is essentially a sociohistorical, that is, a cultural, world. In the life-world, we do not encounter—at least not in the first place—mere corporeal objects, pure perceptual things which can be exhaustively described in terms of what traditionally are called primary and secondary qualities. What we encounter are cultural objects, objects of value, e.g., works of art, buildings which serve specific purposes, like abodes, places for work, schools, libraries, churches, and so on. Objects pertaining to the life-world present themselves as tools, instruments, and utensils related to human needs and desires; they have to be handled and used in appropriate ways to satisfy those needs and to yield desired results.[14] It is the specific sense of their

13. Husserl, *Philosophie der Arithmetik* (Halle: Pfeffer, 1891), chap. 4; *LI*, pp. 236 ff., 241 ff.; *Ideas*, §§ 10 ff.; *FTL* §§ 24, 27 ff., 87; and *Crisis*, § 9 f. See "On a Perceptual Root of Abstraction," in *SPP*.

14. See Heidegger, *Being and Time*, trans. John Macquarrie and Edward Robinson (London: SCM Press, 1962), § 15, about "Zeug" in contradistinction to "Ding," and "Zuhandenheit" as distinguished from "Vorhandenheit." On entirely different grounds, the connection between perception and action has been emphasized by Bergson in *Matter and Memory*, trans. Nancy Margaret Paul and W. Scott Palmer (London: George Allen & Unwin, 1911), chap. 1.

instrumentality which essentially defines those objects and makes them be what they are, that is, what they mean to the members of the sociohistorical group to whose life-world they belong.

By the social character of the life-world more is meant than the presence of persons who perform typical roles and functions in whose terms they are defined and determined. Among the members of a social group, there is a consensus concerning the ways of doing things and the typical behavior to be displayed under typical conditions. It is not necessary that the consensus be explicitly formalized, sanctioned, and enforced. Besides the legal order, there are in every society usages, habits, and mores all of which, without being rendered explicit and explicitly formulated, are silently accepted as matters of course and taken for granted as the natural ways of behaving under typical circumstances. Finally, every society entertains views, beliefs, and interpretations concerning their "world" as well as themselves within their "world." For example, the world is taken by present Western societies as amenable to technological manipulation and control. These beliefs and interpretations, which must not be understood in a strictly conceptual sense and are hardly systematized coherently, vary from one society to the other, vary for the different social strata in a given society, and vary in the course of the society's history. Obviously, the same holds for the consensus as to usages and mores.

Therefore, in starting from the notion of the life-world taken in full concreteness, we find ourselves confronted with a plurality of life-worlds. Consequently, the first sciences to emerge are those which concern themselves with the several life-worlds, both past and present, that is, the sciences which endeavor to reconstruct a life-world of the past or to lay bare and make explicit the particular nature of a present one. In contrast to the traditional view of the stratification of the sciences, the sociohistorical or human sciences appear to precede the natural sciences in the logical order of constitution.

Abiding by the plurality of life-worlds entails endorsing a sociohistorical relativism. For that relativism to be overcome, the question may, and must, be raised of whether there is a world common to all human beings and all sociohistorical groups, a world invariantly the same over and against the diversities of the multiple life-worlds and in that sense "beyond" the latter. To attain that world, an abstractive procedure is required. Starting from any concrete life-world, one disregards the specific interpretation and comprehension it receives in the corresponding sociohistorical group and retains only the remainder which is left after the abstraction has been performed. By this very token, the objects encountered in the life-world are stripped of their cultural senses and values; they lose their instrumental characteristics and become mere corporeal things to be accounted for in terms of both primary and secondary qualities, but in those terms only. In other words, the life-world which is a cultural world undergoes a transformation into a mere thing-world. This distinction is reminiscent of that established in early Greek philosophy between *thesei* and *physei*, by convention and by nature, between what is and what is not man-made.

Husserl's treatment of cultural objects and the cultural world is beset by ambiguity. On one hand, he insists on the cultural sense, e.g., a specific instrumentality's being a property which the object in question possesses in its own right; the cultural sense is "impressed" on and incorporated in the object ("eingedrückt" and "eingeschmolzen") and must not be misconstrued as a psychological occurrence accompanying the perception of a mere thing and being merely extrinsically associated with it.[15] Accordingly, the transition from the cultural world to the thing-world requires an abstractive procedure. On the other hand, Husserl conceives of the thing-world arrived at by means of the abstractive procedure as having precedence and priority with respect to the cultural world.[16] In other words, the thing-world is interpreted by Husserl as being common to all diverse life-worlds in the sense that the latter include and contain the former as a common invariant substratum underlying them.

It seems to us to be more in conformity with the spirit of phenomenology to define priority in terms of priority of access. For that reason, we maintain the priority of the cultural world over the thing-world. Because it is arrived at by a process of abstraction operating on the cultural world, the thing-world proves to be of a "higher" order with respect to the cultural world rather than an underlying and supporting substratum of the cultural world. Differently expressed, we locate the thing-world "beyond" rather than—as Husserl does—"beneath" the cultural world. It is to the thing-world as thus understood that

15. *Ideas*, §§ 27, 117; still more explicitly, *Phänomenologische Psychologie*, § 16.
16. *Phänomenologische Psychologie*, p. 118: "Offenbar ist diese Dingwelt gegenüber der Kulturwelt das an sich Früher."

Husserl's idea of what he calls "Apriori der Lebenswelt" or "Ontologie der Lebenswelt" (*Crisis*, §§ 36, 51) has to be referred.

Utensils and cultural objects in general are transformed into things, and the persons encountered lose the typical characteristics deriving from their social roles and functions and present themselves as living organisms endowed with mental life.[17] The place of psychology as a positive science, abiding by the *natural attitude*, is on this level, although not conceived of in a *naturalistic setting*. Correspondingly, the same holds for those natural sciences which may be called descriptive in the sense of accounting for the subject matter of their studies in its own terms, that is, without reference to an ideal (mathematical) order. If allowance is made (as it must be) for the fact that men live in a society, *any* society, there arises the idea, delineated by Schutz, of a philosophical anthropology setting forth the universal invariant structures of human existence, including its social dimension.[18] The problem of the relation of philosophical anthropology in Schutz's sense to Husserl's "Ontologie der Lebenswelt" cannot be tackled here.

A further step leads from the thing-world as we have described it to the scientific universe in the specifically modern sense, that is, nature as mathematized. For the sake of brevity, we confine ourselves to referring to Husserl's analyses of the genesis of sense and the presuppositions of Galilean science, i.e., science of the Galilean style, and to what others, following Husserl, have written on the subject.[19] We propose to deal with a paradoxical situation which, according to Husserl, arises in this connection (*Crisis*, §§ 34b, 34e). He endeavors to show that the scientific universe—that is, the theoretical constructs in terms of which nature is mathematized—is, in the final analysis, founded upon the "Evidenz der Lebenswelt." The latter provides the ground on which the edifice of the scientific universe is

17. See *ibid.*, p. 119; but there is no reference to social roles and the abstraction from them.

18. Schutz, "Equality and the Meaning Structure of the Social World," *Collected Papers*, II (1964), 229 ff.

19. *Crisis*, § 9; Joseph J. Kockelmans, "The Mathematization of Nature in Husserl's Last Publication, *Krisis*," in *Phenomenology and the Natural Sciences*, ed. Joseph J. Kockelmans and Theodore J. Kisiel (Evanston, Ill.: Northwestern University Press, 1970); and chap. 2, above.

built. Still, the edifice must be distinguished from the ground on which it stands.

Scientific theories and the entities in terms of which they are conceived and constructed are not encountered in, or belong to, the life-world, like trees, houses, and stones. On the other hand, scientific theories are elaborated through mental activities and operations and, therefore, refer to the scientists who produce them and who as human beings live within and belong to the life-world understood as a cultural world. Scientific activities are carried on in the cultural world and their purpose is to provide a systematic rationalization and explanation in mathematical terms of occurrences in the life-world (more correctly in the thing-world to which the cultural world must first be reduced); moreover, Husserl also goes so far as to maintain that, because of their validity for the life-world (whether understood as a cultural world or a thing-world), the theoretical results and accomplishments of the sciences are inserted and integrated into the life-world. The paradox consists in the scientific universe's being constructed by means of special mental operations on the basis of the life-world as specifically different from the latter and yet at the same time apparently proving to be part and parcel of it.

Two distinctions may serve to resolve that paradox. First, theoretical science in the proper sense must be distinguished from the technological use to which it lends itself or, to express it more properly, which may be derived from it. Only the technological derivatives of theoretical science, but not the latter itself, come to be incorporated into the life-world in the form of rules for handling things and acting on them to obtain certain results. Such rules are adhered to because and as long as they yield the desired results.[20] The second distinction is more subtle in nature. One could be tempted to argue that, while the scientists undoubtedly are members of their cultural world and their mental activities belong to that world because they take place in it, this does not apply to the products and results of their activities, namely, the scientific theories which have an autonomous status of their own over and against the mental activities through

20. On the predominance of the pragmatic motive in the world of daily life, see Schutz, "On Multiple Realities," *Collected Papers*, I (1962), 20 ff.; and *Reflections in the Problem of Relevance*, ed. Richard M. Zaner (New Haven and London: Yale University Press, 1970), pp. 5 ff.

which they are arrived at. Legitimate and even necessary though the distinction is between mental activities and their results and products as their intentional or noematic correlates, the complete divorce of the former from the latter is at variance with the intentionality of consciousness, especially when intentionality is defined as noetico-noematic correlation.[21] In fact, the historian studying a certain period, who must take into consideration the scientific work done during that period, cannot avoid making allowance for the results of that work—the scientific views and theories advanced.

The distinction which we have in mind is rather a difference in attitude toward the sciences and their "epistemic claims." [22] A scientist makes claims and must debate about them. He accepts a certain claim, rejects it, or else modalizes it by, e.g., ascribing to it a greater or lesser degree of likelihood. Briefly, he takes a stand with regard to epistemic claims. No such stand is taken by the historian, who may as well be assumed to study the period in which he himself lives. The historian does not accept, reject, or modalize any epistemic claims. To be sure, in dealing with the sciences of the period he studies, he has to take notice of and allow for their epistemic claims. However, while he must recognize those claims as such, his position in their regard must be that of neutrality and abstention from involvement. In a word, the historian takes the sciences merely as cultural facts among other such facts.[23]

If they are approached in this attitude, all of the sciences, including the mathematical sciences of nature, find their place within the cultural world. For that reason, according to Husserl (*Crisis*, p. 237), the cultural or human sciences prove to be all-encompassing, since they also comprise the natural sciences, since nature as conceived of and constructed in modern natural science, i.e., mathematized nature, is itself a mental accomplish-

21. Along Husserlian lines, but going beyond Husserl's formulations, we have endeavored to develop the conception of intentionality as noetico-noematic correlation in our essays "On the Intentionality of Consciousness," in *SPP;* "Towards a Theory of Intentionality," *Philosophy and Phenomenological Research*, Vol. XXX (1970); and below, chap. 9.

22. We borrow this very fortunate, because telling, term from R. M. Zaner, *The Way of Phenomenology* (New York: Pegasus Books, 1970).

23. About the attitude of neutrality with regard to the sciences, see *CM*, § 3.

ment, that is, a cultural phenomenon. The converse, however, is not true. The cultural sciences cannot be given a place among the natural sciences, any more than the cultural world can be reached beginning from mathematized nature or, for that matter, from the thing-world, while, as we have seen, by taking one's departure from the cultural world, one can arrive at the thing-world and the mathematized universe by means of abstraction, idealization, and formalization. In general, then, there is a possible transition from the concrete to the abstract, but not the reverse.

SUMMARY

OUR DISCUSSION has led to the conclusion that the unity of the sciences consists in their common rootedness in the life-world, which exhibits a logicality of its own. The first task which presents itself to a phenomenological theory of the sciences is giving an account of the transition from that logicality—proto-logic—to the logic proper, that is, to the development of a theory of conceptualization, both generalization and formalization. Furthermore, the sciences appear in a certain order derived from their relative nearness or remoteness from the concrete life-world. However, there is no systematic order among the sciences in the traditional sense of stratification, with the "higher" sciences relying on the "lower," i.e., more fundamental, ones and availing themselves of the results of the latter. Differently expressed, the domains of reality dealt with by the "higher" sciences cannot be accounted for in terms of increasing complexity. Finally, the fact that a certain method has proved theoretically fruitful in modern physics in no way justifies considering it as the only scientific method, as the scientific method *par excellence*.

PART II

Contributions to
Constitutive Phenomenology

7 / An Introduction to Constitutive Phenomenology

ONE SHOULD NOT APPROACH A PHILOSOPHY in the manner of an impartial spectator who views its expression as merely literary documents. A summary of proposed solutions is not an introduction. A philosophy is properly introduced by presenting the motives and problems which brought it to life. The ideas must be traced back to their point of origin so that the work is reperformed and re-created. This is as true for historical studies of the sciences as for those of philosophy, and even more true where it is a matter of a living philosophical movement which—and here we agree with Edmund Husserl—is only at the beginning of its development. For this reason, we do not offer a résumé of Husserlian phenomenology or pretend to an exhaustive commentary on his works. To avoid overwhelming the reader with analyses of analyses, our exposition is limited to major points of selected phenomenological theories. Instead of presenting the doctrines as finished products that might seem to have fallen from the sky, we have tried, in a sense, to let

This is a slightly edited translation by Bethia S. Currie of the Introduction and first two chapters of the unpublished book, "Esquisse de la phénoménologie constitutive," which the author was preparing for publication when he left France in 1939. That book derived from lectures on constitutive phenomenology which he gave at L'Institut d'Histoire des Sciences et des Techniques de la Université de Paris (Sorbonne) in 1937, and much of *The Field of Consciousness* is derived from the other two chapters of his manuscript, which are entitled "La Conception de la conscience" and "La Structure du noême perceptif." Mlle. Monique Lippman originally read the text for possible errors in French idiom.

phenomenology be born before the reader's eyes. Proceeding in this way, the author must inevitably exercise a certain arbitrariness and pass over in silence many phenomenological theories no less interesting or important than those chosen for discussion here.

THE PROBLEM OF THE PHILOSOPHY OF CONSCIOUSNESS

The Philosophy of Consciousness as "First Philosophy"

MODERN PHILOSOPHY DIFFERS essentially from that of antiquity and the Middle Ages in concentrating on the conscious grasp of objective being and on the apperception of consciousness itself as a special domain rather than on Being itself. The discovery of consciousness is one of the most notable achievements of Descartes and after him it becomes the principal theme of philosophy.

Descartes does not restrict the *cogito sum* to an axiomatic point of departure for a series of deductions, i.e., to an initial premise. Summing up the analysis and critique of perception he has just performed in the second of his *Meditations*, Descartes concludes that whenever an external body is grasped by an act of consciousness, consciousness itself is disclosed "not only with much more truth and certainty, but also with much greater distinctness and clarity." [1] To be in relation to any extramental object is to be in relation to oneself, i.e., to one's mind. When the conscious grasp of an object is experienced as the object presents itself as actually existing, that very act of consciousness is itself grasped with increased force as a conscious reality. Every act and process of the mind which suggest, correctly or incorrectly, the admission of an external thing as existing, reaffirm the existence of the mind itself. Thus consciousness appears as a domain of being contraposed to its objects. Whatever the object with which the mind is occupied, and whatever the manner in which the mind is conscious of it, there is a necessary reference back to the acts in and by which one finds

1. *The Philosophical Works of Descartes*, trans. Elizabeth S. Haldane and G. R. T. Ross (New York: Dover Publications, 1955), I, 156.

oneself, all at once, in the presence of consciousness, the only domain to resist the universal doubt. The *cogito sum* must therefore be understood as the expression of this discovery of an aboriginal domain of being, prior to any other, alone possessed of indubitable existence, and, in this sense, absolute.

This privilege attributed to consciousness by Descartes persists throughout modern philosophy, especially in the classical English school of Locke, Berkeley, and Hume, and is carried over into nineteenth-century empiricism. These were the first thinkers to subject consciousness to systematic investigation. We shall not concentrate here on the historical reasons governing this new philosophical orientation. We want to show the ground for this privilege assigned to consciousness. This consideration provided the driving force of empiricism and must still be taken into account among the motifs which gave rise to *phenomenology*. Properly speaking, it is no more than a deepening generalization of the idea expressed in the quotation from Descartes above.

The task of a systematic investigation of consciousness was passed on from the Cartesians to the empiricists because of what may be termed the mathematical bias with which the Cartesians are imbued. Malebranche, e.g., while maintaining that we know "more distinctly the existence of our soul than the existence of our body and those around us," nevertheless does not grant that there may be "as perfect a knowledge of the nature of the soul as of the nature of the body." "The idea that we have of extension is sufficient to make us acquainted with all of the possible properties of extendedness." [2] Each particular modification of extension, each shape, each motion, can and must be conceived as a variation of the fundamental idea of extension, as a special case of an ideal generalization, issuing, in accordance with determinate laws, from that idea which guarantees its possibility as well as its necessity. But it is entirely different for the soul, which is not what Husserl calls a "definite multiplicity" (*Ideas*, § 72), because we do not have an idea of the soul but know its modifications only "by the internal feeling that we have of ourselves" or by way of "consciousness."

In this domain, so privileged as to its existence, there are no means for conceiving and embracing a totality of possibility. If someone has never directly experienced a color, warmth,

2. *De la recherche de la vérité*, bk. III, pt. II, chap. 7, §§ 3, 4.

pleasure, sorrow, etc., "these sensations could not be conveyed to him by all the definitions of them that we could muster." He could not even "know whether or not our soul is capable of them." In this matter there is not a fundamental idea which is differentiated and deployed in a system of possibilities. Therefore, it can only be noted that "what we sense is outside of us," i.e., we can record only the presence of data which are produced. But such a knowledge by means of experience does not answer to the mathematical ideal by which Malebranche is guided. In spite of this thesis, which he defends, Malebranche must be counted among those who inaugurated modern psychology. Cassirer characterizes him as "the first genuine *psychologist* in the history of modern philosophy." [3] We shall return to the general orientation Malebranche gave to the embryonic psychology.

The objects which form our surroundings exist for us only by virtue of the acts of consciousness in which they present themselves to us. In and by these acts we are placed in relation to the objects, which thus become accessible and are deployed before the conscious subject, presenting themselves as they are, taking shape for the subject with all of their determinations and qualities. Without such acts of consciousness, we could not discuss objects or have a suspicion of their existence—or even of its possibility. Any property whatsoever, of any object whatsoever, is determined solely by a conscious grasp of that object as it presents itself in its authentic nature. Even when the scientific truth of an object's authentic nature is sought by substituting for the perceivable thing the physical and "objective" body constructed as, for example, in physics, the constitutive acts involved pertain to consciousness and consist in specific activities of the mind by which all of the determinations characterizing the object are conferred on it. In fact, that an object exists means that someone has an actual experience of it, or that, if certain conditions are met, one can then expect to experience those acts of consciousness in which the object in question will present itself. It is possible, of course, to be deceived about an object or even about its existence. Something that has been accepted as existing may subsequently be revealed as mere appearance. But, even in such a case, it is the acts of consciousness which are responsible for the correction of the initial error. Acts which are in some respect more adequate call the prior acts into question

3. *Das Erkenntnisproblem* (Berlin: Bruno Cassirer, 1911), I, 554.

and supplant them. Thus only consciousness itself can modify what has presented itself to consciousness. The existence of a world is relative to consciousness alone, and it is because of consciousness alone that this world presents itself as it is.

Consequently, a philosophical understanding of the world and its component objects requires that one turn to consciousness, for philosophical understanding is a radical comprehension in which no reality is accepted as simply given but must be grasped in its origin in such a way that its existential sense is disclosed. However, the ground of things cannot be found elsewhere than in consciousness, in the acts by virtue of which the things appear and in which they are constituted and present themselves as existing. One must return to these acts in which the specific existential sense is conferred on things, and one must examine them. That is, in order to understand the things, the philosopher must reestablish their modes of appearance and must disengage their formation, constitution, and genesis for consciousness.

Thus, for example, to determine what the material thing and the world of sense in general may be, Hume set himself the task of analyzing perceptions and other acts in and by which this world has its inception. Or, again, in elaborating theories about the genesis of the representation of space, the empiricists proceeded by determining the elements composing that representation and by disengaging the progressive stages of its constitution, thus placing in evidence what space is, bringing to light the very meaning of spatiality.

The world as it is sensed and understood in daily living can be subjected to scientific determinations. Ideas are formed, judgments are made, and theories are elaborated, and all of these are unarguably creations of the mind, springing from the spontaneity of thought. The universe of numbers, mathematical data, and all kinds of relations can and must originate solely in those acts of consciousness by which they are conceived and constituted. Once again, a philosophical understanding of these forms of thought requires a reference back to consciousness as the source from which they stem. The meaning of these creations of thought, the particular existence which belongs to them or, better yet, their specific mode of existence, can be disengaged only by backtracking to their birth in consciousness, by taking by surprise—so to speak—the mental steps by which each such creation is constituted. Thus the philosophical analysis of the nature of numbers leads back to the acts of counting in which the numbers originate. For this reason, the empiricists paid close attention to *abstraction*, establishing psychological theories intended to shed a definitive light on the nature of general notions, which are essential elements of theoretical knowledge. It was the same apropos "belief," a phenomenon in which, to the eyes of the empiricists, the truth of theories, the acceptance of extra-mental objects, and the certainty of all belief in general are reduced.

Thus the whole world, objects of every kind, with all of their determinations and characteristics, all ideas, relations, and other creations of thought, must be regarded as the *correlates* of conscious acts, either of particular acts or of combinations or groups of acts, where it is necessary that a plurality of diverse acts concur in the constitution of an object, whatever the relation that may exist among these acts or the specific character assumed by the group they form. *Transcendental* problems, problems relating to the conditions of the possibility of objects, their unity, their objectivity, their existence, or its meaning, and relating also to the conditions of the truth and validity of everything which presents itself as true and valid, can be approached and carried toward solution only by an analysis of these acts of consciousness of which the objects, notions, truths, and so on, are the respective correlates. Indeed, these conditions of possibility cannot be found except in the conscious life itself. In *transcendental philosophy*, which arises from the conception of objects as correlates of acts of consciousness, reflection on the conscious grasp of an object replaces the straightforward directing of the mind toward the object itself that is the normal attitude in both daily life and the sciences. It would seem, then, that transcendental philosophy must of necessity take the form of a universal psychology.

Whether or not the empiricists were aware of the full implications of the fundamental task in which they were engaged, an enormous philosophical importance accrues to their admirable philosophical radicalism in conceiving such a program of work, even if almost all of their particular doctrines are rejected, as is true for Husserlian phenomenology. But the elaboration of a universal psychology in the service of transcendental philosophy reveals an insurmountable difficulty of principle which endangers the fundamental conception just discussed. This difficulty must now be explained in its most general form.

The Dependence of Consciousness on Objective Entities

We are acquainted with consciousness as human or animal consciousness connected with a central nervous system and in relation to an external world, a relation which is necessarily one of dependence. For example, to explain perception it is necessary to consider, along with some purely psychological factors, the present state of the nervous system and the effects resulting when external stimuli act on this system. In other words, perceptual data appear as responses by consciousness to physical and objective facts, as reactions conditioned by a multiplicity of variables—which necessarily include biological and physical data. Thus, although consciousness can and must be considered as a special reality, it is one reality among others in the collection of realities, existing in the world, by which it is influenced and with which it interacts. An inquiry into consciousness, therefore, takes the form of research bearing on this interdependence and interaction. Indeed, in the psychophysical branch of psychology the task is to establish the relations between changes occurring in the corresponding perceptual data and the physical factors.

In principle, such an investigation of consciousness in its dependent relation to objective data has been carried out by Locke. The soul, which he compares to a blank sheet of paper, is located in a surrounding universe, conceived of in accordance with the physical theories of his time. Physical facts and events exercise effects on the sense organs, so that the simple ideas of "sensation" are inscribed on the "blank paper." [4] Adding ideas of "reflection," Locke seeks to explain the origin of the notions of the human mind and of the qualitative aspect under which physical reality presents itself. His intention is to explain the formation and constitution for consciousness of knowledge and the objects of knowledge, but all of his analyses and constructions rest on the assumption of a real physical universe whose existence he accepts from the beginning without subjecting it to criticism of any kind.

4. See Locke, *An Essay Concerning Human Understanding*, bk. II, chap. 1, §§ 2, 3, and chap. 8, §§ 12, 13.

Consciousness is not, however, dependent on the physical universe alone. Man lives in a particular society in a certain historical epoch of that society. Sociologists, especially those of the Durkheim school, have made us aware of the constraining force of the "social fact." However one may balance out individual initiative and the social fact, i.e., whether personal thought is viewed as merely the stamp of the social fact or as providing the ground for this fact, any study of consciousness would seem to require taking account of the concrete sociohistorical locale of an individual and inquiring into the interplay of the social factors which form the framework within which the human life unfolds and which determine, by their action on an individual, the content of his consciousness.

Thus one arrives at the same result, whether it is the physical universe or the human universe that is being considered. Consciousness, which appeared in the Cartesian investigations as the source of all existence and therefore as a primordial and absolute domain of being, in the sense that "nulla re indiget ad existendum," is now revealed as depending on and conditioned by realities external to it. Consciousness is not, apparently, a closed and Archimedic domain of being beyond the world; it is so much a part of the world that any study of consciousness necessarily leads back to the mundane realities on which it depends.

CONSCIOUSNESS AS HUMAN REALITY

IF CONSCIOUSNESS WERE STUDIED exclusively under its immanent aspect, i.e., as being restricted solely to psychic interiority, there would be no need for recourse to extraconscious realities. The data encountered in consciousness could then be described, analyzed, and classified, but any attempt to explain them would be abandoned.

Descartes takes a first step in this direction with his proof of the existence of God in the Third Meditation. It is not our intention to discuss this proof or to offer an interpretation of Descartes's philosophy from a historical point of view. Certain texts are quoted simply to illustrate his approach to consciousness, which we wish to examine. It should be noted, once again, that the study of Descartes, the first in modern philosophy to analyze consciousness, exercised an influence on later philosophers such that, however great the differences in doctrinal content, the directive idea of Descartes was adopted by thinkers whose specific notions were far afield from those expounded by him.

Having broadened the meaning of the term "cogitations" [5] so that it is synonymous with "data of consciousness," Descartes reviews the content of the newly discovered domain and finds there man's feeling of his own insufficiency, his conception of himself as finite, imperfect, and dependent. Also present in man's consciousness is the idea of God as a being in whom all those perfections man himself lacks, but to which he unceasingly aspires, are united and coincide.[6] Using a causal argument inherited from the Scholastics, Descartes then proceeds with his proof of the existence and veracity of God, and of the reality of the realm of extension. Thus the *cogito sum* performs two functions for Descrates: (*a*) as the special domain of being which is called consciousness; and (*b*) as a point of departure for a deductive argument aimed at demonstrating the existence of the external world.

In its second function, the *cogito* is not regarded by Descartes as simply an experienced act, one fact of consciousness among others. Man's feeling of the lack of perfection in his own nature is not the same as, e.g., a perception. Under the universal doubt, the thing perceived cannot be accepted as existing, apart from being present to consciousness. All that can be certain is that an act of perceiving is experienced, and that a perceivable object presents itself to consciousness. This reductive modification, which is entailed by the universal doubt and which permits the recognition of perception and imagination as absolute and indubitable experienced data of consciousness, does not apply to the feeling of human imperfection. The universal doubt does not apply in this instance, since no reality outside the sphere of psychic interiority is in play. In examining this feeling of human insufficiency, we go beyond the mere confirmation of a simple phenomenon which presents itself to consciousness and grasp a *human reality,* an apperception of ourselves as we actually *are,* incomplete and imperfect. The importance of this datum lies in the fact that it signals something of what we actually are because

5. Descartes, *Philosophical Works*, p. 153. See also *ibid.*, p. 222, Princ. IX.
6. *Ibid.*, pp. 169, 170.

our being is defined by the humanity of the soul, and we are put in direct contact with one of the essential conditions of human reality, one which lies entirely within the province of psychical immanence.

Similarly, the idea of God in human consciousness is confined to psychic interiority, but Descartes invokes the act by which this idea is grasped as more than just one fact experienced among others. As with the feeling of human insufficiency, the idea of God in human consciousness expresses man's reality from another perspective, revealing the second basic condition of his constitution. It is in this sense that Descartes understands the idea of God as innate:

> [O]ne certainly ought not to find it strange that God, in creating me, placed this idea within me to be like the mark of the workman imprinted on his work; and it is likewise not essential that the mark shall be something different from the work itself. For from the sole fact that God created me it is most probable that in some way he had placed his image and similitude upon me, and that I perceive this similitude (in which the idea of God is contained) by means of the same faculty by which I perceive myself. . . . And the whole strength of the argument which I have made use of to prove the existence of God consists in this, that I recognize that it is not possible that my nature should be what it is, and indeed that I should have in myself the idea of a God, if God did not veritably exist.[7]

That is, the incompatibility that Descartes sees between the two conditions of human reality leads him to conclude the actual existence of God.

Limitations of space have led to an oversimplification and exaggeration of the distinction Descartes makes between perceptions, imaginations, and so on, on the one hand, and man's feeling of insufficiency, on the other. While it is true that acts of perception, imagination, and the like are subject to modification under the universal doubt, once modified, these acts become absolute and unquestionable data of consciousness, to which the doubt no longer applies. Considered only as experienced facts of consciousness, the acts, however heterogeneous, are not differentiated as to essence or principle, "but where these ideas are taken as so many modes of thought, I do not recognize any inequality among them, and all seem to me to proceed from me

7. *Ibid.*, p. 170.

in the same way."[8] That is, the acts are established by Descartes as equal and indubitable data of consciousness; and the relation between them and the psychic reality of the soul, as far as Descartes is concerned, is made apparent. It is only by placing the acts in this relation that Descartes is able to examine ideas such as those of substance, duration, number, and so on, as productions of the soul itself, measurable by its capacity insofar as it is human.[9] Thus all acts of consciousness appear in some sense as indexes of the human psychic reality to which they bear witness and with which they are permeated, and they are thus conceived in Cartesian terms as modifications of the soul in the sense of *modes* or *accidents* of a *substance.*

Consciousness, the domain of *cogitations,* is therefore, for Descartes, simply the human soul, the real human individual, abstracted from the body which falls under the universal doubt, and considered as a purely spiritual being, as "a thinking thing . . . insofar as it is preceisely this portion of me now in question which is a thinking thing."[10] Descartes indicates the comprehensiveness of consciousness by establishing the terms "thinking thing," "mind," "spirit," "intellect," and "reason" as synonymous.[11] The reality of consciousness consists in thinking, i.e., in performing acts of consciousness.[12] Thus the central problem of the Third through Sixth Meditations, i.e., that of the relation to something "outside of me," acquires meaning, so that Descartes is able to raise the question of the origin and preservation of the self,[13] and the Cartesians are able to ponder the question of whether the soul is always thinking. They believe the answer must be affirmative, since by their principles it is the actual presence of the acts performed which constitutes the essential and specific nature of man.[14] Therefore, *Descartes conceives of consciousness as a reality, one of the two created substances of which the world is composed. In De la recherche de la vérité,*

8. *Ibid.,* pp. 161–62.
9. *Ibid.,* p. 165.
10. See *ibid.,* p. 169, for context. Freely translated.—Trans.
11. *Ibid.,* p. 152.
12. Descartes, *Oeuvres,* ed. Charles Adam and Paul Tannery (Paris: Librairie Philosophique, J. Vrin, 1964——), VII, 107; cf. IX, 85: "nihil in me, cujus nullo modo sim conscius, esse (potest) [it is not possible that there is in me anything of which I am in no way conscious]."
13. Descartes, *Philosophical Works,* I, 167–68.
14. *Ibid.,* I, 190, 193.

Malebranche views consciousness in the same light when he investigates various kinds of acts—perceptions, imaginations, natural inclinations, and passions—in an attempt to disengage the potential errors within them which endanger man, corrupted as he is by original sin.[15] Here, too, consciousness is examined in the light of the two great conditions of human reality: the fall and the relation between the human soul and God, a relation which opens the way to truth through acts of pure mind (*esprit*) and "vision by means of ideas."

CRITIQUE AND CONSEQUENCES

THE UNIVERSAL DOUBT OF DESCARTES involves not only the existence of the external world but also the certainty of geometry, even of arithmetic.[16] But since it does not apply to the domain of psychic interiority, one part of the world is granted subsistence, the human soul, and thus one of the created substances is saved. Starting from that substance, Descartes seeks to salvage extension, the other created substance, by the circuitous route of the infinite (uncreated) substance.

Husserl's critique is aimed at this point (*CM*, pp. 24, 82 f.). The discovery of the *cogito sum* makes it possible to raise transcendental problems, in the sense indicated earlier. But if Descartes's example is followed, and a "thinking thing" or "mind" or "spirit" is perceived in consciousness, then the transcendental problems are related to the reality of the soul and are posited within the domain of human psychic interiority. But this sphere, by definition, is relative to another domain which is external to it. To consider consciousness as the psychic reality of the human individual is, at the same time, to place this individual on the worldly plane vis-à-vis differing realities, since on this level any reality whatsoever can be contrasted with any other reality whatsoever. Thus the sphere of human psychic immanence is reached only by making a division within the world as a whole—which presupposes the world—and it is only after this step that what remains of the world is related to the sphere thus arrived at and disengaged. Consequently, the transcendental problems are set up and approached on a terrain gained only by interposing,

15. Malebranche, *De la recherche*, Preface.
16. Descartes, *Philosophical Works*, I, 147.

in the very circumscription of this terrain, the world, presupposed as existing. The very setting up of the transcendental problem, in other words, is achieved by a contradictory element, a begging of the principle, since posing transcendental problems in the domain of mundane reality, such as psychic interiority or the human soul, means invoking and presupposing, in the very way in which the question is raised, that which can only follow from the transcendental inquiry.

This critique is aimed at the whole conception of consciousness as human psychic reality and not just at the particular Cartesian doctrine of human nature. We could, for example, replace this Christian conception, which is even more accentuated in Malebranche, with that of Scheler. Scheler perceives, at the heart of man's essential nature, a duality of pure and disinterested, but impotent, spirituality, opposed to vital, but blind, impulsions and forces; the two sides cooperate to give rise to individual human actions as well as to collective and historical events.[17] Whatever conception of nature and of human reality is adopted, basing the philosophical starting point on an anthropological datum which can only be defined with relation to mundanity and on the mundane level inevitably leads to the paradox of referring transcendental problems about the constitution of the world back to one particular part of this very world. Thus the target of the Husserlian critique is the anthropological orientation of Descartes's examination of consciousness. This orientation reappears in later thinkers, in one form or another, and the Cartesian doctrine has been analyzed here only as one example of it.

Even if the anthropological orientation starts from a strictly descriptive point of view, as with Descartes, and studies the data of consciousness without seeking to explain them by extramental facts, the end result will be an abandonment of the initial point of view, since the domain of human psychic interiority can be reached only by separating the realities which make up the world. Ultimately the descriptive and analytical study of the domain of consciousness blurs the lines of demarcation, forcing a recognition of the relationship between consciousness and the data of physiology and physics. Then the problem is to restore the disrupted primordial unity and to reintegrate consciousness,

17. Max Scheler, *Die Wissenformen und die Gesellschaft* (Leipzig: Neue Geist Verlag, 1926), pp. 6 f.

as psychic interiority, into the totality of mundane occurrences, as one reality among others. Considering consciousness in this way makes psychophysics possible.

This line of reasoning can lead to a transformation of psychology into biology or, at the very least, a branch of biology. The data of consciousness are interrelated with all the component data of life. Experienced states, then, may be regarded as vital manifestations, forming one aspect of living reality, with physiological data forming another aspect. To give preference to one of these rather than the other would seem, therefore, to be arbitrary and unjustifiable. Goldstein, for example, contends that physiological and psychological data are by nature incapable of constituting independent, separate levels, and that the problem of psychophysical interdependence and interaction has therefore been incorrectly formulated.[18] What are usually designated as "the physical" and "the psychic" are not actual data; they are instead the results of an abstractive isolating which actually modifies the concrete living reality. Therefore, the terms "physical" and "psychical" must be very judiciously employed.

All of the observed data, from whatever level they may seem to arise, whether or not they are governed by the same laws, must be referred back to the fundamental biological datum which is organismic life. The living organism is an organized whole, and each "part," sector, or region exists in a reciprocal relationship of functional dependence with every other. Any phenomenon, "physical" or "psychic," observed in an organism must be considered as a local or specific symptom of a supervening holistic reaction in the organism that is expressed in this particular sector by the phenomenon in question. At the center of such a holistic organismic reaction, there can be either a physical or a psychic datum; this is why it is as necessary to explain physical data by psychic data as it is to understand the latter by the former.

Goldstein certainly recognizes the characteristic nature of the "physical" and of the "psychic," but he feels that the importance and value of each—whether for any individual organism or for one of its particular reactions—can be evaluated only

18. Kurt Goldstein, *Der Aufbau des Organismus* (The Hague: Martinus Nijhoff, 1934), pp. 198, 202. See our studies, "Le Fonctionnement de l'organisme d'après K. Goldstein," *Journal de psychologie normale et pathologique*, Vol. XXVI (1939), and "Goldstein's Conception of Biological Science," in *SPP*.

in the light of the specific structure of the organism and with reference to its holistic behavior in a given situation. Biological considerations must start, not from an arbitrary and factitious separation of the physical and the psychical, but from that strict and intimate unity in which they exist within the living organism.[19]

This orientation inevitably introduces extraconscious data into the investigation of consciousness. By its own internal logic, the anthropological orientation leads Descartes, after he has rehabilitated the other created substance, extension, in the Sixth Meditation, to the problems of mind-body unity and the nature of the action of the body on the soul.[20] In this inquiry, qualitative data of perception, such as pains, pleasures, and appetites, although data of consciousness, are revealed as arising not from the mind as such but from the union in which the mind exists with the body. Being like signals transmitted by the body to the mind, these data inform consciousness about the needs and necessities of the body and about the dangers which threaten it, rather than about the truth of external things.

These ideas are taken over and developed by Malebranche, who also deprecates perceptions, imaginations, and the like, in favor of the acts of pure spirit. In his explanation of these data of consciousness—which, according to him, cannot attain the status of truth—Malebranche refers to the tendency of the human being to conserve his life, i.e., his bodily existence, and regards the data of consciousness as reactions of the conjoined mind and body to external physical events. These events are conceived just as they reveal themselves to pure mind, i.e., as they are determined by physics, whose constructions pass not only for scientific truth but also as the real world. Thus, in his psychological expositions, which are often highly naturalistic in character, Malebranche starts from the objective reality of the world and then seeks to explain subjective appearances and natural illusions. Although he rejects the very idea of a scientific psychology, to some extent he nevertheless inaugurated that

19. We are not seeking acceptance here of this position in psychology, physiology, or biology. Rather, we merely want to develop the consequences that an understanding of consciousness as human reality entail for the idea of a transcendental philosophy. The antinomy which inevitably springs from the anthropological orientation will be made clear in the next section.

20. Descartes, *Philosophical Works*, I, 190–96.

orientation in which psychology, by the way in which it views things and formulates problems, permits itself to be interpreted as an extension of physics. This orientation was subsequently taken over and developed in the twentieth century. Ernest Mach was the first to contest it, and contemporary psychology, with the advent of Gestalt psychology, tends to abandon it.[21]

THE ANTINOMY IN THE IDEA OF A UNIVERSAL PSYCHOLOGY CONCEIVED AS TRANSCENDENTAL PHILOSOPHY

SUMMARIZING THE PRECEDING DISCUSSION briefly, we see that for the empiricists the transcendental principle can be realized only in the form of a universal psychology. This suggests the need to turn to consciousness in order to reveal, by psychological analysis of its acts, the constitution and formation of objects of every sort, and the disengagement of the existential sense of these objects. Thus the origin and ground of truth—and of the evidence of everything that offers itself as claiming validity in any sense whatsoever—are brought to light.

But in studying consciousness, one cannot help but see the relation of dependence between consciousness and mundane realities. It makes no difference whether these realities are external, forming the objective world from which, according to Goldstein, the living organism selects and develops an environment suitable for its existence; or whether they are concerned with the organism itself and with what constitutes its essence; or whether they are social or historical realities; or indeed—especially important in our context—whether we are dealing with some human reality seated wholly within psychic interiority.[22] All of these realities, however psychically or spiritually their natures may be conceived, are as mundane as any material reality, and each has its existence and its existential sense. Thus, to play a part for us, it must present itself in certain acts of consciousness; and only by virtue of these acts and the intrinsic unity established among them can that human reality itself be

21. The major lines of this evolution have been traced by the author in his essay "Some Aspects and Developments of Gestalt Psychology (1936)," in SPP.

22. Goldstein, Der Aufbau, pp. 58, 78–79.

constituted as such and acquire that consistency by which its special and specific objectivity is assured. In setting up the transcendental problem, we can and must treat this reality like any other mundane reality, and we are therefore led back once again to the examination of consciousness.

Thus, philosophical thought, faced with an alternative, is perpetually oscillating between two contradictory terms. Yet the acceptance of one term entails acceptance of the other. The notion of a radical philosophy conceived as a universal psychology, which was implicit in the discovery of the *cogito sum* and which imposes itself with seemingly incontrovertible clarity, is jeopardized from the beginning. It is not that previous formulations of this notion have been incomplete, or that the methods employed have been somehow deficient. It is simply that the conception itself contains a basic contradiction which calls its very possibility into question.

Escape from this antinomy is essential if philosophical radicalism is to survive, and certainly the transcendental principle must not be abandoned. All oppositions—such as, e.g., authentic vs. inauthentic experience, or necessity vs. absurdity, etc., as well as terms such as real existence, necessary existence, possibility, probability, etc.—do not, and cannot, exhaust their meanings except in acts of consciousness and groups of such acts. Once again, it is because of acts of consciousness that there is an integrated world and the multiplicity of domains of which it is composed—material things, animate beings, human beings, social institutions, works of art, the universe of numbers, general notions, systems of relations, and the like. All these objects are the percepts of our perceptions, the thoughts of our thinking, the understood of our understandings, the created of our creatings, and so on. Man not only lives in the world in fact; at the same time he conceives himself as situated in the world as one reality among others, is conscious of the world, and sees himself, by an inevitable rationale, as obliged to relate the world's constitution to his. But this consciousness seems to be taken into consideration only in the form of human and individual consciousness, bound to the physical organization of a being who exists in the most diverse relations of dependence with the realities which surround it. For this reason, consciousness itself—the prime reality, it is true, special and privileged in one respect or another—reveals itself as nevertheless a mundane reality. From this fact arises the antinomy into which transcendental philosophy conceived as a universal psychology falls—and necessarily so—at its very debut.

There is no hope of emerging from this antinomy without breaking away from the conception of a consciousness which leads to the setting up of transcendental problems on the terrain of a mundane reality. It is therefore essential to develop a conception of consciousness which no longer views consciousness as human reality or as an expression or symptom of that reality. Such a notion of consciousness, no longer implying or presupposing the existence of the world and of mundane realities, is established by Husserl with his theory of the *phenomenological reduction,* which makes it possible to free the philosophy of consciousness from the dead weight of the antinomy and to resolve the profound contradiction which has compromised the very idea of that philosophy. The phenomenological reduction, which unlocks the door to phenomenology, can be characterized only, initially at least, in a negative way, as the most radical possible modification of the *natural attitude*—a term whose meaning must immediately be explained.

The Natural Attitude and the Phenomenological Reduction

The Surrounding World

AT ANY WAKING MOMENT OF LIFE, speaking strictly objectively, we live in a world which we accept as actually existing. Being awake means, simply, having consciousness of the surrounding world and of oneself as situated in this region, circumscribed in a more or less indefinite way by the world which constitutes the environment of the conscious subject. In these surroundings, the subject is presented with a great diversity of objects of many sorts. The relation to these objects cannot always be that of spectator, because pure contemplation is a special attitude which cannot be continuously maintained even by the scientist for whom it has become a habitual disposition. In the usual case, in normal daily life, the subject exists in a concrete situation, within his surroundings, in which he acts and which poses problems of a practical nature that he attempts to solve.

Such a state of affairs is formed by the objects the subject uses or acts on. He views these objects in the light of their function in a given situation and the role they play in it. For example, a hammer presents itself as capable of being utilized in a certain fashion in a particular state of affairs. It is defined by the use to which it can be put. But it is not merely a thing of a certain length, breadth, thickness, and weight, of such a form, with a particular color, and so on. All of these determinations, which are undoubtedly perceived and noted, are important in the practical attitude only as indicating the utility and applicability of an object in question for some end. The objects which make up the surrounding world, and which are dealt with in the practices of daily life, are not primarily characterized by these determinations which, in order to be qualitative and perceivable, must always be designated as objective, in the sense that they belong to the object taken in itself quite apart from any relation to a situation in which it can be utilized. The familiar objects of the surrounding world are not defined by what they are but *by the way in which they serve,* i.e., by what can be done with them. An object previously unknown does not become familiar to us simply by our frequent visual inspection of its objective determinations, but by our discovery of its possible uses and of the way in which to handle it—in the figurative sense of the word—in relation to the intended employment of it in some situation, so that the function it must accomplish is understood.

The nature of the objects which constitute the environs is determined by the "functional values" they take on, either in typical situations or in some particular state of affairs. These values are acquired from the total situation and its structure as a whole. This is why we refer here to *objects of use* or, better still, *functional objects.*[23] In any given situation, the functional objects

23. W. Köhler, "Intelligenzprüfungen an Anthropoiden I," *Abhandlungen der K. Preussischen Akademie der Wissenschaften,* phys.-math. Klasse (Berlin, 1917), pp. 29–32. Besides the observations of Köhler concerning the behavior of the higher apes, we refer, in this much too brief discussion of the functional objects, to those made by Gelb and Goldstein about aphasic problems (see the summaries of their views published in *Journal de psychologie normale et pathologique,* 1933). Gelb and Goldstein note "a *regression* toward a *less abstract, less rational, more immediate and more concrete behavior,* which is in this sense *more primitive*" (*ibid.,* p. 408), a primitiveness which, however, must not be taken as synonymous with that which, according to Lévy-Bruhl, characterizes the mentality

play a role determined by their location in the situation, and their natures and functional values are dependent on their interrelations with the other functional objects conjoined with them as components of the situation. The functional values are thus supported and grounded reciprocally, and it follows that they are not inherent properties of the objects but are assigned to them only by virtue of specific functions in a particular practical situation. This is not to say that the structure of the situation is solely dependent on the objects present and is unaffected by the attitude of the subject. On the contrary, an essential element in the formation of that structure is the subject's atheoretical understanding of the state of affairs in which he finds himself. Such a situation is not to be considered as something apart from the experiencing subject's understanding of it but is only what it signifies to that subject. Its structure is therefore relative to the behavior of the subject and dependent upon his understanding. Thus, if the objects in a situation are determined by their functions in the situation, it is because the subject, in his comprehending—which is constitutive for the structure of the situation—assigns determined roles to the objects, in accordance with his understanding. Ultimately, then, the functional objects owe their location, and therefore their whole being *as* functional objects, to the subject's understanding.

For this reason, a functional object can be different for different people, although in abstraction from its use in a practical situation, when regarded in itself, it remains the same thing,

---

of lower societies (pp. 424–29). Gelb and Goldstein stress the difference between the behavior of aphasics and that of children (p. 474, n.), on the one hand, and the practical attitude of normal subjects, on the other (pp. 413–17). Nevertheless, it seems to us that the investigations into the primitive, childish mentality and into that of aphasics and the behavior of the higher animals have brought to light a certain peculiarity of structure common to these mentalities that is represented in each of them in a specific way. This peculiarity, we believe, is found also in the practical attitude of the normal subject, in which it takes a special form. Here, where it is possible only to allude to it, we must limit ourselves to noting the work still to be done in elaborating that peculiarity and, correlatively, in defining the notion of the object whose structure corresponds to it, an object which would be grounded on a qualifying of the primitive object. This would involve a comparative study in which, of course, any ill-considered analogies and assimilations must be avoided.

objectively speaking. For example, an electric lamp appears under one aspect to someone who uses it and under another to the electrician who installs or repairs it. Or again, a product is viewed by its maker in the light of the manufacturing process, the profit to be gained from its sale, and so on, but the purchaser sees it in relation to the use he will make of it in satisfying his particular needs. If these two people understand each other at all, it is because they meet in a shared situation, i.e., in the market-place—the merchandise is at the center and the two play their reciprocally determined respective roles—and because the orientation to this shared situation is a factor in their attitudes toward their individual places within it. From this point of view, the identity of the functional object as such can be maintained, although it is regarded by each person from a different perspective. But it is not necessary to catalogue the variety of ways in which people view things in order to recognize modifications undergone by the objects as a result of supervening changes in their functional values. There are enough instances where a practical situation, and the problem it poses, can be resolved only by endowing an object with a function different from its initial use in the situation or by introducing a new object with its role to play.[24] In each case, the object assumes functional values it did not previously possess and is transformed in the eyes of the one who manipulates it.

Being in a practical situation and making use of the functional objects involved in it can become an absorbing activity, but never to the point where the existence of the world surrounding the current state of affairs is completely forgotten or lost from view. When writing, for instance, or making something, one retains a certain awareness of the surroundings, of being in this room of this house which is on this street of this city, with something going on outside, but without a knowledge of exactly what or, at least, without any feeling of a need to know. There is a similar vague and approximate awareness of the time of day, of what has gone before the present situation, and of what is about to occur. This is not at all a matter of memories, anticipations, representations, images, and such, which are simply superadded

24. See the examples drawn from the behavior of animals in Köhler, "Intelligenzprüfungen," pp. 81–85, and those given of human activity by Max Wertheimer, *Productive Thinking* (New York: Harper, 1959).

by association to the different acts in which the subject is related to the current situation.

The situation refers, by its very nature, to concerns located outside of it. For example, the enterprise is undertaken initially because of certain goals that may be attained as a result of it; and while it is being carried on there is an orientation toward anticipated situations that one may seek to bring about or to forestall. Each current situation is integrated into the chronological order of the life of the subject, occupies a certain rank in that life, and so on. Admittedly, all these facts arise from the attitude of the subject, which tends to color the situation, but this does not justify denouncing them as "purely subjective." The external references form the horizon of the current situation, assuring its relation to the rest of the world. Through them a context is created such that each particular situation presents itself as a particularization at the heart of a *universe* (*CM*, p. 36) and assumes the character of a mundane state of affairs. It is through such references that the existence of the world is indicated to the subject at any instant of his life. Thus, from the subject's point of view, any activity bearing on only a particular situation occurs within the framework of a world which is always present, not as something added to the state of affairs but as something embracing it in its totality.

What the subject in a present situation is related to can be more or less indeterminate. Indeed, the horizon is always indeterminate in the sense that its limits are not precise and circumscribed, but fade away into indefiniteness (*Ideas*, § 27). There is never a perfectly clear consciousness of every thing in the world any more than there is of every thing in one's past life. What is present in the horizon is only a part of what actually surrounds and is objectively related to the current situation. The horizon is enveloped in a kind of "haze" which even penetrates the horizon at some places, making it somewhat nebulous. As one becomes more immersed in the present situation, the horizon becomes increasingly nebulous, and the details referred to lose their precision and become confused in the haze until we arrive at the limiting case where nothing of the world is given beyond its form and general or, better yet, generic style. But however indeterminate its *continua* may be, the horizon is not, and cannot be, absent from any particular situation, for no such situation presents itself as isolated or cut off from the rest of the world.

ORIENTATION IN THE SURROUNDING WORLD

LIFE IN THE SURROUNDING WORLD, the manipulation of the functional objects existing there, are guided by an understanding which is characterized distinctively by being in no sense theoretical. It is possible to be directed toward social life, responding to the demands it poses, utilizing all the various kinds of possibilities that society puts at the disposal of its members, without having any knowledge whatever of social mechanisms, of the laws governing their functioning, or of the reasons which have led to the rise of just these mechanisms rather than others.[25] Thus, for example, everyone uses what we call money without having to form a notion of the way the metallic disks and engraved notes acquire those properties that fit them for their functions as universal media of exchange. Nor is it necessary to have anatomical and physiological knowledge in order to walk, or to understand the physical laws which govern the function and construction of a machine in order to operate it. All that is needed is a set of operating instructions, containing such information as which lever must be raised or lowered, which buttons pushed, and the order in which such actions must be performed. These guidelines serve as signals to the subject who is involved in the situation, preparing him for events which may occur and stimulating adequate responses in him.

This orientation toward guidelines that one may be tempted to qualify as external, however superficial it may seem compared with scientific thinking, is nonetheless the only useful behavior for someone not concerned with a theoretical explanation of the situation in which he is involved but simply with performing adequately in that situation—responding at the right time and in the right way to changes heralded by certain warning signals. This practical orientation is undoubtedly inferior to scientific understanding, especially to mathematicophysical thought, with respect to rationality, precision, and exactitude. But all of the incontestable advantages of mathematicophysical knowledge do not make it applicable to the solving of problems like those encountered in the surrounding world of everyday life.

25. See Max Weber, "Über einige Kategorien der verstehenden Soziologie," *Logos*, IV (1913), 293–94.

Physical theories lead to a superior understanding of the world and are certainly admirable. But what they do not yield is precisely that knowledge most necessary in performance situations, where the practical orientation makes a successful outcome possible (see *FTL*, § 105). This is not because of some defect in the physical sciences that their subsequent evolution could remedy. The functional object is, and must be, ignored by the physical sciences, because these sciences cannot be constituted until after the functional aspect to which the surrounding world owes its being as such has been excluded, and because the objects constructed by these sciences are totally different in structure and existential sense from the functional objects. But the functional aspect of the surrounding world, once analyzed out cannot be resynthesized. The mathematicophysical intellect is necessarily deployed on a level alien to that of the world of daily living in all respects, not within the compass of the functional objects. This is why it cannot be substituted for the practical orientation—which should not be assessed in terms of mathematical intellect and deprecated in comparison with it, but must be recognized for its cognitive value in the world of daily living. Obviously this is a relative value, because such knowledge is confined solely to the plane of daily living, but it is nonetheless a positive value.

Existence and behavior in the surrounding world most often take the form of automatic habit. We must not assume that this automatism, which is the rule in all practical conduct or know-how, is merely a blind mechanism at its inception. Formal theoreticians have demonstrated that, for a habit to become completely automatic after a period of conditioning, a complete reworking or reorganization of perception is required.[26] With this reorganization, an object involved in a certain situation becomes phenomenally and psychologically different to the eyes of the experiencing subject than it was before the habit was formed. This reworking of perception is only the attribution of a functional value to an object which may have had none or quite a different one. The role that object must play in the situation is thus disclosed, as has been noted with reference to becoming acquainted with a hitherto unknown object. These transforma-

26. See especially Paul Guillaume, *La Formation des habitudes* (Paris, 1936), chap. 3.

tions of objects express the structure of the performance situation itself, which, in such processes, takes on the definitive form under which it will present itself subsequently to the experiencing subject. It is in this sense that the attitude, disposition, understanding, and other factors, ordinarily taken as being purely subjective, contribute to the constituting of a performance situation.

It is in and through the practical orientation that such a situation assumes its specific functional aspect and becomes what it is for the subject located within it. The knowledge accompanying and directing experience in the world of daily living is nothing more than the apprehension of functional objects in their places within a given situation, the discovery of the general and special structures of the situation, and the progressive adaptation to these structures. This knowledge consists simply in following the references which exist among the objects in such a situation. These references form the structure of the situation, assuring its context and lending it its particular aspect. Moreover, the more familiar a situation becomes, the more the manipulation of the functional objects becomes a stabilized and automatic habit, the more this special and specific character fades out—in the sense that the perception of the situation and of the effects that the activity of the subject brings about within it is superseded by the proprioception of the activity itself, that is, the kinesthetic sensibility progressively supplants the perception.[27]

THE HUMAN SCIENCES

LET US NOW EXAMINE the contemplative attitude, which cannot be permanently adopted and can be applied only to one domain of the surrounding world at a time (no matter how this region may be delimited) so that the chosen domain may then become the object of scientific inquiry. In dealing with a past epoch, we must reconstruct the surroundings as they were for those living then. In this orientation of scientific thought, the mechanisms of the environment in question must be established,

27. *Ibid.*, pp. 121–24.

the laws determining their functions must be ascertained, the formations of social institutions and the changes they have undergone in the course of history must be studied, and the conditions of their origin, expansion, and decline must be investigated. Thus the historical, archaeological, philological, economic, sociological, and similar sciences are constituted. In these moral or human sciences, the objects are not considered in terms of their physical and chemical determinations or according to their purely qualitative and perceivable properties—even when they are objective, as in the case of material things. Instead, the objects are considered in their locations within the surroundings, not as they are in themselves but according to the functions assigned to them by those who utilize them. That is, *in the human sciences, the objects remain functional objects.*

Thus, for example, an economist does not think of iron as a material body characterized by certain physicochemical properties but as something having economic value and importance in an economic system. If the physicochemical properties enter into the economist's considerations, it is only indirectly, as the ground of technical possibilities which, in their turn, have an economic value. Therefore, these properties play a role only if something relating to the economy is present in them. For this reason, it must be maintained that iron is not the same object for the economist as it is for the physicist. Or, again, for the linguistic sciences, a human utterance is not a purely auditory datum produced by the superposition of certain undulatory motions of the air, where it is only a question of establishing the physiological conditions of wave emission. Contemporary linguistics (*the phonological school,* especially, attempts to beat a path in this direction) considers the sound in the place assigned to it in the phonological system of a given language, studying it from the point of view of its contribution to differentiating the significance of verbal units (words and phrases).[28] Thus the sound is not so much regarded in terms of its effective realization as in terms of the intention and imagination of the speaking subjects when they utter it. It is considered in the role it plays in the linguistic consciousness of a community.

28. See Prince N. Trubetskoy, "La Phonologie actuelle," *Journal de psychologie normale et pathologique* (1933). See also J. Vendryès, "Sur les tâches de la linguistique statique," *ibid.* We have analyzed these two works in *Revue philosophique de la France et de l'étranger* (1935), pp. 427–32.

THE PHYSICAL SCIENCES

HOWEVER, science is not required to respect the specific aspect of the surrounding world. If, by a purely mental operation, one cuts away and suppresses the relations and the references from which an object draws its character and its existential sense as a functional object, what remains is the physical thing, characterized solely and exclusively by perceivable and qualitative determinations, such as length, breadth, depth, color, shape, weight, hardness, and so on. It is the material thing understood in this sense to which Descartes applies his analysis and critique of perception, and which Locke attempts to construct from his simple elements of "sensation." [29]

But the physical sciences do not stop at the physical thing. In these sciences, the material thing with its perceivable properties is replaced by the physical entity, which is defined by such notions as atoms, ions, electrons, energy, and the like, which can be characterized only by mathematical expressions (*Ideas*, § 40). The physical entity is located in a space which is not the visual and tactile space familiar to us as our field of action. The space of the physical sciences is mathematical space, which allows only those determinations which spring from the axioms of geometry. In constructing the universe of physics, one does not, therefore, as Locke believed,[30] separate the so-called secondary qualities of a thing from its perceivable spatial properties and retain only the latter, which are then accepted as the true physical reality of the thing. On the contrary, the physical entity is at every point transcendent to the material thing, none of whose perceivable determinations enter, as such, into the constructions of physics.

The universe as physics constructs it is presented as *the scientific truth of the world*. But the constructions of physics must not be taken as images more or less approximating the *authentic reality* of the world, an underlying, hidden reality veiled from us by our psychophysical organization, which inevitably leads us into natural illusions, so that this reality appears to us under the specious form of the perceivable world (*Ideas*,

29. Descartes, *Philosophical Works*, I, 154 ff.; Locke, *Essay*, bk. II, chap. 12, § 6, and chap. 23, §§ 6, 14.
30. Locke, *Essay*, bk. II, chap. 8, §§ 15–23.

§ 52). The procedure followed in the physical explanation of qualitative data is quite different from the insertion among observed facts of other facts susceptible of observation but not yet observed—for example, certain problematical planetary motions have been explained by assuming the existence of a planet presently unknown but perhaps observable in the future. In principle, this method of procedure is like that of the archaeologist who, on the basis of some excavated ruins and literary accounts, conceives the architectonic plan of an ancient building, expecting later documentation to confirm his hypothesis.

All data—observed, calculated, and assumed—are on the same level, which is not overstepped at any stage of the reasoning. However, in the explanation of qualitative data, the physicist places himself on the plane of the perceivable world and never abandons this level, because his goal is to predict the events occurring in the world of natural things whose perceivable and qualitative determinations are used by him as instances of verification of his theories. But he transcends this plane when he translates the data into physical terms by making a material body situated on the specifically natural level correspond to the physical entity, so that certain mathematicophysical determinations pertain to the physical entity only insofar as the material body presents corresponding qualitative properties. Thus the physical entity appears as an X which bears physical determinations which are accessible only in and through the qualitative properties of the material thing. Therefore, the entities of physics can be constructed only if the qualitative determinations are given in advance. The perceivable world underlies the constitution of the physical universe as its ground and buttress. In this respect, the universe of physics must be considered as higher than the world of perception.[31] However, this superiority must not be given a realist interpretation, as if the physicist, by some happy instinct, successfully penetrated behind the natural appearances of naïve life, and grasped some in-itself, i.e., things as they really are.

By such an interpretation, the entities of physics would be taken as things to which a sensibility not subject to the con-

31. A level of being, A, is higher than a level of being, B, if the completed construction of B is a prerequisite for the construction of A. This is the formal definition of "higher," which can be expressed in diverse ways.

ditions of human psychophysical organization would have direct and immediate perceptual access, while the human being would be reduced to merely indirect and symbolic representations of these genuinely real things. If the thing is the objective correlate of perceptual life, then its existential sense is determined only in relation to that life. But the construction of physical entities, since it is completely grounded in the appearance of the perceivable world, cannot be carried out without the intervention of acts of categorial thought, especially those of mathematico-physical reason. Even if the creations of categorial thought are at the lowest level of such thinking, they cannot be transformed into perceptual data and must on no account be considered as capable of lending themselves to pure perception or as susceptible of being grasped by acts other than those of categorial thought. To confer on the entities of physics the existential sense of physical objects—which is an inevitable result of substituting these entities as "absolute realities" for the perceivable world—is to falsify the meaning of the existence of the physical universe, no matter what definition may be given of this meaning.

The realist thesis accepts the statement that "nature is in itself mathematical" as a matter of course. In so doing, it avoids the true problem which the physical sciences pose for philosophy. For if a philosophical problem is raised by these sciences, it is not by virtue of their results but of their very existence (*Crisis*, § 9). The "given nature"—the transformation of functional objects into physical things that have already occurred—not only contains qualitative facts but, above all, does not recognize exact determinations. Even the spatial and temporal forms are vague and unstable. They admit only determinations of a type which allows some latitude for variation. This given nature is related to the universe of ideal mathematical objects, is considered in the light of these objects, and is conceived as realizing mathematical relations which the physicist seeks to determine with progressively more accurate approximation. The realist thesis conceals this transition from the given nature to the mathematized nature, because in the realist thesis the mathematized, or at least mathematizable, nature is substituted for the given nature from the beginning.

But the philosophical problem of the physical sciences lies in this very transition. In becoming the object of physics, the given nature undergoes an idealized transformation relating it to mathematical objects. This transformation is accomplished through acts of consciousness, in processes and operations of which the mathematizable and mathematized nature (the universe of physics) are revealed as the products or, better yet, as the objective correlates. The existence of the physical sciences therefore no longer imperils the principle, advanced earlier, according to which every object and every level of being must be conceived relative to the acts of consciousness in which they are constituted and of which they are the objective correlates. On the contrary, one must refer to these acts—to the operations of consciousness and to the motives of these operations—in order to clarify and explain the presuppositions implicit in the historical formation of the physical sciences. These have not been recognized *as* presuppositions because, for the most part, they were transmitted from the tradition of geometrical thought. Only with the help of such mediations can we disengage the existential sense of the *universe of physics* as objective correlate of the acts in which it is constructed—an objective correlate of a higher degree, because it is conceived and elaborated by starting from that other objective correlate of consciousness which is the *world as we perceive it*. Only thus can the origin and specific nature of the evidence which is characteristic of the physical sciences be grasped.

THE GENERAL THESIS OF THE NATURAL ATTITUDE

THE STATEMENTS CONCERNING ATTITUDES which have just been made are fragmentary in a twofold sense: they are incomplete;[32] and they must be discussed in greater depth.[33] However, this is not our present task. Seeking to break a trail toward constitutive phenomenology, which can be approached by means of the phenomenological reduction, we are interested more in what these attitudes have in common than in the differences among them.

In each of these attitudes, however they may differ from one another, the objects with which one deals, at whatever level of being they may appear, present themselves with an *existential*

32. Thus, e.g., the artistic attitude is excluded.
33. We only wish to stress here the interest in penetrating more deeply the structure of the functional object, a notion which, in our opinion, must be fundamental in the theory of the human sciences.

character (*Ideas*, § 30). Thus, in the given surroundings, whether one adopts the active attitude of daily living or the contemplative life of the human sciences, the functional objects as well as the social formations offer themselves as being there. In elaborating the universe of physics, we not only presuppose the existence of the material things which serve as a basis for that construction, we also confer a specific existence on the universe itself, on the entities which are its components. It is the same for pure mathematics. The mathematical objects, numbers, functions, equations, geometrical forms, and so on, present themselves as given. In the mathematical attitude, they are considered as existing, no matter how that existence may ultimately be understood. The system of mathematical deductions, drawn with ever increasing complexity from axioms, presents itself as valid; and this validity is also an existential character. It is the specific form that the general notion of existence assumes in the domain of thought. The specific sense of existence is differentiated according to the level of being; it therefore varies from one level to another among those we have considered, and also among those we have not been able to include in this discussion. But at every such level, the objects offer themselves as bearing this existential character, which can be expressed by the phrase "simply being there."

Certainly the existence of an object can become doubtful in a particular case. However, being doubtful or problematic, and being possible, probable, and so on, are also existential characters and must be understood as variations of the fundamental existential character which is existence pure and simple (*Ideas*, § 104). What is more important is that it is only a particular object whose existence becomes problematic or doubtful. But this object presents itself in a more or less inclusive context along with other objects which retain their existential character. It should be noted especially that the level of being itself from which these objects arise is in no way involved with any alteration of the existential character which may occur with reference to a particular object. This remains true as long as the subject does not philosophize but acts in a naïve manner, in one attitude or another, on the ontological level in question.

Therefore the adherence of an existential character to objects, and, correlatively, the belief in the existence of these objects, are a quite general fact, no matter what levels of being are involved, although the meaning of the existence may not always be the same. Consequently this fact does not constitute a privilege which distinguishes one attitude, such as that of daily living, from some other, such as the scientific attitude. Rather, it dominates and supports all special attitudes. The general *existential thesis* is present in every mental activity, no matter in which of these attitudes it may be performed, and therefore this thesis is a kind of common denominator of all these attitudes.[34] It is because of the presence of the general existential thesis in each of them that all the attitudes are grouped under the common title, "the natural attitude."

But the general existential thesis is not explicitly posited. The subject who is living in the natural attitude accepts the thesis and makes use of it but does not expressly take account of it, or at least can dispense with so doing. The thesis can intervene in the constitution of the natural attitude, and be effective there, and yet be subconscious, not perceived but concealed and, so to speak, forgotten. This thesis confronts us with one of those phenomena of daily life which present themselves only in an *implicit form,* phenomena which make an essential contribution to the interpretation of certain data and yet do not lend themselves without special effort to the directing of intellectual attention on these data, which can be grasped and made explicit only by specific reflection. As we shall see, one of the principal methods of phenomenology consists in explaining these implicit phenomena—which are not, however, all of the same type.

THE PHENOMENOLOGICAL REDUCTION

THE GENERAL EXISTENTIAL THESIS is subject to radical modification by the phenomenological reduction. This change in the very thesis itself is not a matter of replacing one of the particular attitudes noted above with another. By the same token, the new attitude that results from the phenomenological reduction must on no account be regarded as just one attitude among others. Because of the very radicalism of the modification which gives rise to the new attitude, it stands in contrast to all the natural attitudes.

In the phenomenological reduction, the existential character

34. See E. Fink, "Vergegenwärtigung und Bild," *Jahrbuch für Philosophie und phänomenologische Forschung,* XI (1930), 248–49.

adhering in objects is not doubted, for that would be no more than substituting one given existential character for another. But there is no plausible motive for casting doubt on the existence of all objects and levels of being. Furthermore, it is not that existential belief is denied in general, as with the characteristically dogmatic negation of skeptical philosophy. In the phenomenological reduction, the modification of the general existential thesis consists in exercising a certain abstention, an epochē with regard to that thesis, in not carrying out the act of existential belief; and, most important, this takes place without the disappearance or even the setting aside of that belief (*Ideas*, §§ 31, 32; and *CM*, § 8). *The belief in question is suspended and correlatively the existential character is placed between parentheses;* it is *inhibited*, but inhibition is not suppression.

The objects are not in themselves modified by the phenomenological reduction. They remain at every juncture just as they were known in the various natural attitudes. All of their determinations, properties, qualities, structures, and so on, are safeguarded. Even the existential character with which an object presents itself remains intact, and, especially, no different existential character is substituted for it, nor is it cancelled a fortiori. Each object continues to be that genuine, hypothetical, possible, problematic, or apparent reality that it was before the phenomenological reduction. What the phenomenological reduction does do is put the existential character out of play, out of action, so that it is no longer in use. Thus, in the phenomenological attitude, an object which continues to offer itself to consciousness as existing is considered not simply as existing, not as such and such a reality, but as presenting itself *as* existing, as laying claim to existence.

In the natural attitude, the subject is convinced that he is in the midst of a real world, confronted by other levels of being whose objects also comport themselves as existing in one form or another. This conviction is not shaken; it persists when the subject adopts the phenomenological attitude. But the conviction is no longer effective in that it no longer plays the role of *a living conviction* [*conviction vivant*] but only that of *a past conviction* [*conviction vécue*]. Consequently, in phenomenological meditations no statement which translates such a conviction or one of its possible variations—which therefore expresses an existential character—is admitted as a premise. Similarly, a logical or mathematical theorem in no way loses its character of validity by the phenomenological reduction but continues to present itself as derived from certain axioms and as having a determinate place in a system of conclusions. But this theorem is not employed in phenomenological considerations and does not ground these considerations, which make no recourse to it. It enters into and plays a role in them only as a datum appearing to consciousness—exactly the same datum as it was in the natural attitude—but, once it is under the governance of the phenomenological reduction, no use is made of its validity.

Thus, the phenomenological reduction is less concerned with the objects themselves, or with the convictions the subject has about them, than with the way in which these objects and convictions enter into phenomenology, the position phenomenology takes with respect to them. With the existential character out of play and its import suspended, all the objects are transformed into phenomenal objects, even while continuing to subsist as they are. At the same time the levels from which these objects arise become *levels of phenomenal existence.* This modification pertains especially to the existential character which the objects bear, which is transformed into a phenomenal datum while still integrally safeguarded between the parentheses which bracket it. It is as a phenomenal fact, as an experienced datum, but solely as this, that an existential character and, consequently, also the statement translating it, can play a role in phenomenology. This modified attitude, once taken, will not be abandoned, and the investigations which it makes possible are called phenomenological investigations.

Because of the modification it brings to the general existential thesis, the phenomenological reduction is universal in scope. It pertains to all objects of any level whatsoever (*Ideas,* §§ 56–60) with the single exception of acts of consciousness as experienced data. Like the universal doubt of Descartes, and for the same reason, the phenomenological reduction makes no imprint on these acts. But *these acts escape the phenomenological reduction only as experienced facts and phenomenal data, and not in any sense as symptoms, expressions, or the like, of a human reality, even a purely psychical one.*[35] Every such reality is subject to the

35. The Cartesian origin of the phenomenological reduction is evident. But while, in Descartes, it is a matter of a kind of universal negation—the objects are presumed to be nonexistent and illusory, and the convictions are taken as false—the reduction of Husserl is only an abstention, an epochē.

phenomenological reduction (*CM*, § 11). In the phenomenological attitude, the subject continues to conceive of himself as man, as an individual, as a social and historical being, and so on. He remains the concretely real and empirical self that he was before, with no diminution of the wide range of determinations belonging to him. But this human reality, with all of its component elements, cannot serve as a point of departure for phenomenological meditations or as a given with an effective existential character, just as the judgments which translate it are not admitted as premises, arguments, and so on, any more than would be the case for any other mundane reality. The concrete human self also becomes a phenomenon. It can enter into phenomenology only as a datum appearing to consciousness and presenting itself there through acts which have reference to it and by which it is grasped along with its essential characteristics. It is in this sense that Husserl speaks of "a *splitting of the Ego:* in that the phenomenological Ego establishes himself as '*disinterested onlooker,*' above the naïvely interested Ego" (*CM*, p. 35). Obviously this formula must not be taken too literally.[36] It expresses metaphorically the distinction to be made between the real concrete self, as constituted objective correlate, and the consciousness to which this self presents itself.

Consciousness can be understood in two ways: (*a*) as in the biological and psychological sciences, in its relation to mundane realities, as pertaining to the concrete human self, therefore impregnated with human reality; or (*b*) as a pure field of experienced acts which are related to objects, acts by which the real concrete self, among other objects, is itself grasped and in which the real concrete self, among other objects, is itself grasped and in which it is constituted. This is why consciousness possesses that absolute character assigned to it by Descartes and reaffirmed by the phenomenological reduction.[37] Therefore, no anthropological element may be allowed to enter into phenomenological considerations. One of the fundamental reasons for the phenomenological reduction is that it carves an impassable gulf between phenomenology and every species of philosophical

36. "Obviously it can be said that, as an Ego in the natural attitude, I am likewise and at all times a transcendental Ego, and that I know about this only by executing phenomenological reduction" (*CM*, p. 37).

37. Concerning this absolute character of consciousness, see *Ideas*, §§ 44, 46, 49, 54.

anthropology.[38] At the same time, the difference between phenomenology and psychology becomes apparent, since in psychology consciousness is accepted as one reality among others and is studied in its dependence on extraconscious data. The matter of these two sciences is obviously the same, since consciousness is a unity. This is why psychology and phenomenology are connected by such intimate bonds, and why the results of psychology, especially the descriptive results, acquire great importance for phenomenology. Inversely, psychology can derive much profit from phenomenology by taking account of its results, of its methods, and of the way in which problems are formulated by it. Psychology is the only science to which phenomenology is bound in this intimate fashion, but this special relationship should not gloss over the great difference of principle between the respective points of view from which the two consider their shared domain of inquiry, that is, consciousness.

When the phenomenological reduction is effected, what is retained is the reduced consciousness, i.e., consciousness viewed solely in terms of the appearing and constituting of objects before it. Reduced consciousness is defined as a field of experienced acts which refer to objects. Although transformed into phenomenal objects, the objects remain as they were, apart from the modification to which their existential character is subject. Thus the duality between acts and objects enters into the very definition of reduced consciousness, inasmuch as the phenomenological reduction does not cause the objects to disappear or be set aside.

The phenomenal objects acquire a teleological function in the investigations of phenomenology (*Ideas,* § 86; *CM,* § 21). As goals toward which phenomenological inquiries must be directed, they serve as a guiding thread for these analyses. The simply given object is conceived as the ready-made product of consciousness, which in both "natural" and scientific life remains hidden and veiled and can be brought to light only by special efforts. Starting from the object, we must ask ourselves what

---

38. This observation certainly does not apply to anthropology as a positive science from which, when it is a matter of comparative psychology, phenomenology can draw, as with all positive psychological work, considerable profit. Here we have not hesitated to make use of some of its results. But we must avoid, when philosophical and transcendental problems are related to an area apropos of which the same problems must be raised, falling inevitably into the antinomic situation discussed earlier.

acts and complexes of acts have to be experienced or be capable of being experienced, what processes and operations must occur, to ensure that the objective correlate of this ensemble of data of consciousness should be just that particular object in question. Once the particular acts are disengaged, it becomes a matter of studying the groups they form and the syntheses and forms of unity established among the particular acts because of their relation to a given object. In this way, it becomes possible to follow the progressive formation and constitution of the object until, once again, it is encountered as it was known in the natural attitude.[39] These investigations are thus justly qualified as transcendental, because they deal with the conditions of the possibility of objects, and these conditions can be located only in consciousness.

The phenomenological reduction makes it possible to set up transcendental problems on a terrain where only the reduction can prevent philosophical thought from falling into the antinomy discussed earlier. Our initial reflections in this essay led to the view that each object is the correlate of certain acts of consciousness. This principle must now be made more explicit: *Any object whatsoever*, as concerns its existential sense, *is relative— relative to the reduced consciousness, but not to consciousness viewed as human psychical reality* and thus embraced by the entire world. The same principle gives rise to the notion of the philosophy of consciousness as first philosophy, which will consequently take the form not of a psychology but of a *universal phenomenology*.

39. Although the expositions given in the characterization of the natural attitude of the structure of some types of objects are much too incomplete, they indicate certain directions in which the investigations of constitutive phenomenology must move. But the present framework restricts us here and prevents the detailed discussion of special problems.

8 / Some Fundamental Principles of Constitutive Phenomenology

WE HERE UNDERTAKE to survey some of the general principles of constitutive phenomenology, that phenomenological idealism which Husserl introduced in a well-developed form with the *Ideas* of 1913 and thereafter continued to elaborate, deepen, and expand.

One should not regard phenomenology as a "philosophical system" in the usual sense of the term. The principles we shall attempt to present express nothing less than a sort of *profession of personal, philosophical faith*. They derive their value from the fact that they open a vast field for research and inspire concrete analyses of particular phenomena—an analytical labor by which these principles become concrete and manifest. Thus phenomenology does not present itself as a philosophy which is complete at the outset, which springs in an accomplished form from the mind of its author, and which only translates his personal manner of viewing the world—in the fashion, say, of the speculative systems of the so-called German idealism.[1]

Phenomenology can be realized only as a collective effort, i.e., by means of the cooperation and coordinated attempts of

This essay was originally written in French during 1937 under the title "Quelques principes fondamentaux de la phénoménologie constitutive" for *Recherches philosophiques*. The proofs were read, but the journal unfortunately suspended publication before the essay could appear. This translation is by Jorge García-Gómez.

1. See Husserl, "Philosophy as a Rigorous Science," in *Phenomenology and the Crisis of Philosophy*, trans. Quentin Lauer (New York: Harper & Row, Torchbooks, 1965), p. 76.

generations of investigators. Renouncing all desire for *personal* originality, phenomenologists strive instead to transform their discipline into a positive science in conformity with the conditions for scientific progress. Hence any result of such analyses is, in a sense, provisional, since it stimulates further investigations. These investigations do not completely abandon the achieved results, but rather seek to deepen them and to place them in more encompassing contexts, inevitably leading us to modifications and completions. But this is precisely what takes place in any positive science.

On this occasion, we cannot enter into such investigations in detail, and even less can we attempt to advance them. Instead, we limit ourselves to outlining the framework within which such investigations are to be conducted.

The Equivalent of Consciousness

Each object, whatever its nature—physical thing, tool, value, work of art, historical fact, social institution, etc.—becomes accessible to us only by means of certain acts of consciousness which we are actually experiencing or can experience. In these acts, which are all related to the object and form a group with reference to it, the object presents itself now from one side, now from another, now under one aspect, now under a different one; now we are conscious of it in one way, now in another. Progressively experiencing these acts and coming back to those already lived through in order to connect them with present experiences, we successively grasp the moments, attributes, and properties which pertain to the object and make up the unity of its nature. This unity corresponds to and depends on the harmonious agreement among experiences, and it is in virtue of this unity that all those partial experiences join to form the whole experience of the object in question.

Without the experiences through which the object displays its nature, presents itself from various sides and under various aspects, constitutes and constructs itself step by step, and discloses the sense of its being or existence, it would be nothing. Moreover, were the synthetic unity which encompasses the partial experiences to fail, then it would no longer be a true object but only the fading shadow thereof (*Ideas*, p. 383). Even when the direct apprehension of an object by means of a suitable experience is denied us, be it for technical or practical reasons or because of the structure of our minds, it is by means of specific experiences relative to other objects and especially through meditations on these experiences that we are entitled to posit the object and to confer a determinate nature on it. Thus every concealed property and structure of an object at least indicates the possibility of acts to be experienced and performed, because there is no access to any object except through the acts relating to it and in which its being is disclosed. An object can come under consideration only to the extent that it can be apprehended and insofar as it figures in these acts of apprehension.

This conception is not infected with subjectivism. One is justified in distinguishing between the subjective appearance and the being-in-itself of an object or in substituting—as is done in the natural sciences—the "true reality" of an object for the object as it appears to our senses. Yet this objective reality refers us to the acts in which it is constituted, such being the acts into which the experience of the subjective appearance is integrated as a partial and one-sided experience, because it is the appearance corresponding to a certain point of view or obtained in a special orientation—hence as an experience subject to completion. Again, as is the case in physics, perceptual experience is the basis for constructive acts by which the physical object is conceived, a construction guided by the perceptual experience such that the physical object qua object of a higher order is fashioned on the basis of the perceptual object and its elaboration is oriented by it (*Ideas*, §§ 40, 52).

The existence of any object whatsoever is thus necessarily linked to the possibility of a subject's performing quite determinate experiences under certain conditions which, perhaps, cannot be fulfilled. It is in these acts of consciousness that the object unfolds and discloses itself for what it is to the subject who becomes conscious of it. Acts of consciousness which confer its nature, structure, and sense of being on the object have a constitutive function in relation to it. We may thus regard the object as the *correlate* of a group of acts related to it or, reciprocally, we may regard that group of acts as *the equivalent of consciousness* of the object (*Ideas*, p. 422).[2]

---

2. *Ideas*, p. 402: "'Object' is for us at all times a title for essential connections of consciousness" (translation modified).

In order to conceive of the object as the correlate of acts, we need not reduce it to consciousness. Even though in every particular act the object presents itself under one aspect or from one side, what is grasped in any such act is not an aspect, a side, or any part of the object but, rather, the whole object appearing in a determinate way (*Ideas*, p. 383). On the one hand, since this object is the same one which, by means of another act, offers or will offer itself under a different aspect, it goes beyond and transcends each and every one of these particular acts, in the sense that it is not a real ingredient of any act. On the other hand, the object cannot be identified with the totality of particular acts which collectively form the group relating to it, for the object—over and against the multiplicity of such acts considered individually—is one, identical, and identifiable (*Ideas*, p. 133 and § 97; *CM*, §§ 17, 18). The acts which form such a group can and must be considered under an aspect other than that of their relationship to the object.

Each of these particular acts, insofar as it is a lived event, occupies its own place in the order of subjective, immanent, or phenomenal time, i.e., in time as it is felt and lived through by the conscious subject.[3] The relations of agreement which arise among particular acts and the synthetic unity established among them are also produced in phenomenal time. This harmony, which obtains among a multiplicity of acts and on which the unity and, so to speak, the consistency of the object common to all of these acts depend, is brought about by means of temporal phases and extents. Now, the object is entirely independent of these temporal structures as well as indifferent to the places which particular acts relating to it occupy in phenomenal time. Moreover, the object transcends the duration of these acts, for duration is another phenomenon that belongs to immanent temporality. If the object continues throughout a certain period of time, its duration is of a physical or cosmological order and would have nothing to do with phenomenal duration. Since the object is alien to the phenomenal temporality which defines the psychological facticity of experiences, it is not a real fact of consciousness or even a group of such facts. Insofar as the object is a correlate of consciousness, it is not a real ingredient thereof.

3. Husserl has devoted *The Phenomenology of Internal Time-Consciousness*, trans. James S. Churchill (Bloomington: Indiana University Press, 1964), to the temporality of consciousness.

Thus we have learned that the object appears before consciousness without being a part of consciousness, that the acts which relate to it do not include it as a really inherent part, that the object remains identical over and against the many acts which relate to it, and that in all these acts the identity of the object is sensed and experienced. This state of affairs has led Husserl to his theory of the intentionality of consciousness, a theory which brings about a truly revolutionary change in the concept of consciousness.

THE OBJECT AS TRANSCENDENTAL CLUE

THE CORRELATION between an object and a group of acts opens a field of research. With regard to any given object, the problem arises of determining its equivalent of consciousness, i.e., the question of knowing which acts must or should be experienced in order for the object to exist and to be such as it presents itself.

Since the object is being displayed in these acts, the contribution which each act makes is predetermined by the fact that every act involves our becoming conscious—if only partially— of the object in question. It is necessary for an object that possesses a given nature to present itself by means of some acts rather than others. Despite the differences obtaining among these acts, they must all converge to produce a total consciousness of the object and to constitute the object for what it is. This is why any change ascertained in the bearing of an act, if it does not break up the synthetic unity of the total consciousness of the object and therefore destroy the unity of the object itself, points to a modification of the object or at least to a variation of the aspect under which it appears—in the latter case, referring to a different manner of appearance where this change is absent (*Ideas*, pp. 283–86). There is thus nothing arbitrary or fortuitous in such acts, except the passage from the potentiality or pure possibility of being experienced to the present performance of the act (i.e., to the psychological actuality) and the fact that the passage takes place at one point in time rather than another.

The object with its individual nature thus includes a law regulating the acts in a binding fashion so as to ensure the existence of the object or, in other words, the possibility of a total consciousness of the object. By experiencing one such act, we are able to anticipate the contributions of future acts and the aspects under which the object will present itself in them (*CM*, § 19). Undoubtedly, the object may be only slightly known or may be given in an extremely indeterminate way. This would be reflected by an almost complete indecisiveness and imprecision in our anticipations, which may sometimes be so vague and indistinct as to lack any special contents. But even then there would necessarily be some anticipations: We would anticipate at least the style of experiences to be performed and the form and type of what the future acts will and must contribute (*Ideas*, pp. 148 f.). For instance, when one looks at a physical thing from the front, one may not know how it will present itself from the back. What is certain, however, is the fact that the thing may be seen from that side, and that the contribution of such acts will complete that of our present perception, so that all of them will join to form a total experience of the thing (*Ideas*, pp. 137–39). These more or less explicit and determinate possible anticipations—no matter how indecisive and vague—cannot be missing, qua conscious and lived facts, from the perception of a physical thing, for in the very nature of a physical object we find the requirement that it appear only under one aspect and from one side in any given perception. Accordingly, this one-sided appearance itself refers to further acts which will bring the present consciousness to completion (*Ideas*, §§ 40, 149).

These anticipations can in no way be regarded, therefore, as events which are only accidentally attached to the act actually being performed. What we find is that they are the means of making explicit what the present act contains only in a concealed manner. Although we cannot, in this context, enter into even a superficial exposition of the general characteristics as well as the typical forms of these "implications," let us at least stress the fundamental fact which the existence of such implications—among other conscious phenomena—indicates.[4] The manifold acts which relate to one and the same object should not be considered as merely juxtaposed, for they are internally

---

4. See our essay, "The Phenomenology of Perception: Perceptual Implications," in *An Invitation to Phenomenology*, ed. James M. Edie (Chicago: Quadrangle Books, 1965).

related; these acts indeed form an order, an organization, even a hierarchy (*Ideas*, pp. 416–18). Since they frequently confirm, complete, and continue one another, we may say that they support each other. For this is to be the case, it is irrelevant whether the acts in question are actually performed or merely possible, since in the latter case what would actually be lived is the possibility itself. Accordingly, the acts form a system which has a well-determined structure of its own and is regulated by *a principle of unity*. This principle endows the system with coherence and, on the other hand, guarantees and conditions the unity of the object which corresponds to the system, for the unity is nothing but the objective equivalent of this coherence.

Beginning with the object, one is thus *regressively* led toward its equivalent of consciousness. The tasks which arise in such an orientation are: to analyze the particular acts which belong to the system in question; to make explicit whatever they imply; to establish the relations which connect them; to penetrate the nature and structure of the system they form; and to determine the elements on which the unity and existence of the object depend. In order to deal with these problems, we must try to disengage the conscious life to which the object is correlative and in which it appears somehow as a complete product; we must disclose, step by step and layer by layer, the *phenomenological constitution of the object for consciousness*. In these investigations, any particular act is conceived of less for what it is in itself than as it is envisaged "from the 'teleological' standpoint on its function in making 'synthetic unity' possible" (*Ideas*, p. 252; translation modified). In other words, the acts should be viewed in terms of the places they occupy and the roles they play in the system which they form, and according to their contribution to the constitution of the object. In such a regressive meditation, the object which we take as our point of departure becomes our *"transcendental clue"* (*Ideas*, § 150; cf. *CM*, § 21) in an investigation which can also claim to be transcendental, for, beginning with the given and existing object, it bears on the necessary conditions for the nature, unity, and existence of the object.

Likewise, we must raise transcendental questions about *the ontological nature of the object*, i.e., about its own specific sense of being. Every object calls for acts of a kind which is correlative to the category to which the object belongs. It is such a category that predetermines the sense of the object's existence. Accordingly, an object belonging to a given category can be grasped only by acts of a certain determinate sort. The category of objects and the kind of acts correspond to one another reciprocally (*Ideas,* pp. 83 f., 395 f., 411 f.). Just as a color can be given only in visual experience, a tone in auditory perception, and a physical thing in perceptual acts, and just as every particular perceptual act cannot exist without necessarily implying a reference to further perceptual acts, no tool, work of art, or social institution can be grasped except through acts which are specifically suitable. Phenomenological research is hence confronted with the tasks of identifying the different kinds of acts, of penetrating their essential structure, and of discovering their characteristic and distinctive traits. Such explorations will not be complete until they yield the result that the correlate of a certain kind of act and, above all, of a certain kind of act-system cannot be anything but an object endowed with a quite determinate sense of being.

THE GENERAL STRUCTURES OF EVIDENCE

AMONG THE ACTS that make up the system which is the equivalent of consciousness of an object, we find some that are endowed with a special privilege. Such acts are those marked with the character of *evidence,* for in them an object is not merely apprehended in some fashion or other, but so that "an affair, an affair-complex (or state of affairs), a universality, a value, or other objectivity [appears] in the final mode: 'itself there,' 'immediately intuited,' 'given originaliter'" (*CM,* p. 57; cf. *FTL,* § 59). By experiencing any such act, the subject does not regard the thing in a more or less empty, symbolic, or indirect way; rather, he encounters the thing itself and grasps it directly with the consciousness that he is confronted with it immediately. Evidence is neither a secondary fact accompanying certain thoughts and produced under certain conditions nor a subjective feeling of belief attaching itself to some acts but absent from others (*Ideas,* § 21 and p. 399). On the contrary, it is the essential feature of certain acts, and, correlatively speaking, it is an especially privileged mode of presentation before consciousness.

Evidence is a fundamental form of conscious life, and any

act which has not yet taken it tends toward this form. Actually, any act which is not an evidence needs to be confirmed and justified by a "parallel" act which would provide *modo originali* whatever has been regarded only in an indirect fashion in the nonevident act. An identifying synthesis between two acts will take place insofar as an act marked by the character of evidence fulfills a symbolic and indirect "intention." Such a synthesis certifies the claim of the nonevident act to disclose something about the object in question. In the identifying synthesis, the object reveals itself as it has been foreseen, presumed, predicted, or suspected to be; now it presents itself as it was represented.[5]

The verification which nonevident acts require and which is intimately connected with the possibility of such identifying syntheses is therefore the phenomenon of evidence. Any philosophical analysis of truth, as well as of the notions grouped under the heading "reason" (*Ideas*, Pt. IV, chap. 2), necessarily leads to this phenomenon. The only source from which such notions may be derived is the set of privileged acts by which the object in question presents itself "in person" (*Ideas*, p. 83; *FTL*, p. 158). That is why all conscious life necessarily directs itself toward reason (i.e., theoretical, practical, or aesthetic reason). Whether we are dealing with the truth of assertions, the validity of values, or claims of any kind whatsoever, *evidence has a universal and teleological function in conscious life.* Reciprocally, conscious life owes its tendency toward reason to the role played by evidence.[6]

The fact that nonevident acts are in need of verification is a conscious event: These acts are experienced with such a need and inasmuch as they have this need. By its very nature, then, every nonevident act refers us to the evidence which corresponds to it and in some way implies it—without, however, requiring that the evident parallel act be a real part of the nonevident act. This implication should not be conceived on the model of the way in which a particular perception of a physical thing encompasses further perceptions. Nonevident acts, such as those of memory, expectation, and representation, have the essential

5. In the *Logical Investigations*, Husserl has devoted vast and penetrating studies to the fulfillment by evidence of an empty intention.

6. *FTL*, p. 159; see *CM*, p. 57: evidence "is a possibility—and, more particularly, one that can be the aim of a striving and actualizing intention—in the case of anything meant already or meanable."

and intrinsic characteristic of being modifications of the evident acts parallel to them, for they present in an "improper" way the same objects as the originary consciousness which is the corresponding evidence—in our example, perception has this function for physical things (*Ideas*, § 99). On this basis, they can be regarded as deriving from evidence through the mediation of "ideal operations"; they accordingly appear as "ideal operational transformations" of an experience which, for this reason too, should be characterized as originary (*Ideas*, p. 220). The non-evident acts imply the parallel evident act in such a determinate way that any modification implies the originary and unmodified state of what is so modified.[7] In conformity with this, the non-evident acts do not have originary legitimacy, for they derive their legitimacy from the parallel acts called on to confirm them.[8] Thus, the evident acts form a separate group within the system of acts that is the equivalent of consciousness in relation to an object of any sort—a group which is somehow the kernel of the whole system.

In transcendental phenomenology, which begins with the object and turns toward the corresponding act-system in order to disclose the constitution of the object for consciousness, the evident acts can still be regarded under an aspect different from that which we have just mentioned, for the evident acts are, above all, originary forms of consciousness and authentic *experiences*.

We should not take the term "experience" in its traditional sense, i.e., as synonymous with perceptual or sensory experience. Husserl endows the term with a broader sense: What is essential to experience is the mark of authenticity and the originary character of a privileged form of consciousness through whose discrete acts the object appears "in person" and as existing.[9] Far

---

7. Besides this kind of implication, there is also the relationship obtaining between *simple belief* and presumption, suspicion, questionability, doubt, etc. All such acts are intrinsically characterized as variations of simple belief. See *Ideas*, §§ 103 f.

8. Quite apart from the special form which the legitimating procedure may adopt and which we have examined in this context, Husserl has analyzed two other forms. See *ibid.*, § 141.

9. The originary character of experience is obviously not taken by Husserl in a chronological or biographical sense, as if it signified the moment in which a subject becomes conscious of an object for the first time. Here we are dealing with an internal and essential

from being an arbitrary and merely terminological innovation, this broadening of the meaning of "experience" becomes necessary when we want to express the most general and fundamental function which the acts in question have in conscious life. In this new usage, the traditional sense of experience (i.e., qua sensory experience) is to be regarded as a special case of experience-in-general, namely, as the originary form of consciousness of physical things.[10]

In the performance of an authentic experiential act, the object in question does not merely appear as the correlate of thought or as *cogitatum;* it is, rather, apprehended in its own being, i.e., as truly existing. Experience, therefore, has the value of being an originary formation for the consciousness of the object, and the veritable existence of the object—as opposed to a merely presumptive, suspected, or proposed existence—depends on the special structure which distinguishes the privileged acts.[11] And, since experience has this role of primordially constituting the object, evidence can be the foundation of the parallel nonevident acts (*FTL*, p. 158).

As the most fundamental fact of conscious life, evidence thus appears in a twofold way, either as an instance of verification or as authentic experience (i.e., as the originary consciousness of objects). Regarded from the second standpoint, the phenomenon of evidence is basic to the notion of existence, since any examination of this notion ultimately leads to such a phenomenon. There is, therefore, an intimate connection between the notion of truth (and, more generally, of reason) and the notion of existence, such that veritable existence and the reality which is a particular case thereof are the correlates of reason.[12] This corre-

---

structure of some privileged acts which, in principle, can be reiterated.

10. *Ideas,* § 19; *CM,* pp. 57 f. Even though one must be careful not to assimilate experience in general to perceptual experience, it is quite useful to begin with perception and regard it as a paradigm for experience in the broadened sense.

11. "In principle . . . *to every 'truly existing' object* there corresponds *the idea of a possible consciousness,* in which the object itself is *originarily* and thus *perfectly adequately* graspable. Conversely, when this possibility is truly accomplished, *eo ipso* the object truly exists" (*Ideas,* p. 395; translation modified).

12. *Ideas,* p. 395; and *CM,* p. 60: "It is clear that truth or the true actuality of objects is to be obtained only from *evidence,* and that it is evidence alone by virtue of which an 'actually' existing,

lation is one of the great themes of Husserlian phenomenology (see *Ideas,* Pt. IV; and *CM,* Third Meditation).

According to the ontological diversity of objects or the different regions to which they belong, evidences become differentiated and divided into several diverse kinds that have in common only their general function, i.e., the presentation of the object. A certain special structure of evidence thus corresponds to every particular region of being. It is that structure which, in a way, is reflected in the specific ontological sense of objects pertaining to the region of being in question (*Ideas,* pp. 385 f., 395 f.; *FTL,* pp. 159–62). The kind of evidence and the ontological category of objects correspond to each other, refer to and condition one another. Assuming the privileged status of evident acts over and against parallel nonevident acts, we can see that the source of the general correlation between the kind of acts and the category of objects is none other than the correspondence between the essential structure of a kind of evidence and the specific ontological sense of a region of being.

The nonevident acts can be perfected. This is likewise true of acts already invested in some way with the privileged character of evidence (*Ideas,* §§ 67 f.; *CM,* pp. 14 f.). The perfecting process can be conceived of as the approximation to an ideal which varies according to the given region of being. In such a process, it is thus necessary to abide by the essential structure of the kind of evidence which corresponds to the objects in question. For this reason it would be absurd, for example, to try to substitute, in the field of physical things, a rational cognition for perceptual experience, on the grounds that apodicticity (i.e., the impossibility of conceiving of the nonexistence of the object) and other perfections are lacking in such a form of experience.

It is by virtue of the privileged performances called "evident acts" that we confer on the object the ontological sense which is its own and with which it exists in our conscious life and that we grasp the object as veritably existing in the mode of being which is specific to the ontological region to which it belongs (*FTL,* § 61). No object is anything but what it reveals itself to be in and by means of those acts which are originary and authentic forms of consciousness for such an object; hence the object can

---

true, rightly accepted object of whatever form or kind *has sense for us*—and with all the determinations that for us belong to it under the title of its true nature."

be regarded as the objective correlate of the special group of evident acts which exist within the relevant act-system. If one seeks to have a philosophical understanding of an object, and especially of its sense of being, then one is accordingly led toward a structural analysis of those experiences in which the object presents itself, for it is from nowhere else that the object may derive its nature, its ontological sense, and anything else which it is for us. And it is because the nature of consciousness allows for a diversity of kinds of evidence that the different regions of being which we in fact encounter exist for us.

Objects and Consciousness

DESPITE THE FUNDAMENTAL IMPORTANCE of the relationships existing between objective being and consciousness, they should not be employed to cover up the cleavage or abyss between the two realms. Every object—regardless of the ontological region to which it belongs—becomes accessible to us through some phenomena in which it appears. As an identical unity and the objective correlate of a system of acts, the object stands over and against the manifold acts which relate to it; hence it is not to be identified either with individual acts or with the totality thereof. In every such act, the object indeed presents itself under aspects or in ways which change or could in principle change, but it nevertheless appears as identically the same.

In the realm of consciousness, however, a parallel distinction between phenomena and what is offered in and through phenomena has no sense whatever.[13] The being of a conscious act is identical with its being performed, that is, with its appearing. In reference to one and the same object, it is always possible to perform many acts which would complete one another, in such a fashion that one act would disclose an element of the object which would not be accessible through a prior act. But this does not apply to the conscious acts themselves. To reperform an act so as to determine whether any property not as yet discovered in such an act in fact belongs to it is not at all possible. Actually, we would be engaging in the performance of a new act, which would refer to the same object as the former. It is true that such

13. See *Ideas*, §§ 42, 44 f., for Husserl's contrast of consciousness and objective being.

acts can resemble one another, but, even were the similarity to increase to the greatest possible degree, it would be absolutely impossible for them to be identical. Hence there is no repetition of the act. We must therefore avoid inferring something about one act on the basis of what we experience in another; that is, we must resist the temptation to conclude that a feature was present in an act simply because we find it in another, arguing that, although such a feature was not directly and immediately observable in the original act, it was nevertheless present in an unperceived form.[14] An act of consciousness is only such as it presents itself; there are no concealed elements in it and there is nothing to look for behind it. When the subject reflectively turns toward his conscious life, when he engages in so-called inner perception, he grasps each of his acts as something absolute which does not take variable forms and aspects and for which the opposition between unity and multiplicity—which is essential to the apprehension of objects—plays no role.

Since objects are constituted in conscious life, they depend on it in the sense that they need conscious acts to confer their nature, specific being, and veritable existence on them, and also in that they are to be regarded as the objective correlates of such acts (*Ideas*, § 47). We have already insisted that the existence of any object is connected to actual—or at least potential—acts. These acts are characterized as experiences of objects, the objectivity of which results from the agreement established among such acts, according to the general principle that the category of objects and the kind of acts correspond to one another. It follows that, if an abnormal consciousness is unable to perform acts of a certain kind, for that consciousness the corresponding objects will not exist. If we were to find that the acts corresponding to certain objects could not be performed by any possible consciousness because of their essential structure, then we would see that such objects would be chimeras which can neither exist for nor be conceived of by consciousness. However, if everything necessary for the appearance of a coherent universe and the theoretical account thereof were to be produced on the side of consciousness, then it would be absurd to conceive of the eventual nonexistence of such a universe (*Ideas*, pp. 151 f.).

14. See our essay, "Some Aspects and Developments of Gestalt Psychology," in *SPP*.

Consciousness, on the contrary, depends on no region of objective being, since it does not presuppose the existence of the universe of physical things. A dissolution of this universe—such that it would no longer be possible for us to characterize and explain things in the fashion peculiar to the natural sciences (*Ideas*, pp. 147–48)—is perfectly conceivable, provided that it would affect neither the existence of physical things as identical unities standing opposite the manifold acts pertaining to them nor the stability they have from the coherence and agreement among such acts. We could even imagine a much more radical dissolution (*Ideas*, § 49), for the following situation is certainly possible: Suppose that, as experiences unfold, we encounter a vast number of incompatibilities and contradictions which we are unable to harmonize; as a result, no identical and objective unity could be constituted; only vague outlines of things would arise and immediately disappear, thus bringing about the annihilation of the universe. Such an event would not, however, entail the end of consciousness; it would only imply a modification of it. And this would be the case in either of the two situations presented—whether the universe vanished because the motives for constructing a physical universe out of the perceptual world disappeared, or because the agreement among acts which guaranteed the coherence and stability of perceivable things was no longer produced. Yet, despite those eventualities, consciousness would continue to exist. It would certainly become other than it is in fact, but its existence would remain untouched either by the dissolution or by the annihilation of the world. For, in point of fact, this dissolved or annihilated world would ultimately be the objective (or, if one prefers, the quasi-objective) correlate of the modified consciousness. We may thus conclude that *even though the objective world qua constituted is in need of an actual or possible consciousness,* since its existence is only an existence for the consciousness constitutive of it, *consciousness itself is absolute in the sense that* "nulla re indiget ad existendum."

The existence of any object depends on consciousness. This relationship of dependence specifically points to characteristics inherent in those acts to which we have referred as experiences of the object in question. Objective being thus presents itself as in a sense secondary, for it is relative to consciousness and therefore depends on something other than itself. Such a dependence is particularly salient in the case of physical things, the veritable existence of which is intimately connected with the agreement and harmony obtaining among all the acts making up the perceptual life and having a bearing on the real world. And this is so much so that the existence of such objects can never be completely established, since it is always possible that the experiences pertaining to one such thing fail to be confirmed by further experiences or even come to be denied and contradicted by them. Should this take place, the thing would dissolve or, at least, become manifest as other than what we believed it to be.

Objective being is thus always open to possible doubt, even in the form of experiencing the need to go back to an already acquired evidence and reestablish it by a new act, also characterized as evident. The being of consciousness, on the contrary, is set apart by the feature of indubitability, which Descartes ascribed to *cogitationes* (*Ideas*, § 46; *FTL*, p. 251). Whatever the value of an act's contribution when considered from the standpoint of reason, one thing remains indubitable, namely, the fact that it has actually been performed. Whenever we reflectively turn to an act actually performed, we apprehend a being devoid of the need or the possibility of being confirmed or falsified. We thus find an absolute being, i.e., one for which it is impossible not to be.

Since objects are constituted, we are entitled to say that they depend on the consciousness which constitutes them. Inasmuch as objects are objective unities and "unities of sense" (*Sinneseinheiten*), they presuppose the consciousness which endows them with unity and sense (*Ideas*, § 55). Looking upon consciousness as having a constituting function, as being "the sphere of absolute origins" (*Seinssphäre absoluter Ursprünge*), and as "the source of all reason and unreason, all right and wrong, all reality and fiction, all value and disvalue, all deed and misdeed" (*Ideas*, p. 251; translation modified), we have to say that consciousness itself, on the contrary, presupposes nothing which exists apart from it and owes its sense of being to nothing other than itself. The acts of consciousness are thus relative only to themselves.[15] We have therefore found a sense marked as absolute.

15. Husserl, "Nachwort zu meinen Ideen . . ." in *Jahrbuch für Philosophie und phänomenologische Forschung*, XI (1930), 562.

THE PHENOMENOLOGICAL REDUCTION

WE MUST NOT, however, confuse consciousness qua transcendental with the consciousness to which the naïve reflection of everyday life has access or with the consciousness which traditional scientific psychology conceives of as connected with a physical organism and as belonging to an ego which has its own life, evolution, and personal tendencies and lives in the midst of one or another social group during a certain historical phase of the development of such communities. In the context of constitutive phenomenology, consciousness is not regarded as being subject to the actions and influences which have their source in the real world. In a word, consciousness is not taken as part of the real world and as one reality among others (*Ideas*, §§ 53 f.; *CM*, § 11; *FTL*, pp. 251–54). We have a right to characterize consciousness as absolute only to the extent that we conceive of it exclusively as a medium and, so to speak, as the theater in which the constitution of all sorts of objects—including psychical and human realities, such as the soul, the mind, the ego, the personality, our social and historical being, etc.— takes place.

We arrive at this manner of conceiving consciousness by means of the phenomenological reduction. This is a radical modification of attitude, which consists in suspending and parenthesizing the existential character of the entire world and of the objects belonging to every ideal region. In the reduction, of course, we neither deny the existential character nor subject it to doubt; it is merely inhibited and put out of play. The reduction does not result in any modification of the objects or in any special interpretation of the being of objects, after the model of one or another traditional philosophical conception. The only transformation to be noted is this: The objects and the world become *phenomena*. The existential characters with which objects present themselves and continue to present themselves after the phenomenological reduction has taken place are merely put out of action. This means that they still appear in an unaltered fashion in the ensuing phenomenological investigations, although they are not employed any longer as premises for the philosophical meditation being undertaken.

The existential characters become phenomena and themes

to which special and indeed quite important analyses are devoted. Objects of all kinds and descriptions remain, therefore, such as they are. Meanwhile, no phenomenological employment of their existence is made, for the phenomenologist strictly abides by what he finds in pure and reduced consciousness—the appearing, for example, of a real world before consciousness—and carefully refrains, regardless of grounds, from basing any of his results on a reality different from consciousness itself. Any such reality may be regarded as a phenomenon appearing before consciousness, but it should never be taken as a veritable reality to be used as a point of departure or even as a supportive element for phenomenological investigations. In this group of realities we must certainly include those characterized as human.[16]

At this point it is proper to insist that consciousness, as a result of the performance of the phenomenological reduction, cannot be philosophically regarded as human consciousness, for the latter would require that we take into account the biological, social, and historical being of man and everything else which plays a role in his humanity. The phenomenological reduction thus excludes philosophical anthropology or, if one prefers, it bars the choice of philosophical anthropology as the foundation of philosophy. Precisely this consequence is one of the justifications for the phenomenological reduction. In effect, to consider consciousness as human is to place it qua real being within the context of all realities which surround man, on which he depends, and on which he acts. Such a procedure would be tantamount to assuming as constituted that which it is a question of constituting. Only the phenomenological reduction allows us to avoid the vicious circle intrinsic to the attempt to raise transcendental questions about the constitution of the world on the basis of a part of the same world.

Regarded from the standpoint attained by the phenomenological reduction, consciousness becomes manifest as a self-enclosed region of being which nothing can enter and from which

16. For reasons of space, we must restrict our presentation of the phenomenological reduction, which Husserl has discussed in *Ideas*, pt. II, chaps. 1, 4, "Nachwort," and *CM*, §§ 8, 15, 40, 41. See Eugen Fink, "Vergegenwärtigung und Bild," *Jahrbuch für Philosophie und phänomenologische Forschung*, Vol. IX (1930), § 4; our "Critical Study of Husserl's 'Nachwort'" and other essays in *SPP*; and chap. 7, above.

nothing can escape. Consciousness appears as a domain which is first in itself and prior to any other region of being (*Ideas*, p. 152). When we proceed on this basis to compare Husserl's view[17] with Descartes's own,[18] we soon realize that transcendental phenomenology may be correctly characterized as "a neo-Cartesianism, even though it is obliged . . . to reject nearly all the well-known doctrinal content of the Cartesian philosophy" (*CM*, p. 1). Indeed, certain notions of Descartes, which until the advent of constitutive phenomenology had not displayed their full force, are now taken over in a radical fashion (*Ideas*, p. 145).

CONCLUSION

CONSTITUTIVE PHENOMENOLOGY can be defined as the systematic and methodic exploration of consciousness, regarded from the point of view of its presentational function. Accordingly, consciousness is not taken as a totality of real psychical facts and events; it is, rather, viewed from the standpoint whereby objects stand in front of and exist for it. It is in and by means of conscious acts that objects are constituted such as they are for conscious life. The general theory of intentionality is devoted to this capital and fundamental fact of consciousness.

Phenomenology divides into several special branches according to the different regions of objects. Every ontological category points to a special phenomenological discipline, the purpose of which is to explore the constitution and formation for consciousness of objects encompassed by such a category. Only by going back from the different kinds of objects to their origin in consciousness can we be ready to disengage their ontological structures and to arrive at a final and definitive philosophical

17. "But what if the world were, in the end, not at all the absolutely first basis for judgments and a being that is intrinsically prior to the world were the already presupposed basis for the existence of the world?" (*CM*, p. 18).

18. *Meditationes de Prima Philosophia*, in *Oeuvres*, ed. Charles Adam and Paul Tannery (Paris: Librairie Philosophique, J. Vrin, 1964——), VII, 33; and XI, 26: "Toutes les raisons qui servent à connoître et concevoir la nature de la cire, ou de quelque autre corps, prouvent beaucoup plus facilement et plus évidemment la nature de mon esprit."

understanding of the essential nature of every kind of object. On that basis, we are able to see in what sense and with what right phenomenology can and should aspire to universality.

The different regions of being are not merely juxtaposed with one another. Indeed, there are kinds of objects the structure of which requires that they be constituted only if other, simpler objects are already constituted. We may thus say that the higher-order objects derive from the more primitive ones through the mediation of certain mental operations. These relationships of dependence may take many forms, according to the case in question. Unfortunately, we cannot examine them here. Suffice it to say that they are at the root of the genetic phenomenology which is to complete the investigations initiated by static phenomenology.

All such phenomenological investigations should be undertaken and conducted in the phenomenologically reduced attitude, which alone guarantees their philosophical value and allows us to elude the anthropological paralogisms.

9 / Husserl's Theory of the Intentionality of Consciousness in Historical Perspective

THOUGH HE WAS NOT A HISTORIAN, either by temperament or by training, Husserl repeatedly and most emphatically insisted on the continuity of his endeavors with the great tradition of Western philosophy, especially modern philosophy, which began in the seventeenth century. His insistence appears most explicitly in several of his writings of the 1920s and 1930s published in the course of the last decade.[1] Even as early as 1913, in the first volume of the *Ideas*—the only volume published during his lifetime—Husserl speaks of his phenomenology as the "secret longing" of the whole of modern philosophy, referring especially to Descartes, Hume, and Kant (*Ideas*, p. 183). Finally, it is significant that one of Husserl's presentations of phenomenological philosophy as a whole—a presentation in a highly concentrated, condensed, and, in comparison with the *Ideas*, abbreviated form (notwithstanding the discussion of the problem of intersubjectivity, which is not contained in the *Ideas*)—bears the title *Cartesian Meditations*, that is, meditations carried out in the manner of Descartes.

The phrase "secret longing" expresses Husserl's claim to have

This essay originally appeared under the same title in *Phenomenology and Existentialism*, ed. Edward N. Lee and Maurice Mandelbaum (Baltimore: Johns Hopkins Press, 1967). Two paragraphs, on William James and Franz Brentano, respectively, have been transposed from "Towards a Theory of Intentionality," *Philosophy and Phenomenological Research*, Vol. XXX (1970).

1. *Erste Philosophie*, *Husserliana* VII (The Hague: Martinus Nijhoff, 1956), pt. I; and *Crisis*.

brought the intentions of his predecessors to fulfillment. This in turn implies that, on the one hand, their intentions were substantially the same as his, but that, on the other hand, they were unable to realize those very intentions and therefore did not reach the level or dimension of transcendental constitutive phenomenology. Thus, in his opening remarks in *Cartesian Meditations* (p. 1), Husserl characterizes his phenomenology as "a neo-Cartesianism," though he rejects nearly the whole doctrinal content of Cartesian philosophy—for the very sake of radicalizing Descartes's ultimate intentions.

We therefore find ourselves confronted with a twofold task. First, we must formulate what Husserl considers to be the fundamental intention which guides and dominates the whole of modern philosophy. In the second place, we must raise the question of why, prior to Husserl, this intention could not find adequate fulfillment and satisfactory realization. We take our departure from Descartes, to whom Husserl repeatedly refers as having given modern philosophy its distinctive character and physiognomy by orienting it toward transcendental subjectivism.

HISTORICAL ROOTS OF HUSSERL'S PROBLEMS

Descartes's Subjective Orientation and Its Generalization

DESCARTES'S DISCOVERY OF CONSCIOUSNESS (as his *sum cogitans* may be interpreted) amounts to and may even be said to consist in the disclosure of a double privilege pertaining to consciousness. There is, in the first place, its indubitability in the well-known sense. Whatever else may be, and is, open to the universal doubt, the existence of consciousness as such and as a whole—of actually experienced particular acts of consciousness of every description, the existence, finally, of the experiencing and conscious ego itself, to the extent to which it is conceived merely and exclusively as a conscious being (*res cogitans*)—is not engulfed by the doubt but, on the contrary, withstands such engulfment.

Of still greater importance in the present context is the second privilege of consciousness, which Descartes indicates at the end of his Second Meditation when he summarizes his famous analysis of the perception of a piece of wax.[2] According to this analysis, we become assured of the existence of the piece of wax by the fact that we see it, touch it, hear the sound it emits when struck, etc., and bring further mental faculties into play, especially that faculty which Descartes calls inspection of the mind (*mentis inspectio*). At the end of the Sixth Meditation, Descartes points out that it is the convergence, concordance, and agreement among those mental operations and their yieldings which make us accept the objects thus encountered as really existing and which differentiate them from figments of the fancy and dream occurrences.[3] It follows that, in becoming convinced of the existence of any extramental objects, such as the perceived piece of wax, we are a fortiori assured of the existence of the mental operations in question by means of which we come to accept those extramental objects as real and existing.

To express it differently and in a more general manner, so as not to lay the main stress on the problem of existence and reality, Descartes's analysis of the perception of the piece of wax sets forth and makes explicit the essential reference of objects to consciousness, namely, to those acts of consciousness through which the objects present themselves. Descartes's analysis discloses consciousness as necessarily involved in whatever objects are encountered and dealt with. It may appear a truism to say that we cannot deal with objects in any manner except actually dealing with them and that such dealing denotes mental activities and operations of various kinds. However, what appears to be a truism expresses a profound and momentous discovery, namely, the insight into the nature of consciousness as the universal medium of access to whatever exists for us and is considered by us as valid.

As Husserl interprets Descartes's discovery of consciousness as to the indubitability of its existence and to its function as a universal medium of access, this discovery implies the principle of a subjectively oriented philosophy. It implies a goal pursued by Descartes himself as well as by the subsequent development of modern philosophy, a goal that is also the goal of Husserl's own endeavors. All that is required is a generalized expression of the reference of objects to acts of consciousness and to conscious

2. *The Philosophical Works of Descartes*, trans. E. S. Haldane and G. R. T. Ross (New York: Dover Publications, 1955), I, 156 f.
    3. *Ibid.*, I, 198 f.

life as a whole and the formation of that reference in sufficiently radical terms.

First of all, the term "object" must be understood in the widest possible sense. It is meant to apply to perceivable things encountered in everyday common experience; to things of cultural value and significance such as utensils, books, musical instruments, and the like; to all real beings both inanimate and animate, e.g., our fellow men with whom we deal in highly diversified social situations, where they play the roles of employees, teachers, doctors, partners, collaborators, rivals, and so forth. Taken in this all-inclusive sense, the term "object" may also apply to the constructs of the several sciences, such as matter, energy, force, atom, electron, etc., and furthermore to ideal entities of every kind and description, such as the general notions considered in traditional logic, propositions and systematic concatenations of propositions, relations of all sorts, numbers, geometrical systems, etc. Finally, the term "object" may also denote specific social realities, such as the opinions and beliefs held in a certain society at a certain period of its historical development, political institutions, legal systems, and so on.

Every object—understood in this wide sense—presents itself to us through acts of consciousness as that which it is for us, as that which we take it to be, in the role which it plays and the functions assigned to it in our conscious life, with regard to our several activities, practical, theoretical, and other, e.g., artistic. In and through specific acts of consciousness, the object displays its qualities, properties, and attributes. It exhibits the components that contribute toward determining its sense, including the sense of its specific objectivity and existence—which obviously is not the same in the case of numbers and other ideal entities as it is in that of perceivable material things. Because of their essential reference, in the sense which has just been described, to acts of consciousness, objects may be said to "depend on" or—as we should prefer to express it—to be relative to consciousness. Hence a problem of a very general nature and of universal significance arises.

Given an object of any category whatever, we must set forth and analyze descriptively those acts of consciousness in their systematic interconnectedness and interconcatenation through which the object displays and presents itself—acts of consciousness in and through which all its sense-determining components and constituents accrue to the object. Hereby the task of constitutive phenomenology is defined, though in a somewhat sketchy way. It rests on the principle that, for an object of any class and sort to be what it is and to have whatever existence, objectivity, or validity pertains to it, acts of consciousness of a specific kind, as well as typical organizational forms in which those acts are united and concatenated with one another, are required. Constitutive phenomenology translates into concrete terms the essential reference of objects to conscious life (a reference that Descartes had expressed in a more or less abstract and general way) insofar as it makes every object arise, so to speak, out of the relevant acts and operations of consciousness as accomplished (*geleistet*) by them and, in that sense, as their product. Hence Husserl speaks of an "equivalent of consciousness" related to every object (*Ideas*, p. 422; translation modified), and he describes it as the task of constitutive phenomenology to lay bare and make explicit the correlation which a priori obtains between objects of the different varieties, on the one hand, and systematically organized groups of specific acts and operations of consciousness, on the other.[4] For reasons that cannot be discussed here, precedence in the order in which the constitutive problems are to be tackled belongs, according to Husserl, to the real perceptual world, the existents it comprises, and the events taking place in it.

Obviously, it is only by means of generalizations and radicalizations going far beyond not only Descartes's explicit statements but also his actual intentions that the program of constitutive phenomenology can be derived from his discovery of consciousness. As a matter of fact, what Husserl interprets as the central motif of Descartes's thinking was, for Descartes himself, rather a means to an end and stood in the service of a different purpose. Descartes's main intention was the validation of the incipient new science of physics, the justification of a tenet whose boldness we, the heirs to a scientific tradition, can appreciate only with considerable difficulty. This is the tenet that an external, extramental, and extraconscious world exists, but that this external world is in reality not as it appears in everyday perceptual experience but as it is conceived and constructed in mathematical terms in the new science. This explains why

4. *Crisis*, §§ 46, 48; and *Phänomenologische Psychologie*, ed. Walter Biemel, *Husserliana* IX (The Hague: Martinus Nijhoff, 1962), §§ 3b, 3e.

neither Descartes himself nor any of the Cartesians proceeded to exploit the momentous discovery of consciousness—whose exploitation did not begin until Locke's *Essay Concerning Human Understanding.*

Having made the preceding remarks for the sake of the accuracy of the historical record, we must insist on the legitimacy of isolating the discovery of consciousness and developing it in its own right. Understood along the general lines of Husserl's interpretation, though of course not in the sense of his extreme radicalization, Cartesian philosophy takes on its fundamental significance within the course of the subsequent development of modern philosophy. It can be considered as the first historical expression of what was to become the ultimate intention of the whole of modern philosophy.

We have mentioned that, in Husserl's judgment, neither Descartes nor any of his successors, whom Husserl considers as his own predecessors, has succeeded in adequately realizing the intention in question. Husserl points to what he calls "transcendental psychologism" as one of the main reasons for that failure. Succinctly stated, the task is to account for objects of every kind and description—in the first place, the real perceptual world and whatever it contains—by reference to subjective conscious life. Acts and operations of consciousness are, as a matter of course, interpreted as mundane events alongside other such events. They pertain to sentient living organisms, e.g., human beings, which are obviously mundane existents occupying determinate places within the spatiotemporal order of the real world. We thus seem to be caught in a circular reasoning, insofar as the very terms in which the world is to be accounted for are themselves affected by the sense of mundanity.[5] This situation leads to, motivates, and even necessitates the transcendental reduction as a methodological device whose function is to strip conscious life of the sense of mundanity.

Undoubtedly, the transcendental reduction is of utmost importance for the foundation and consistent elaboration of constitutive phenomenology. Still, it is not along that line of thought that we shall pursue our discussion. We wish to point out a second and no less important reason for the failure referred to.

5. Concerning the paradox of transcendental psychologism, see *Phänomenologische Psychologie,* pp. 287 ff., 328 ff. Concerning Husserl's objection to Descartes in this respect, see *CM,* § 10; *Crisis,* §§ 17 ff.

To do so, we raise the question of whether the theoretical means at the disposal of Descartes and his successors in the classical tradition of modern philosophy were sufficient for an adequate realization of what, following Husserl, we consider their ultimate intention to be. In other words, we turn to examining the general conception of consciousness as laid down by Descartes and taken over, almost as a matter of course, by his successors. Such an examination will enable us to see in its true proportions the radical and revolutionary innovation which is Husserl's theory of the intentionality of consciousness.

CARTESIAN DUALISM AND THE THEORY OF IDEAS IN THE "REPRESENTATIVE VERSION"

REALITY AS WHOLE IS DIVIDED BY DESCARTES into two domains. The domain which withstands universal doubt is the domain of consciousness (*cogitatio*), while the other domain, that of extension, is at first engulfed by universal doubt and subsequently reconquered and, so to speak, reinstated in its rights. Throughout, Descartes emphasizes the thoroughgoing heterogeneity of these two domains. To be sure, with respect to both domains Descartes uses the term "substance." However, the defining attributes of these substances are so utterly different, the two substances have so little in common, that the distinction between them amounts to a profound dualism dividing reality.

As, in Descartes's view, a corporeal thing is nothing but a delimited portion of space and, in this sense, a mode or modification of extendedness, so is a mental state, a *cogitatio*, nothing but a modification of consciousness or, in more modern parlance, an occurrence in conscious life. Because of the heterogeneity of the two domains, each is completely self-contained and self-sufficient, at least with respect to the other. Such self-sufficiency justifies denoting both domains as substances within the meaning of the specific Cartesian definition of that notion.

On account of its self-containedness and self-sufficiency, the domain of consciousness forms a closed sphere—the sphere of interiority or subjectivity. All mental states, which by definition belong to the mental sphere, are on the same footing, for whatever differences may obtain between them in any other respect, they are all modes of consciousness, subjective occurrences, events taking place in conscious life. This holds also for the particular class of mental states which Descartes singles out under the heading, "Ideas," [6] whereby are meant such mental states as have a presentifying function, that is, make present a man, a chimera, the heavens, an angel, or God, to abide by the examples Descartes gives in the *Meditations*. Ideas by means of which or, more correctly, by the means of *some* of which—as will presently be explained—contact is established with what pertains to the other domain, that of externality, are, to begin with, subjective occurrences and events, not different from other mental states, e.g., a feeling of pleasure or pain, a desire, a hope, and the like.

At this point, we may formulate two tenets that are connected with and characteristic of both the theory of Ideas and the interpretation of consciousness as a closed sphere of interiority. In the latter respect, the mind is confined to its own states. Only its own experiences, its modes and modifications, are directly and immediately given to the conscious ego. Differently expressed: *The only immediate and direct objects of knowledge are our own mental states.* It is not Descartes himself who defined Idea as that which is in our mind or thought,[7] but—as far as I can see— Antoine Arnauld, who was the first explicitly to lay down that principle which has become a general and fundamental doctrine accepted in the whole subsequent development of classical modern philosophy.[8] Even thinkers who, like Hume and Kant, depart considerably from Descartes maintain that, as Hume expresses it, "Nothing is ever really present with the mind but its perceptions or impressions and ideas";[9] or, as Kant has it, all our

6. We capitalize "Idea" when that term is to be understood in the general sense, as it is used by Descartes; we use "idea" when we refer to the specific sense that Hume gives it.

7. Letter to Mersenne, June 16, 1640: "par le mot *Idea*, j'entends tout ce qui peut être en notre pensée . . . ."

8. See E. Bréhier, *Histoire de la philosophie* (Paris: Presses Universitaires de France, 1962), II, 219 f. John Locke says: "Since the mind, in all its thoughts and reasonings, has no other immediate object but its own ideas, which it alone does or can contemplate, it is evident, that our knowledge is only conversant about them" (*Essay Concerning Human Understanding*, bk. IV, chap. 1, § 1).

9. *A Treatise of Human Nature*, ed. L. A. Selby-Bigge (London: Oxford University Press, 1888), p. 67; see also pp. 197, 206, 212.

representations, whatever their origin and nature, are nothing but modifications of the mind (*Gemüt*) and therefore belong to inner sense.[10]

The second doctrine is of a less general significance, because, in contrast with the first one, it is not essential to the theory of Ideas as such but only to a special version of that theory, the version advocated by Descartes. As noted, Descartes's goal is to prove the real existence of the external world, conceived to be of a mathematical, especially geometrical, nature, and to show that certain particularly privileged Ideas correspond to, and are in conformity with, corporeal things. Still, the Ideas in question are subjective occurrences in the sphere of interiority. Furthermore, on the strength of what has just been shown, the mind can never leave that sphere of subjective interiority but remains forever moving, so to speak, within it—that is, among its own states. If, owing to the privileged Ideas, contact is to be established with extramental corporeal things, the contact can only be a mediated one. The Ideas in question must be considered as intramental representatives of extramental, i.e., extended, objects. (We are avoiding the expression "representation" deliberately, because the meaning of that term as usually understood in the psychological sense is too narrow.) Being representative is meant to denote substituting for, standing in the place of, acting and functioning on behalf of, and therefore mediating. The conception of consciousness as the universal medium of access acquires an additional meaning, insofar as "medium" comes to be understood with respect to the mediating function that is attributed to certain mental states, i.e., those that are representative.

At this point we must raise the question of how to account for the representative function by virtue of which certain Ideas play the role of mediators between the conscious ego and extramental corporeal things. The question concerns nothing less than the cognitive significance and objective validity of the Ideas under discussion. We are in possession of some knowledge concerning the extramental world of extension. Such knowledge is acquired by means of privileged Ideas and, more generally, through processes and operations of consciousness which—to repeat and stress it once more—are and remain subjective events occurring

10. *Critique of Pure Reason*, trans. Norman Kemp Smith (London: Macmillan, 1961), A98 f., see also A189 ff. = B234 ff. and A197 = B242.

in the sphere of interiority. How, under those conditions, is it to be understood that subjective events within the sphere of interiority can have reference to, and significance for, what on principle lies outside that sphere? How do the role and function of mediators accrue to the Ideas in question?

Let us briefly recall Descartes's well-known reasoning. Among the totality of Ideas he singles out a special class, namely, those which exhibit clearness and distinctness. Whatever formal definition Descartes gives of clearness and distinctness,[11] in view of the use he makes of these notions in actual practice, we may say that clear and distinct Ideas are in the first place mathematical, particularly geometrical, Ideas. At least, these alone are relevant within the present context. The special emphasis on geometrical Ideas is in conformity with Descartes's goal of vindicating the incipient new science. However, clearness and distinctness—whatever privilege they may bestow on the Ideas concerned—are not the same as, and do not even imply the objective reference of, those Ideas. Descartes is fully aware of the necessity of establishing a connection between clearness and distinctness, on the one hand, and, on the other hand, objective reference—that is, reference to what is extramental. He must establish the principle that whatever is clearly and distinctly perceived is true, i.e., has objective reference and validity. For the establishment of that principle, Descartes, as is well known, resorts to the veracity of God. Divine veracity guarantees the existence of the external world.[12] In guaranteeing that principle, divine veracity also guarantees the validity of the mathematical conception of the external world—its interpretation in purely geometrical terms. Finally, although divine veracity does not guarantee the cognitive value of common perceptual experience, it does confirm its reliability for the practical conduct of life. This reliability rests on the inner consistency and coherence exhibited by that experience.[13] By a veritable *tour de force*, Descartes has cut the Gordian knot; but in effect, the problem of the objective reference and significance of subjective events and occurrences in the sphere of interiority proves to be insoluble in the representative version of the theory of Ideas.

11. *Principia Philosophiae*, pt. I, §§ 45 f.
12. *The Philosophical Works of Descartes*, trans. Elizabeth S. Haldane and G. R. T. Ross (New York: Dover Publications, 1955), I, 190 f.
13. *Ibid.*, I, 198 f.

For lack of space, we cannot enter into a detailed analysis of the work of Locke, who also advocates the theory of Ideas in the representative version. A few remarks will have to suffice. Locke sets out to study what may be called the natural history of the human mind and of human knowledge in particular. He carries this study out on the basis of Newtonian physics, which he unquestioningly accepts as a point of departure. This acceptance appears most clearly in his concept of the role of primary qualities. On the one hand, they pertain to "ideas of sensation," which are psychological events, occurrences within the mind. On the other hand, they are assumed to correspond to and even to render faithfully the true state of affairs—that is, the state of affairs which, in the physics of Newton, passes for the true one. Whereas the objective reference of subjective events is seen by Descartes as a genuine problem—though he could find no solution to it except by a *tour de force*—for Locke that reference is no longer a problem at all but is taken for granted and underlies the elaboration of his whole theory. One may be tempted to say that divine veracity has been replaced in Locke by the authority of Newton—by the prestige and authority of Newtonian science. This is not merely a *bon mot*. The difference between Locke and Descartes seems to us to reflect the development of modern physics, in the course of the seventeenth century, from its incipient phase at the time of Descartes to the systematically developed form it had attained in Locke's time with the *Principia Mathematica Philosophiae Naturalis*. Needless to add, when the objective reference of certain mental states is taken for granted and assumed as a matter of course, the problem—as we have tried to set forth—which is involved in and besets that reference is overlooked rather than solved.

THE NONREPRESENTATIVE VERSION
OF THE THEORY OF IDEAS

IN THE VERSION OF THE THEORY OF IDEAS to which we now turn, objects and Ideas are not opposed to, or even distinguished from, but on the contrary equated with, one another. Hence there can be no question of Ideas functioning as representatives of extramental objects. The nonrepresentative version of the theory of Ideas was first formulated by Berkeley and fully elaborated by Hume. We shall here concentrate on Hume's theory, the analysis of which will lead to the disclosure of a problem that is of utmost importance for the subsequent development of our argument.

According to Hume, "Almost all mankind, and even philosophers themselves," unless they are engaged in philosophical speculations, "take their perceptions to be their only objects, and suppose, that the very being, which is intimately present to the mind, is the real body or material existence." [14] The terms "object" and "perception" (Idea, in the sense defined above) can be interchanged, since both denote "what any common man means by a hat, or shoe, or stone, or any other impression, conveyed to him by his senses." [15] The identification of objects and perceptions follows, according to Hume, from the fundamental principle of the general theory of Ideas. In fact, if the only data immediately given to consciousness are its own mental states—in Humean parlance, its impressions and ideas—the consequence is that it is "impossible for us so much as to conceive or form an idea of any thing specifically different from ideas and impressions." [16]

All mental states, whether "passions, affections, sensations, pains and pleasures, are originally on the same footing; . . . whatever other differences we may observe among them, they appear, all of them, in their true colours, as impressions or perceptions." [17] This also holds for their temporality or, as Hume puts it, for their being "perishing existences" and appearing as such.[18] No perception, once it has passed, can ever recur. A new perception may arise that is very similar to and even perfectly like the former one. Yet, as a new perception, that is, as one that occupies a different place in the order of time, it cannot be identified with the former perception and must not be mistaken for the recurrence of the former perception. On the other hand, we are convinced that the object with which we are dealing now is identically the same as that which we encountered on a previous occasion. If objects are considered as nothing but perceptions and the latter are "perishing existences," how can the

---

14. *Treatise*, p. 206.
15. *Ibid.*, p. 202.
16. *Ibid.*, p. 67.
17. *Ibid.*, p. 190.
18. *Ibid.*, p. 194.

consciousness of the identity of the object arise and how can that consciousness be accounted for?

Stating our problem in terms of consciousness, we follow the general direction of Hume, who does not ask whether bodies have in fact "an existence distinct from the mind and perception"—or even a continued existence, i.e., whether they continue to exist when they are not perceived—but, rather, how we come to believe in their continued and distinct existence.[19]

To account for the consciousness of the identity of an object, Hume refers to the high degree of resemblance between the perceptions arising on successive occasions—as when, for instance, in observing an object, we alternately open and close our eyes, or when, after an absence of shorter or longer duration, we return to the object in question, e.g., our room.[20] Because of that resemblance, the mind passes readily, easily, and smoothly from perception to perception. Its disposition hardly differs from that in which it finds itself when it observes an invariable object for a certain length of time without any interruption. The smoothness of the transition makes us oblivious of, or at least inattentive to, the interruptions that are actually taking place. In this way there arises the illusion of the identity that the imagination ascribes to the multiple perceptions separated from one another by shorter or longer intervals of time. The consciousness of the identity of the object is due to the imagination's mistaking a succession of perceptions for the continuous and uninterrupted presence of an unvarying perception.

However, the obliviousness required for the consciousness or illusion of identity cannot endure indefinitely. As soon as we become aware of being confronted with multiple perceptions which, however similar and even alike, are different because they succeed on one another, the awareness of the true state of affairs conflicts with the propensity of the imagination to ascribe identity to the multiple perceptions. To reconcile this conflict, the imagination is led to contrive the fiction of the "continued existence" of perceptions. Finally, the conflict and contradiction, according to Hume, give rise to what we have called the representative version of the theory of Ideas—namely, the distinction between objects and perceptions, or, as he calls it, the hypothesis of "the double existence of perceptions and objects."[21] Under this

19. *Ibid.*, pp. 187 f.
20. See *ibid.*, pp. 202 ff.
21. *Ibid.*, pp. 214 ff.

hypothesis, identity or continuance is ascribed to the objects and interruptedness and multiplicity to the perceptions which, precisely as representatives of the objects, cannot coincide with them.

Our main concern is not with the details of Hume's theory but with the terms in which he formulates the problem of identity. As our sketchy exposition of his theory shows, Hume considers the "notion of the identity of resembling perceptions, and the interruption of their appearance" as "contrary principles," exclusive of one another.[22] Overcoming the conflict and the perplexity to which it gives rise requires "sacrificing" one of the two principles to the other. By contriving the fiction of a "continued existence" of perceptions even when they are not actually given, we disguise the interruption as much as possible or, rather, remove it entirely.[23]

Hume's formulation of the problem, however, proves to be at variance with the phenomenal state of affairs. Having been absent from our room, we return to it and find the same furniture that we perceived before leaving. To make that identity explicit, far from having to become oblivious or even inattentive to the difference between the occasions on which we perceived the objects in question, we must on the contrary make that very difference explicit. Verbally expressing our explicit awareness of the identity of the object, we say that the object with which we are dealing now is the same as that which we encountered on previous occasions and to which as identically the same we may, under certain conditions, return as often as we wish. The consciousness of the identity of the object arises not in spite of but, on the contrary, in explicit reference to the multiple perceptions of the object. Identity and multiplicity are indeed opposed to one another; however, they are not opposed as contradictory or in any sense incompatible terms but, rather, as correlative ones which mutually require and demand each other.

Hume's analysis of the notion of identity leads to the same result. According to Hume, the uninterrupted presence of an invariable perception conveys the idea of unity but not of identity. For the latter to arise, time or duration must be taken into account. "We cannot, in any propriety of speech, say, that an object is the same with itself, unless we mean, that the object existent

22. *Ibid.*, p. 206.
23. *Ibid.*, p. 199.

at one time is the same with itself existent at another." [24] Hume's analysis is inadequate insofar as he ascribes to "a fiction of the imagination" the participation of the unchanging object or perception in the flux of time. When we are actually confronted with an uninterrupted and unvarying perception, e.g., when the same musical note resounds over a certain length of time, we are aware of its duration; our auditory experience passes through different temporal phases.[25] Since what we experience is an identical note resounding for a certain length of time and not a sequence of notes that are all of equal pitch, intensity, and timbre, we are again confronted with the problem of the identity of the note in opposition and with reference to a multiplicity, in this case not of discrete occasions separated from one another by temporal intervals but of phases that pass continuously into one another, exhibiting various temporal characteristics.

The problem that appears in Hume's theory is of universal significance and goes far beyond perceptual experience. Consider one more example. Yesterday we were reading a fairy tale about a mythical person and today we resume our reading, taking the identity of the mythical person for granted without even making it explicit, though we are always free to do so. On the grounds of Hume's theory, we are presented with two ideas or, if one prefers, two sets of ideas; one is related to the present reading, the other is the memory of yesterday's reading. However similar those ideas may be to one another, it is hard to see how they can yield the consciousness of an identical mythical person.

As this example, as well as the preceding analysis of Hume's theory, show, the problem concerns the consciousness of the identity of any object whatever, understanding "object" in the broad sense in which we initially introduced it. The problem is insoluble within the framework of the theory of Ideas, that is, on the basis of the principle that its own mental states alone are directly and immediately given to the mind. Its insolubility appears still more clearly if allowance is made for the further development that Hume has given to the theory of Ideas in emphasizing that the mental states (the "perceptions," in his

24. *Ibid.*, pp. 200 f.
25. See Husserl's detailed analysis of that phenomenon in *The Phenomenology of Internal Time-Consciousness*, trans. James S. Churchill (Bloomington: Indiana University Press, 1964), §§ 10 ff.; and *EJ*, § 23.

terminology) form merely a one-dimensional temporal order, or, as he expresses it, "The successive perceptions only . . . constitute the mind." [26] How indeed can a mere succession of mental states ever yield the consciousness of the identity of anything?

It can also be shown that the problem in question does not find a solution within the context of Kant's *Critique of Pure Reason,* but let us merely refer to other writings of ours in that regard.[27]

The importance of the problem in question was clearly seen by William James, who formulated it, under the heading "the principle of constancy in the mind's meanings," as follows: "The same matters can be thought of in successive portions of the mental stream, and some of these portions can know that they mean the same matters which the previous portions meant." [28] However, it is not sufficient simply to establish that principle, even while recognizing it as "the very keel and backbone of our thinking," as "the most important of all the features of our mental structure." James could content himself with proceeding in this way because, writing as a psychologist, he deliberately abstained from entering into any problem concerning the possibility of knowledge. From the point of view of *psychology as a positive science,* knowledge can, and even must, be admitted and taken for granted as an "ultimate relation" between the "mind knowing" and "the thing known," two "irreducible" elements between which a "thoroughgoing dualism" and a "pre-established harmony" obtain.[29] If, however, the problem of the possibility of knowledge is raised, as it must be within a philosophical context and even within that of a radicalized psychology, the "principle of constancy in the mind's meanings" cannot be stated alone but must be inserted into a general theory of consciousness. In view of the failure of Hume's endeavors, such an insertion cannot mean reducing the consciousness of identity to something else or accounting for it in terms of something else. On the contrary, the fact that the same object presents itself as identical through multiple acts must be made the cornerstone of the theory of

26. *Treatise,* pp. 252 f.
27. "The Kantian and Husserlian Conceptions of Consciousness," in *SPP;* and "Der Begriff des Bewusstseins bei Kant und Husserl," *Kant-Studien,* Vol. LV (1964).
28. *The Principles of Psychology* (New York: Henry Holt & Co., 1890), I, 459 f.
29. *Ibid.,* I, 216 ff.

consciousness, that is, the theory must start from it and throughout remain centered on it. Finally, the fact in question cannot simply be stated and postulated, as James may be said to have done. Rather, it must be disengaged and disclosed through a descriptive analysis of acts of consciousness.

OUTLINES OF THE THEORY OF INTENTIONALITY

IN THE COURSE OF THE PRECEDING DISCUSSION, two problems have emerged. The first, which arose from the analysis of some of Descartes's tenets, concerns the objective and, we may say, objectively cognitive significance of mental states, their reference to extramental facts, events, and items of any kind. Perhaps of still greater importance is the second problem with which the critical examination of Hume's theory presents us—namely, the problem of the consciousness of any object given as identically the same through a multiplicity of mental states, experiences, or acts. Because of its fundamental importance, we shall begin by considering the problem of the consciousness of identity, which—we submit—has found a solution in Husserl's theory of intentionality. After that theory has been expounded, at least in its basic outlines, the first problem mentioned will no longer present any considerable difficulties.

The notion of intentionality plays a major role in all Husserl's writings except *Philosophie der Arithmetik*. Here we can obviously not enter into a study of the development which that notion has undergone along with that of Husserl's thought in general. Since we approach the theory of intentionality from a specific point of view, namely, the problem of the consciousness of identity, we shall have to overemphasize certain aspects of that theory or, more correctly, to emphasize them more than Husserl himself did. In doing so, however, we remain faithful to the spirit of Husserl's theory and its leading intentions. Finally, we shall exclude from our presentation a few doctrines, especially the notion of sense data and the egological conception of consciousness, which play a certain role in Husserl's theory of intentionality. Not endorsing those doctrines, we may abstain from dwelling on them, because they do not seem to us to be of crucial importance for what we consider most essential to the concept of intentionality.[30] The justification of our departure from Husserl would lead us too far afield to be attempted here.

THE NOTION OF THE OBJECT
AS MEANT OR INTENDED (THE NOEMA)

FROM THE CRITICAL EXAMINATION of Hume's theory, it has become clear that the consciousness of identity cannot be accounted for in terms of the theory of Ideas, that is, on the grounds of the traditional conception of consciousness. Hence a totally new and radically different conception is required in which the consciousness of identity no longer appears as an explicandum but is, on the contrary, made the defining property of the mind, that essential property without which the mind could not be what it is. For that reason it is insufficient, though true and valid as a first approximation, to define intentionality as directedness, saying that in experiencing an act of consciousness we find ourselves directed to something—e.g., in perceiving we are directed to the thing perceived, in remembering we are directed to the event recalled, or in loving or hating to the person loved or hated, and the like. Directedness merely denotes a phenomenal feature of the act, inherent and immanent, a feature that appears and disappears along with the act to which it pertains. If intentionality is thus defined, the question remains unanswered as to how we can become aware of the identity of the "something" to which the multiple acts are directed, considering that each one of those acts possesses directedness as a phenomenal feature of its own. Therefore the theory of intentionality must be based on the notion of the "something" that we take as identical and whose identity we may disclose and make explicit by the appropriate considerations.

At this stage of the discussion, the advance of Husserl's theory of intentionality over that of Brentano can be clearly stated. According to Brentano, all psychic phenomena, and only psychic phenomena, are characterized by the "intentional" or

30. See "Phenomenology of Thematics and of The Pure Ego" and "A Non-Egological Conception of Consciousness," in *SPP;* and *FC*, pp. 265 ff.

"mental inexistence of an object." [31] "Inexistence" is here meant to be understood in the Latin sense of *inexistentia*, existence within. Brentano also speaks, though somehow hesitatingly, of a "relation to a content," a "direction to an object," "an immanent object" (*immanente Gegenständlichkeit*). Each psychic phenomenon "includes something as object within itself, although not always in the same way. In presentation [*Vorstellung*] something is presented, in judgment something is affirmed or denied, in love, [something is] loved, in hate, [something is] hated, in desire [something is] desired, etc." If the "intentional object" is said to be included or contained within the act or psychic phenomenon, that is, to form a real part of it, or if the relation or directedness to an object is conceived of as a phenomenal feature of the act, the problem recurs that arose in our analysis and criticism of Hume's theory. Any phenomenal feature of an act as well as any part which is contained or included in the act as one of its constituents shares the temporal fate of the act as a whole. Landgrebe has pointed out that, on the grounds of Brentano's theory, it is hard to see how the intentional directedness of one act of consciousness can be like or equal that of another act, descriptively different from the first.[32] Likeness and equality require a point of reference with respect to which they obtain. While such a point of reference is lacking in Brentano's theory, Husserl's theory provides it with the concept of the noema. Two or more descriptively different acts agree in their intentional directedness if, and only if, the same noema corresponds to all of them.

Let us now take up the special case of the understanding of meaningful verbal expressions, a phenomenon whose analysis forms the subject matter of the first investigation of Husserl's *Logical Investigations*.[33] To lay bare what is involved in the understanding of meaningful expression, let us contrast our ex-

31. *Psychologie vom empirischen Standpunkt* (Leipzig: Felix Meiner, 1924), bk. II, chap. 1, § 5; see the translation by D. B. Terrel, in *Realism and the Background of Phenomenology*, ed. Roderick M. Chisholm (Glencoe, Ill.: The Free Press, 1960), pp. 50 ff.

32. "Husserls Phänomenologie und die Motive zu ihrer Umbildung," *Revue internationale de philosophie*, I (1939), 281. See Herbert Spiegelberg, *The Phenomenological Movement* (The Hague: Martinus Nijhoff, 1960), pp. 39 ff., 107 ff.

33. Vol. II; cf. Marvin Farber, *The Foundation of Phenomenology* (Cambridge, Mass.: Harvard University Press, 1941), chap. 8.

perience in hearing a phrase like "the victor of Austerlitz" or "New York is the biggest city in the U.S.A." with the experience we have when we hear a noise in the street, a sound like "abracadabra," or an utterance in a foreign language with which we are not familiar. In the latter cases, we have merely an auditory experience. In the former cases, we also have an auditory experience, but one which supports a specific act of interpretation or apperception by means of which the auditory experience becomes a vehicle of meaning or a symbol. The same holds in the case of reading, except for the immaterial difference that the visual experience of marks on paper takes the place of the auditory experience.

The specific acts that bestow the character of a symbol on perceptual objects may be called acts of meaning apprehension. Like all other acts, they, too, are psychological events occurring at certain moments in time. By means of the reasoning we used in the critical discussion of Hume's theory, we come to establish the distinction between the act of meaning apprehension and the meaning apprehended. We remember that on numerous occasions we have uttered or heard the phrases mentioned. Recalling those occasions, we recall them as different from one another because of their different temporal locations. At the same time, we become aware of the fact that what we meant and had in view on those occasions and what we mean now is the same: On all these occasions there presents itself to, and stands before, our mind "the one who won the battle of Austerlitz," or Napoleon as the victor of Austerlitz, or New York under the aspect of its number of inhabitants in comparison with the other American cities. Furthermore, we take it for granted that all who listen to our utterance, provided they are familiar with the symbolic system used—in this case, the English language—apprehend the same meaning. Each person experiences his own act of meaning apprehension which he cannot share with anyone else. Yet through all these multiple acts, distributed among any number of persons, and for each person, varying from one occasion to the other in the course of his life, the same meaning is apprehended. If this were not so, no communication, in the mode of either assent or dissent, would be possible. For a proposition to be accepted or rejected, it must first be understood.

The identical entity that we call "meaning" may be defined as a certain person, object, event, or state of affairs which presents itself, taken exactly as it presents itself or as it is intended.

Consider the two phrases: "the victor of Austerlitz" and "the initiator of the French legal code." Though both meanings refer to the same person, Napoleon, they differ from one another insofar as in the first case Napoleon is intended under the aspect of his victory at Austerlitz and in the second with regard to his role in the establishment of the French legal code. The difference in question has been expressed by Husserl as that between the "object *which* is intended" and the "object *as* it is intended" (*LI*, p. 589). It is the latter notion which we identify with that of meaning. For a further illustration, we mention another of Husserl's examples (*LI*, p. 590). In hearing the name "Greenland," each one of us has a certain thought or representation of that island; that is, the island presents itself and is intended in a certain fashion. The same holds for the arctic explorer. Both he and any one of us intend the same object. However, Greenland *as* intended and meant by some of us, with our sketchy, very vague, and indeterminate representation, obviously differs from Greenland *as* meant by the arctic explorer, who has been to the island and knows it thoroughly.

Two multiplicities, each related to an identical entity, must be distinguished from one another. On the one hand, we have the multiplicity of acts through all of which the same meaning is apprehended; on the other hand, there is the multiplicity of meanings, of "objects as intended," all referring to one and the same "object which is intended."

For the sake of simplicity, we have confined ourselves to such meanings as refer to real objects, persons, or events. This simplification makes it easy to see that meanings cannot be identified with physical objects and occurrences any more than with psychological events. From the fact that a plurality of meanings can refer to the same object, it follows that none of the meanings coincides with the object. Real events, like the battle of Austerlitz, take place at a certain moment in time. But it is absurd to assign a temporal place to the meaning of the phrase "the battle of Austerlitz" and to ask whether it precedes, succeeds upon, or is simultaneous with another meaning, though all the acts through which the meaning is apprehended occupy definite places in time. There are no spatial relations between meanings any more than there are causal effects exerted by meanings either on one another or on anything else. We are confronted with entities of a special kind—aspatial, atemporal, acausal, and hence irreal or ideal—which have a specific nature of their own.

Between these entities obtain relations of a particular sort whose like is nowhere else encountered. As a simple example, we may mention the relations, studied in logic, that obtain between propositions as a special class of meanings.

Our results can easily be generalized. For brevity, we limit ourselves to perceptual experience. When we perceive a thing, e.g., a house, we do so from the point of observation at which we happen to be placed, so that the house appears under a certain aspect: from one of its sides, the front or the back, as near or far, and the like. It appears, as Husserl expresses it, by way of a one-sided adumbrational presentation (*Ideas*, § 41; *CM*, § 17). Maintaining our point of observation, we may alternately open and close our eyes. We then experience a sequence of acts of perception, all differing from each other by the very fact of their succeeding on one another. Through all of these perceptions, not only does the same house appear, but it also appears under the same aspect, in the same orientation—in a word, in the same manner of adumbrational presentation. Again we encounter an identical entity, namely, that which is perceived exactly as it is perceived, the "perceived as such" (*das Wahrgenommene als solches*). It stands in the same relation to the acts of perception as does the meaning apprehended to the acts of meaning apprehension. One may generalize the term "meaning" so as to use it beyond the domain of symbolic expressions and speak of perceptual meanings. Husserl also denotes the "perceived as such" as "perceptual sense" (*Wahrnehmungssinn*), because by virtue of it a given perception is not only a perception of a certain thing but also a determinate perception of that thing—that is, a perception through which the thing presents itself in this rather than another manner of adumbrational appearance (*Ideas*, § 88). Husserl's most general term here is that of noema (*Ideas*, pt. III, chap. 3), a concept that comprises meanings in the conventional sense as a special class. "Noema" denotes the object as meant and intended in any mode whatsoever and hence includes the mode of perceptual experience.

Having distinguished the perceptual noema from the act of perception—the *noesis*—we have further to distinguish it from the thing perceived. The latter may be seen from different points of view—it may appear under a variety of aspects: from the front, the back, one of the lateral sides, and the like—while the perceptual noema denotes the thing perceived as presenting itself under *one* of those possible aspects. Again, we must apply the distinction between the "object *which* is intended"—the thing perceived—and the "object *as* it is intended"—the perceptual noema, or the thing perceived *as* it is perceived. A multiplicity of perceptual noemata are related to the same thing as, in the previous example, a multiplicity of meanings were seen to refer to the same object.

Let us now consider the difference between the perceptual noema and the thing perceived from a different point of view. The house may be torn down, but none of the pertinent noemata is affected hereby (*Ideas*, § 89). Even after its destruction, the house may still be remembered, and it may be remembered as presenting itself under one or the other of the aspects under which it had previously appeared in perceptual experience. To be sure, the noema is no longer a perceptual one but is rather a noema of memory. The point is that two or even more noemata, their difference notwithstanding, may have a certain stratum in common, a stratum that Husserl denotes as "noematic nucleus" (*Ideas*, § 91). Within the structure of every noema, the distinction must be made between the noematic nucleus and "noematic characters," which, incidentally, belong to several dimensions (*Ideas*, §§ 99, 102 ff.). By means of this distinction, it is possible to account for the verification of a nonperceptual experience by a perceptual one. When, in actual perceptual experience, a thing proves to be such as it had been assumed, thought, believed, etc., to be, it is that the nucleus of the nonperceptual noema is seen to coincide and even to be identical with that of the perceptual noema, while the noematic characters indicating the mode of givenness of presentation remain different on either side (*LI*, pp. 563 ff., 694 ff.). Both the identity of the noematic nucleus and the difference concerning the characters are required for and essential to the phenomenon of verification.

CONSCIOUSNESS DEFINED AS NOETICO-NOEMATIC CORRELATION

IN THE CENTER OF THE NEW CONCEPTION stands the notion of the noema, of the object meant and intended, taken exactly and only as it is meant and intended. Every act of consciousness is so essentially related to its noema that it is only with reference to the latter that the act is qualified and characterized as that which it is, e.g., that particular perception of the house as seen from the front, that determinate intending of Napoleon as the victor of Austerlitz and not as the defeated of Waterloo. Traditionally, consciousness has been interpreted as a one-dimensional temporal order, a conception whose most consistent elaboration lies in Hume's theory. To be sure, acts of consciousness are psychological events that take place and endure in time and stand under the laws of temporality to which Husserl has devoted detailed analyses. Though temporality undoubtedly denotes a fundamental aspect of consciousness, that aspect is not the only one.

The temporal events called "acts of consciousness" have the peculiarity of being actualizations or apprehensions of meanings; the terms "apprehension" and "meaning" are understood in a very general sense beyond the special case of symbolic expressions. It pertains to the essential nature of acts of consciousness to be related and to correspond to noemata. Rather than being conceived of as a one-dimensional sequence of events, *consciousness must be defined as a noetico-noematic correlation,* that is, a correlation between items pertaining to two heterogeneous planes: on the one hand, the plane of temporal psychological events; on the other, the plane of atemporal, irreal, that is, ideal entities that are the noemata, or meanings understood in the broader sense. Furthermore, it is a many-to-one correlation, insofar as an indefinite multiplicity of acts can correspond to the same noema. Correlated terms demand and require each other. To establish the identity of the noema we had to contrast it with, and hence to refer it to, a multiplicity of acts. Conversely, it can be shown (though this is not the place to do it) that no account of the temporality and especially the duration of an act of consciousness is possible without reference to the noema involved.[34] Thus the conception of consciousness as noetico-noematic correlation brings to light the indissoluble connection between consciousness and meaning (*Sinn*). It shows consciousness to be essentially characterized by an intrinsic duality which is to take the place of the Cartesian dualism.

To evaluate the historical significance of the innovation, let us consider in which respect it constitutes a break with the

34. See "On the Intentionality of Consciousness" and "William James' Theory of the 'Transitive Parts' of the Stream of Consciousness," in *SPP.*

tradition. In the first place the theory of Ideas is relinquished, especially the principle that the mind is confined to its own mental states, which alone are directly and immediately given to it. Undoubtedly the mind lives exclusively in its mental states, its acts. Each act, however, is correlated to a noema which—as we have stressed—is itself *not* a mental state, an act of consciousness, a psychological event. Relatedness to essentially nonmental entities is the very nature of mental states. Furthermore, the noema is defined as the "object as it is intended," i.e., as the object in question appearing in a certain manner of presentation (under a certain aspect, from a certain point of view, etc.), an object capable, however—we must now add—of appearing in different manners of presentation. The definition of intentionality as directedness can now be given its legitimate meaning. Experiencing an act of consciousness, we are directed to an object insofar as, in the structure of the noema corresponding to the act, there are inscribed references to further noemata, to different manners of presentation of that object. Objective reference of mental states is no longer an insoluble problem as with Descartes; nor is it to be explained and accounted for subsequently. On the contrary, it proves essential to the acts of consciousness—not as an additional phenomenal feature of the acts, of course, but rather in the sense of the conception of consciousness as a noetico-noematic correlation.

As a consequence, consciousness can no longer be interpreted as a self-sufficient and self-contained domain of interiority. This interpretation follows from the Cartesian dualism, the severance of *res cogitans* from *res extensa* to which Descartes was led in endeavoring to lay the foundations of the incipient new science. It must be stressed that nature, in the sense of modern physics, is not the same as the world of common, everyday experience. In the latter world, things not only present spatial forms, stand in spatial relations to one another, and change those relations in the course of time; they also exhibit specific qualities, the so-called secondary qualities, and are endowed with characters which, like those of instrumentality, utility, and cultural value, refer to human purposes and activities.[35] Quite generally, in the world of common experience, the corporeal, in the spatiotemporal sense, is intertwined and inter-

35. See *Crisis*, §§ 66 ff.; and *Phänomenologische Psychologie*, §§ 16 ff.

woven with the mental and the psychological in all its forms. Nature in the modern scientific sense is the result and product of an artful method applied to the world of common experience. That method consists, among other things, in abstracting spatiotemporal extendedness to the disregard of whatever is mental or psychological, relegating the latter to the purely subjective domain. In this way one arrives at one single coherent and self-contained context encompassing all spatiotemporal things and events.

The success of this abstractive procedure suggests its application in the opposite direction, namely, a counterabstraction of what is "subjective" to the disregard of what pertains to the spatiotemporal, hence "objective," domain. However, the attempt at such a counterabstraction fails to yield a self-sufficient and self-contained domain of interiority. Turning to and concentrating on the life of consciousness, one does not discover occurrences that take place in a closed domain and merely succeed upon one another, as Hume's theory of the mind would have it. Rather, one encounters apprehensions *of* meanings; perceptions *of* houses, trees, fellow human beings; memories *of* past and expectancies *of* future events; and the like. Generally speaking, one encounters dealings in several manners and modes with mundane things and events of the most diverse description as well as with nonmundane entities, like numbers and geometrical systems, which are not mental states or psychological occurrences any more than they are mundane existents. The very failure of the counterabstraction discloses the essential reference of acts of consciousness to objective entities of any kind, hence also to mundane, i.e., spatiotemporal, objects. This failure marks the breakdown of the Cartesian dualism.

Being based on the theory of intentionality, phenomenology must not be identified with or even too closely assimilated to intuitionistic philosophy or introspectionism as advocated by Bergson.[36] For consciousness to be grasped and studied in its authentic and aboriginal state, it must first, according to Bergson, undergo a purification from whatever contamination or admixture has accrued to it by way of contact with the objective external world, which is not only a spatial but also a social world. Obviously, such a methodological principle presupposes the

36. *Time and Free Will,* trans. F. L. Pogson (New York: Harper & Row, Torchbooks, 1960).

Cartesian dualism. What Bergson considers a contamination of consciousness appears, in the light of the theory of intentionality, as an expression of its genuine nature. Insistence on that difference, profound as it is, must not, however, preclude the recognition that many of Bergson's analyses have phenomenological significance or, to speak with greater prudence, may be given phenomenological significance by a proper reinterpretation.

Because of the intentionality of consciousness, we are in direct contact with the world. Living our conscious life, we are "at" the world, "at" the things encountered in that world. This should be seen as a consequence of the theory of intentionality rather than taken for original, as happens in subsequent existentialistic philosophies. A glance at the phenomenological theory of perception makes that clear. We recall the definition of the perceptual noema as the thing perceived appearing from a certain side, under a certain aspect, in a certain orientation—briefly, in a one-sided manner of adumbrational presentation. The decisive point is that, notwithstanding the one-sidedness of its appearance, it is the thing itself that presents itself and stands before our mind, and with which we are in contact. Noetically speaking, perceptual consciousness is an originary—albeit incomplete, because one-sided—experience of the thing perceived appearing in "bodily presence" (in *Leibhaftigkeit*). Perceptual consciousness must not be interpreted in terms of profoundly different modes of consciousness, as, e.g., by means of images, signs, symbols, and the like (*Ideas*, § 43). Accordingly, the perceptual noema must not be mistaken for an Idea in the Cartesian sense, that is, the substitute for or representative of a reality only mediately accessible. With the phenomenological theory of perception, we submit, the traditional theory of Ideas is definitively overcome.

On the Notion of Objectivity

There remains the task of defining the relationship between the perceptual noema and the thing perceived. While actually appearing in a determinate manner of adumbrational presentation, the thing is capable of appearing in other manners. It actually so appears in the course of the perceptual process, when, e.g., we walk around the thing and, in general, perceive it under various conditions of different sorts. In the course of that process, the thing is perceived as identically the same, presenting itself from different sides, under varying aspects, in a variety of orientations. The thing cannot be perceived except in one or the other manner of adumbrational presentation. It is nothing besides, or in addition to, the multiplicity of those presentations through all of which it appears in its identity.[37] Consequently, the thing perceived proves to be the group or, more precisely put, the systematically organized totality of adumbrational presentations. Both the difference and the relationship between the thing perceived and a particular perceptual noema can now be defined in terms of a noematic system as a whole and one member of that system. This is in agreement with the previous formulation that every particular perception, its incompleteness and one-sidedness notwithstanding, is an originary experience of the thing perceived appearing in bodily presence. In fact, it is the perceptual apprehension of a noematic system as a whole from the vantage point of one of its members.

Two questions arise. One concerns the organizational form of the noematic system; the other, the manner in which its membership in the noematic system is inscribed in the structure of every particular noema. Both questions can only be mentioned here (see *FC*, pt. IV). At present, we must confine ourselves to stressing that the thing perceived also proves to have noematic status. As a noematic system it is a noema itself—but a noema of higher order, so to speak.

Just as the theory of intentionality involves a new conception of consciousness or subjectivity, so, too, it entails a reinterpretation of the notion of objectivity. Traditionally, the objective has been opposed to the subjective as entirely alien to it, so that, for an object to be reached in its genuine and authentic condition, all mental, i.e., subjective, activities and their contributions must be disregarded if not eliminated altogether. In the light of the theory of intentionality, this conception of objectivity, which derives from the Cartesian dualism, can no longer be upheld. The objective reference that is essential to acts of consciousness corresponds to a no less essential relationship of objects to acts of consciousness, especially to their noemata. The disclosure of the thing perceived as a noematic system, that is, an intentional correlate,[38] is in perfect conformity with the general conception

37. See *Phänomenologische Psychologie*, pp. 152 f., 178 f., 182 f., 430 ff.
38. See *ibid.*, p. 184.

propounded here of consciousness as a correlation. Furthermore, several levels of objectivity must be distinguished from one another, and consequentially the notions of subjectivity and objectivity prove to be affected by a certain relativity.

Every particular meaning or noema as an identical entity can be considered as objective in contrast to the multiple subjective acts that are correlated to it, especially if it is remembered that those acts may be distributed among a plurality of persons. A particular perceptual noema, defined as the thing appearing under a certain aspect, is in turn to be characterized as subjective with respect to the perceived thing itself, of which the former is a one-sided perceptual adumbration, with respect to the noematic system of which the particular noema is a member. The things perceived and perceivable form, in their totality, the perceptual world, the world of pure experience, or, as Husserl calls it, the life-world. It is the world such as it is understood, conceived, and interpreted by a certain social group which unquestioningly accepts it as reality. The life-world is an essentially social phenomenon.[39] Accordingly, it differs from one social group to the other and also for a given social group in the course of its historical development. At every phase of this development and for every social group, the respective life-world counts as objective reality.

Over against this multiplicity of life-worlds, the question arises of a world common to all social groups. This is an objective world in a second, more profound sense. More precisely, the question concerns a set or system of invariant structures, universal insofar as they are by necessity exhibited by every socio-historical life-world.[40] Of this common world, which perhaps should not be called life-world but rather the world of pure perceptual experience, the diverse life-worlds in the proper sense appear as varieties to be relegated to the status of merely subjective worlds. Finally, there is objectivity in the specific sense of modern science—the objectivity of the scientific or scientifically true and valid universe as constructed on the basis of perceptual experience by means of mental operations and procedures, into whose analysis we cannot enter here. From the point of view of the universe of science, the world of perceptual experience in turn appears as subjective.

39. See chap. 5, above.
40. See *Crisis*, §§ 36 f.; and *Phänomenologische Psychologie*, §§ 7 ff.

Sketchy and incomplete though these remarks are, they may perhaps suffice to illustrate, if not substantiate, the thesis that what is to be meant by "objective" must not be conceived as severed from the life of consciousness. Moreover, the ascent to higher levels of objectivity, far from requiring the progressive elimination or, at least, disregard of mental activities and operations, on the contrary involves them in increasing complexity; it involves syntheses of consciousness of ever widening scope. As an intentional correlate, an object of any kind or level proves to be an accomplishment (*Geleistetes*) whose clarification, especially the clarification concerning its objectivity and existence, requires that it be referred to the accomplishing (*leistende*) mental operations. Accounting in this manner for an object of whatever sort is tantamount to disclosing its "equivalent of consciousness."

CONCLUSION

OUR DISCUSSION HAS RUN FULL CIRCLE. By generalizing and radicalizing Descartes's discovery of consciousness, Husserl was led to conceive the program of constitutive phenomenology, which is to account for objects of all possible kinds in terms of subjective conscious life. A superficial survey of some levels of objectivity could give an idea of the extent of that tremendous task. For the sake of completeness, we mention in passing the sense of objectivity which pertains to the ideal orders of being and existence in the Platonic sense or, in Husserl's parlance, to the eidetic realms. In the theory of intentionality, we have the theoretical instrument both necessary and sufficient for the realization of that task. Herein appears the historical significance of that theory.

We could as well have started from the theory of intentionality, conceived as a theory of the mind in a merely psychological setting, regardless of philosophical interests. The radical innovation which that theory entails for the conception of the mind and thus for psychological thinking defines its historical significance in a further respect. Consistently developing the theory of intentionality conceived in a psychological orientation, and pursuing it in its ultimate consequences, would have led us to the idea of constitutive phenomenology in a way Husserl has followed himself in the Amsterdam lectures and the article for

The Encyclopaedia Britannica. The theory of intentionality thus serves both as a motivating force, as far as the conception of the idea of constitutive phenomenology is concerned, and as the theoretical instrument for its realization. In other words, provided proper allowance is made for the transcendental reduction, the full elaboration of the theory of intentionality proves co-extensive and even identical with the philosophy of constitutive phenomenology.

10 / Perceptual Coherence as the Foundation of the Judgment of Predication

IN THREE BOOKS which pertain to the last period of his life, namely, *Formal and Transcendental Logic, The Crisis of European Sciences and Transcendental Phenomenology,* and *Experience and Judgment,* Husserl has laid down the program for a phenomenological theory of logic (understood in a very broad sense) and the sciences, especially physics, and has taken decisive steps toward its implementation. According to this program, these disciplines and their phenomenological origin or genesis of sense (*Sinnesgenese*) have to be traced back to perceptual consciousness (see *FTL*, § 86). The guiding idea is that perceptual consciousness contains the germs or the roots of whatever entities are the subject matter of study in the mentioned disciplines and that those entities are brought to full development and given their definitive shape by means of specific mental operations.

We propose here to take up again the problem already dealt with by Husserl in *Experience and Judgment,* namely, the problem of the phenomenological origin of the judgment of predication, i.e., the judgment of the form "this S is p" as exemplified by "this table is brown." We shall be led to modify Husserl's account in some respects, however, because we shall avail ourselves of results which we have established in the phenomenological theory of perception. Therefore, it is necessary to begin by

This essay was originally published under the same title in *Phenomenology: Continuation and Criticism, Essays in Memory of Dorion Cairns,* ed. Frederick Kersten and Richard Zaner, *Phaenomenologica* L (The Hague: Martinus Nijhoff, 1973).

[241]

discussing some problems related to perception and to dwell on those problems at some length.

GENERAL OUTLINE OF THE ADUMBRATIONAL THEORY OF PERCEPTION

ALL PHENOMENOLOGICAL DISCUSSION of matters pertaining to perception must take its departure from the adumbrational theory of perception which Husserl has developed in several of his writings (*Ideas* §§ 41 ff., 149 ff.; *CM*, §§ 17 ff.; *Crisis*, §§45 ff.; and *EJ*, § 8). According to this theory, every particular perception is a one-sided apprehension of the thing perceived. The latter appears from a certain side, under a certain aspect, in a certain orientation (as far or near, as centrally or peripherally located, and the like); it displays some of its properties and its behavior under the given conditions. At the same time, the thing presents itself as capable of appearing under different aspects, of exhibiting other qualities than those it exhibits at present, of displaying a different behavior under other more or less well-specified conditions. Furthermore, the thing perceived through a particular one-sided perception is encountered[1] as identically the same over and against the mentioned possible variations concerning its manner of appearance.

Two implications of the adumbrational theory of perception must be traced. First, perceptual consciousness yields an immediate and direct access to and contact with the thing perceived. In perceptual encounter we are at the thing itself, and there is no need or room for any intermediary to mediate be-

---

1. Following the suggestion of R. Sokolowski, *The Formation of Husserl's Concept of Constitution*, Phaenomenologica XVIII (The Hague: Martinus Nijhoff, 1964), pp. 4 f., we use "encounter" as the English equivalent of *Erfahrung* and "experience" as that of *Erlebnis*. We encounter whatever is "transcendent to subjectivity," that is, things and objects in the widest possible sense, so as to include not only material things but also ideal entities of every description, like propositions and concatenations of propositions, numbers and relations between them, geometrical systems as well as historical events, social situations, political and legal institutions, and so on. What we experience are our own mental states, among them those through which we encounter objects. To express it briefly, we encounter objects and experience our encounters.

tween the act of perception and the thing perceived through that act. Because it is essentially characterized as intentional, consciousness must not be conceived of as an isolated and secluded domain, severed by an unbridgeable gulf from whatever is exterior to that domain. In experiencing acts of consciousness we do not, so to speak, move within a self-contained domain of interiority; on the contrary, we are in contact with the objects encountered.[2] To be sure, not every encounter takes place in the distinguishing mode of originarity, which is the privilege of perceptual consciousness though not of that consciousness exclusively. In the present context, it suffices to note that perceptual encounter is an originary apprehension of the thing perceived offering itself in bodily presence, in flesh and blood, so to speak, and we do not have to enter into a discussion of the relations of derivative modes like memory, expectation, and the like to the originary mode of perception. At any event, we wish to stress again what we have repeatedly emphasized elsewhere:[3] The insight that in our perceptual life we are directly and immediately at the things and at the world, far from being due to the subsequent emergence of existentialist philosophy, must be seen as a consequence following from Husserl's theory of the intentionality of consciousness, especially perceptual consciousness.

Second, because of its one-sidedness, every particular perception, though a direct and immediate apprehension of the thing perceived, is incomplete and insufficient, that is, in need of complementation. Its insufficiency and limitation are not ascertained from a point of view beyond or outside the particular perception in question, as though to find it incomplete the experiencing subject had, so to speak, to step out of his perception —that is, rather than living it, had to look back at it in retrospective reflection, in a word, had to thematize and objectivate it. Here as everywhere reflection consists in nothing other than rendering explicit and disengaging what had pertained to the act reflected on, albeit in an undisclosed fashion, previously to and independently of its being reflected upon. Incompleteness

2. *Ideas,* § 43; *FTL,* pp. 141, 206, 248; *Phänomenologische Psychologie,* ed. Walter Biemel, *Husserliana* IX (The Hague: Martinus Nijhoff, 1962), app. VII; *Crisis,* pp. 233, 235.
3. See chap. 9, above, and "Towards a Theory of Intentionality," *Philosophy and Phenomenological Research,* XXX (1970), 366 f.

244 / CONSTITUTIVE PHENOMENOLOGY

and insufficiency denote a phenomenal feature inherent and immanent in every particular perception, a feature which manifests itself in that perception as pointing and referring to further perceptions through which the thing perceived will appear under different aspects and from other sides, will present properties and qualities which it does not display at present, and will exhibit its behavior as varying along with the changes of the concomitant circumstances. Noetically speaking, every particular perception is pervaded and permeated by anticipations and expectancies to be fulfilled by further perceptions.

These expectancies may be, and are, affected by indeterminacy to a greater or lesser degree, depending on the comparative familiarity or unfamiliarity of the thing perceived as well as on the conditions (e.g., of illumination) under which it is perceived. What is seen in the dusk of the evening at some considerable distance appears to be a quadruped, but not until we come nearer will we be able to tell what kind of animal that quadruped is. Similarly, the house in front of which we are standing presents itself as a residential building whose interior architectural arrangement and organization remain more or less indeterminate; in the case of a building we have never entered before, it is even highly indeterminate, as far as present perception goes. Still, by whatever indeterminacy the anticipated yieldings of further perceptions, to which the present one points, may be affected, those yieldings are subject to the condition of being in agreement and conformity both with one another and with what the present perception yields. Differently expressed, every thing perceived is encountered in the light of a certain typicality, it presents itself as a thing of a certain kind or type which, however, is delineated and determined in a more or less schematic way—more correctly stated, along more or less generic lines. What is indeterminate is the special and concrete manner in which the type is realized. However indeterminate the yieldings of anticipated further perceptions may be, the condition imposed on them is their fitting into the generic pattern and framework which define the typicality in whose light the thing appears through the present perception (see *FC*, pp. 234 ff).

This is borne out when, instead of abiding by it, we change the standpoint from which we observe the thing, by having it move with regard to us, by moving ourselves, or by doing both. In so doing, we make the thing appear under varying aspects and from different sides. Anticipations which had accompanied the initial perception find fulfillment; indeterminacies are brought to determination; properties and qualities which the thing had not thus far exhibited now present themselves, and among these properties are unexpected ones which likewise fit into the generically delineated framework of the type in question. For the sake of simplicity we deliberately exclude the case of a later perception being at variance with and nullifying a former one, as when, on entering the house which had appeared as a residential building, we discover that it is a medical one, so that the initial perception turns out to have been deceptive.

It follows that an individual perceivable thing is related to a multiplicity of perceptions, not to a single one. That multiplicity is not merely a succession of disconnected perceptions, isolated one from another. On the contrary, every further perception makes what had only been anticipated appear in the mode of originarity, yields a determination of what thus far had been comparatively indeterminate, and so on, and thus the particular perceptions come to be united with one another.[4] They coalesce into one sustained and coherent process of which the particular perceptions are experienced as phases. The unity of this process depends on its intrinsic coherence, that is, on its phases' harmoniously enlarging, continuing, and confirming one another. The unity and identity of the thing perceived depends on the harmony and agreement between the phases of the perceptual process to which the thing in question is related; its existence depends more specifically on the mutual corroboration of the successive phases of the process (*FC*, pp. 202 ff., 287 ff.).

As the incompleteness of every particular perception and its need of complementation manifest themselves in the anticipatory references to further perceptions, so the actual complementation takes place in the course of the perceptual process's evolving in a smooth and harmonious fashion. Still, that complementation is never fully consummated. However far the perceptual process may have developed, it always remains susceptible of further continuation. That is, the perceptual process to which an individual perceivable thing is related proves to be infinite (*Ideas*, §§ 44, 149). For this reason, the idea of a complete and adequate perceptual apprehension of a perceivable thing is termed by

---

4. In this respect, Husserl speaks of a "synthesis of unification" (*Einigung*) in preference to the phrase "synthesis of identification" used in earlier writings (*Crisis*, p. 158).

Husserl an "Idea in the sense of Kant," i.e., the idea of an infinite process exhibiting intrinsic coherence—in the sense just mentioned—between all of its phases, the past ones as well as those which are to come (*Ideas*, § 143). Since the existence of the thing depends on the agreement and confirmation by the future phases of the perceptual process of both one another and the past phases, the existence of the thing has the sense of presumptiveness (*Ideas*, § 46; *CM*, § 28). In other words, no perceivable thing may be posited as truly existing and as being in reality such as it has appeared to be thus far, except with the provision that the further course of the perceptual process related to the thing in question will not necessitate revisions, corrections, or nullifications. This must not be construed to mean that the existence of perceivable things, rather than being certain, is only more or less likely or probable. Rather, it must be understood as the clarification of the very sense of the existence of those things and of the contingency by which their existence is affected in principle.

NOEMATIC ORGANIZATION AND INTERNOEMATIC UNITY

ACCORDING TO THE THEORY of the intentionality of consciousness, corresponding to every act there is an intentional correlate or noema, that is, the object intended ("object" understood in the widest sense), taken however exactly as, and only as, it is actually intended through the act under discussion.[5] For instance, if we think of Shakespeare as the director of the Globe Theatre, the corresponding noema is not the real historical person who was born in 1563, died in 1616, wrote the *Sonnets*, *Hamlet*, *King Lear*, and other plays, was director of the Globe Theatre, and so on. Rather, the noema is that historical person under the aspect of his role and function with respect to the Globe Theatre. Correspondingly, the perceptual noema is not the thing encountered per se with all the properties, qualities, modes of behavior under specified conditions (causal properties) which belong to it regardless of whether or not they are actually perceived and regardless of whether they are already known or still to be discovered. The perceptual noema is rather the thing as it pre-

5. For the general meaning of "noema," see *Ideas*, pt. III, chap. 3.

sents itself through the given particular perception, that is, the thing as appearing under a certain aspect, from a certain side, in a certain orientation—briefly, in a certain manner of one-sided adumbrational presentation.[6] Among the constituents of the perceptual noema must also be counted aspects under which the thing does not appear at present, properties which it does not exhibit through the given perception but to which the latter contains anticipatory references—however, only insofar as, and to the extent to which, those aspects and properties are actually referred to and play a role for the perception in question. In a word, the analysis of the perceptual noema (as, for that matter, of any noema) must follow a strictly descriptive direction (*FC,* pp. 231 ff.).

A plurality of perceptual noemata severally correspond to the successive phases of the perceptual process in the course of which the identical thing presents itself under varying aspects. To preclude possible misunderstandings, a distinction between two cases must be made. In one case we repeatedly perceive a thing appearing in the same manner of adumbrational presentation—as when, while abiding by the same point of observation, we alternately open and close our eyes, or when, after an absence from a certain point of observation, we return to it—so that the same noema corresponds to a multiplicity of acts. We are not interested here in this case—of which, in several of our writings, we have availed ourselves as a point of departure for defining intentionality as noetico-noematic correlation.[7] Rather, we are concerned with the second case, in which an identical thing appears in the course of the perceptual process in varying manners of adumbrational presentation, so that a plurality not only of acts but of noemata as well is involved.

At once the problem arises of the noematic counterpart of the unity of the perceptual process. *What kind of noematic organization and internoematic unity corresponds to the coalescing of the successive acts of perception into one sustained process of which, because of the intrinsic coherence prevailing among them, they become phases?* Obviously, the multiple noemata belong together by virtue of their common relatedness to the same thing. We are

6. For the notion of perceptual noema or, as it is also called, perceptual sense (*Wahrnehmungssinn*), see *Ideas,* §§ 88 f., 97 f.; and *Phänomenologische Psychologie,* §§ 34, 36.

7. See above, n. 3; and "On the Intentionality of Consciousness," in *SPP.*

then confronted by questions. What is the identical thing in contradistinction to the multiple noemata which all differ from one
another? How is their relatedness to the identical thing and also
to one another to be understood? To formulate our problem in a
still more precise way: *What makes each one of the noemata in
question be one particular adumbrational appearance of a thing
which as identically the same is susceptible of presenting itself
under different aspects and from different sides? On what is the
consciousness of the identity of the thing in the face of the
multiple perceptual noemata founded?* The same question can,
and must, be raised with regard to the properties: What makes
the different qualities and properties, visual, tactile, causal, etc.,
be properties and qualities of one and the same thing?

Husserl has dealt with this problem by analyzing the noema
in general. First he makes a distinction between what he calls
the "noematic sense" or—as we may also say—the noematic
what and the noematic characters, especially those concerning
the mode of givenness, such as given in perception, in memory,
in clear intuition (*klar anschaulich*), in thought (*denkmässig*),
etc.[8] Disregarding the characters which indicate the mode in
which we are conscious of something, we retain the noematic
sense, that is, that of which we are conscious, taken in a strictly
descriptive orientation exactly such as it presents itself.[9] The expressions to be used for the description of the noematic sense or
noematic nucleus may be formal-ontological in character, like
"object," "property," "state of affairs"; or material-ontological, like
"thing," "figure," "cause." They may furthermore, have material
content (*sachhaltig*)[10] like "rough," "hard," "colored"; and finally,
they may include indeterminacies, as when, in describing a thing
as it presents itself in perceptual encounter, we accurately say
that its back side, not seen at present, will have some color,

8. *Ideas*, §§ 99, 130. In the terminology of the *Logical Investigations* (pp. 586 ff.), the distinction is between the matter (*Materie*)
and the quality of an act. We may also mention the doxic or,
noematically speaking, existential characters (*Seinscharaktere*), like
real, likely, presumable, questionable, and doubtful (*Ideas*, § 103),
although Husserl does not refer to them in *Ideas*, § 130.

9. Sometimes Husserl calls the noematic sense the "noematic
nucleus," a term we have used in *FC*, pp. 179 f. However, he also
gives the term "nucleus" a somewhat different meaning in *Ideas*,
§ 132.

10. For the rendering of *sachhaltig* by "having material content,"
we are indebted to Dorion Cairns.

though which particular color remains indeterminate.[11] This justifies the designation of the noematic sense as the noematic *what*.

At the second stage of his analysis, Husserl discerns within the noematic sense a central core—more correctly, a central point of unity or connection, a "carrier of predicates," a "carrier of sense," a carrier which is but a pure X, devoid in itself of all determinations, yet capable and even in need of being determined. The "determinable subject of its possible predicates, the pure X apart from all predicates" is to be distinguished from the very predicates (*Ideas*, § 131). The terms "subject" and "predicate" must not be construed as logical categories; rather, they are to be understood to express perceptual structures, since all logical categories derive from underlying structures of perceptual encounter. For this reason, we prefer Husserl's terminology in *Phänomenologische Psychologie* (§ 35) and, in the further exposition and discussion of his theory as developed in the text of the *Ideas*, we shall replace "subject" by "substratum" or "substratum-pole" (Husserl's phrase), and "predicate" by "property," "quality," or "attribute" (*Merkmal*).

Though they must be distinguished, substratum and attributes cannot be severed or separated from one another. Because it is devoid of all determinations, the substratum as a pure X calls for attributes by which it is determined. Conversely, the attributes as attributes of "something" require a substratum-pole in which they inhere. Every noematic sense as a one-sided adumbrational presentation of a thing susceptible, i.e., encountered as susceptible, of appearing in different manners of adumbrational presentation, must contain the pure X, the substratum-pole which alone makes the distinction between the "noematic object" *simpliciter* (*schlechthin*) and that object as determined in a particular manner of presentation (*Gegenstand im Wie seiner Bestimmtheiten*) possible. On the other hand, since no thing can be encountered except in a certain manner of adumbrational presentation, there can be no substratum-pole without attributes inhering in it, no carrier of sense without a noematic sense which it carries.

---

11. Concerning "open" in contradistinction to "problematic" possibilities, see *EJ*, pp. 35 f., § 21c, and p. 306; Alfred Schultz, "Choosing among Projects of Action," § 7, in *Collected Papers* (The Hague: Martinus Nijhoff, 1962–66), Vol. I (1962); and *FC*, pp. 245 ff.

By pointing out a special noematic element, Husserl seems to provide an answer to the questions raised before. If multiple properties and qualities are encountered as attributes of the same thing, it is because the several noemata, of which the properties in question are constituents, have, all of them, the same central noematic element in common. In general, noemata which differ from one another as to their noematic sense and also as to their mode of givenness (some corresponding to perceptions, others to memories) are related to the same thing, and hence, also to one another, by virtue of the same pure X's being contained in every one of them. The internoematic unity, which is based on the presence and the unifying function of an identical element in all the noematic senses concerned, is the noematic counterpart of successive perceptions' coalescing into the unity of one sustained process. The consciousness of the thing perceptually encountered as identically the same, of which the multiple noemata are various adumbrational presentations, depends on the presence of that element. In the course of the perceptual process, the noemata involved prove to agree as to their central element or, as Husserl puts it, their determinable Xs come to coincidence (*Deckung*) with one another.

The question can and must be raised whether the central noematic element actually corresponds to ascertained and ascertainable phenomenal findings or is not, rather, posited as a theoretical construct. Examining a noema, we indeed find the difference between the noematic *what* or sense and the noematic characters. However, we do not discern a central element, a pure X, a mere carrier of sense within the noematic sense. To be sure, there is consciousness of the identical thing, which in the course of the perceptual process appears under varying aspects and from different sides and to which various noemata are related. But it does not follow that the consciousness of the thing's identity must be based on an identical element common to all noemata related to that thing. The consciousness in question may depend on the form in which the pertinent noemata are organized with respect to one another, on the specific form of unity prevailing in the group or system which they compose and to which they belong—a form of organization which, in the final analysis, is rooted in the specific organization of each particular noema.

Although he has introduced and emphasized the notion of the

noema and has devoted extensive analyses to it in *Ideas,* Husserl has not explicitly dealt with problems concerning noematic and internoematic organization.[12] In the context under discussion, he finds himself confronted with an organizational problem. The descriptive analysis of the noematic sense yields a set (*Inbegriff*) of formal-ontological and material-ontological terms (*Prädikate*) and, finally, such terms as have material content to a greater or lesser degree of determinateness. Within this set and among its terms there prevails unity which, however, Husserl points out, is not "unity in the sense in which any complex, any combination [*Verbindung*] . . . would be called unity" (*Ideas,* p. 365; translation modified). We take that to mean that the set in question is not a mere sum, a mere aggregate of terms. Rather than entering into an analysis of the structural organization of the set, Husserl resorts to positing a special noematic element, namely, the pure X or pure carrier of sense, which has no other function than that of bestowing unity on the set by serving as a substratum or pole of inherence for its terms.

In this respect, Husserl's theory is somewhat reminiscent of Locke's notion of substance which is assumed by us because the qualities, which we cannot conceive could subsist by themselves, require a substratum in which they inhere; but the latter has no further function and serves no further purpose, since the perceived thing is to be accounted for exclusively in terms of its qualities.[13] With respect to Husserl's theory, the question must be raised as to what distinguishes the pure X as central element of all the noemata related to a house from the central element common to the noemata to a tree—with all determinations being yielded and all anticipations being motivated by constituents of the noematic sense or perceptual sense (*Wahrnehmungssinn*)

12. With the possible exception of *Ideas,* Husserl's analyses move for the most part along noetic rather than noematic lines. This does not mean that the noematic aspect of consciousness is disregarded or neglected but that it is almost always approached from the noetic side and with closest reference to the latter, and not sufficiently in its own right. This holds for Husserl's writings subsequent to *Ideas,* both those published in his lifetime and those posthumously published. Obviously, it holds for the *Logical Investigations,* in which the notion of the noema is not yet explicitly formulated, though amply prepared.

13. *An Essay Concerning Human Understanding,* bk. II, chap. 23, §§ 1 ff.

other than the pure X.[14] The conclusion that the pure X as a mere carrier of noematic sense is the same for all perceivable things appears to be as unavoidable as it is unacceptable.

Gestalt theory provides the theoretical means for dealing with the problems of both noematic organization and internoematic unity. Elsewhere (FC, pp. 114 ff., 132 ff., 144 ff.), we have introduced the notions of functional significance and Gestalt coherence for the descriptive characterization and analysis of a Gestalt contexture (one of the simplest examples is a melody) whose constituents mutually determine and qualify one another. A constituent of a Gestalt contexture is phenomenally defined and made to be what it is by the role which it plays for, and the function which it has within, the Gestalt contexture as a whole, that is, with respect to the other constituents. The constituents of a Gestalt contexture may be said to be present or to be contained within one another, if "being contained" is understood in the sense of their mutual qualification and determination, such that a constituent loses its phenomenal identity and ceases to be what it was by being isolated from its own or inserted into another Gestalt contexture in which it would have a different functional significance. Both cases amount to a sometimes most radical phenomenal transformation.

Another way of expressing the same state of affairs is to say that the Gestalt contexture as a whole is present in every one of its constituents, insofar as each constituent realizes the whole contexture at the specific place which it holds within it. We thus come to be confronted with a kind of unity—unity by Gestalt coherence—which is not due to a supervenient special factor's bestowing unity on materials which, because they are lacking unity by themselves, are in need of being unified from without. *Unity by Gestalt coherence* denotes, on the contrary, *an internal unity* which consists in nothing other than *the constituents of a Gestalt contexture deriving their functional significance from, and assigning it to, one another in thoroughgoing reciprocity.* It is unnecessary to stress that this unity by Gestalt coherence is totally different from categorial unity established merely by thought, namely, by taking together and colligating any un-

14. Our objection is borne out by Husserl's own discussion of the empty horizon of anticipated properties—partly highly indeterminate, partly even unknown—of the thing perceived as a character pertaining to the substratum-pole; see *Phänomenologische Psychologie*, pp. 181 f.

related elements which are first juxtaposed, and which derive no phenomenal feature whatever from their being taken together.[15] Categorial unity is here mentioned merely for the sake of completeness.

The notions of functional significance and Gestalt coherence may be employed for the analysis of the structure of the perceptual noema (*FC*, pt. IV, pp. 228 ff., 273 ff.). Within the perceptual noema, the distinction must be made between those constituents which are, and those which are not, given in direct and originary sense encounter. The latter constituents are the noematic correlates of the anticipations and expectancies which pervade and permeate the present perception. All the constituents mutually determine and qualify one another.

Suppose we perceive a building presenting itself from the front side. That perceptual encounter could not be what it is were it not for references to other sides of the building, not seen at the moment, which contribute toward determining the noematic sense of the present perception as one-sided adumbrational appearance of the building from its front side. Moreover, the front side appears as an architectural form requiring a specific total architectural configuration into which it fits. On the one hand, the perceptual appearance in question arouses, or rather motivates,[16] certain expectancies concerning the total architectural configuration—or, noematically expressed, it predelineates and pretraces the total architectural configuration along more or less indeterminate but specifically generic and typical lines. On the other hand, the total configuration determines the front side of the building as an architectural detail occupying a specific place within the total architectural configuration. In this sense, the latter may be said to be present in each and every detail; conversely, each and every detail makes its specific contribution toward the architectural configuration as a whole.

The phenomenon under discussion is by no means confined to perceptual encounters which pertain to the same realm of sensibility. At night we hear a noise as emanating from a passing automobile which we do not see. The noise is experienced as an

15. Husserl, *Philosophie der Arithmetik* (Halle: Pfeffer, 1891), pp. 77 ff.; and *LI*, pp. 480 ff., 819 ff.
16. "Motivation" is meant in the strict phenomenological sense defined by Husserl in *Ideas*, §§ 47, 140.

auditory encounter of an automobile.[17] Again, that which is given in genuine sense encounter is determined as to its sense, significance, or "meaning" by what is accessible in the mode of originarity through perceptions other than auditory ones.

Now it is possible to answer the questions raised before in a different way than Husserl has. All perceptual noemata related to the same thing mutually qualify and determine, even demand and support, one another. That is, the noemata in question form a system which has unity by Gestalt coherence. As to the *perceived thing*, it is—we submit—*nothing other than the internoematic system itself, i.e., the system of the multiple adumbrational presentations and of the properties and qualities exhibited in those presentations.*[18] Since the unity in question is unity by Gestalt coherence, no special unifying factor or agency is required any longer, and the pure X or mere carrier of sense, which is a theoretical construct rather than being phenomenally ascertainable, proves dispensable.

In other words, *Husserl's account of perceptual encounter in terms of inherence is replaced by an account*, derived from results of Gestalt theory, *in terms of coherence.* The consciousness of the thing perceived as identically the same throughout the perceptual process and in the face of the various noemata concerned is not founded on a special element common to all those noemata. Rather, it is the consciousness of the very identity of the internoematic system itself. The difference between a particular perceptual noema and the thing to which that noema is related proves to be that between a member of a system and the *system itself* which *as a whole is present in each of its members*, in every one-sided adumbrational presentation, in every property exhibited.

The term "substratum" is either to be eliminated altogether from the phenomenological account of perceptual encounter or,

17. See Maurice Merleau-Ponty, *Phenomenology of Perception*, trans. Colin Smith (New York: Humanities Press, 1962), pp. 229 f.

18. According to Merleau-Ponty, "An object is an organism of colours, smells, sounds, and tactile appearances which symbolize, modify and accord with each other according to the laws of a real logic" (*ibid.*, p. 38). See also Jean-Paul Sartre, *Being and Nothingness*, trans. Hazel E. Barnes (New York: Philosophical Library, 1956), p. 186: "The fluidity, the tepidity, the bluish color, the undulating restlessness of the water in a pool are given at one stroke, each quality through the others; and it is this total interpenetration which we call the *this*."

if retained, is to be given a different meaning, so as no longer to denote the relationship of inherence but rather that of pertaining to a "part" of a "whole." The latter is the very system of its "parts," each one of which is made to be what it is by virtue of the functional significance it has with respect to the other "parts" of the system (see *FC*, pp. 144 ff.). Herein we see the noematic counterpart of the organizational structure of the perceptual process whose phases mutually continue and confirm one another (*FC*, pt. IV, chap. 1). That which is given in an enveloped form within the structure of a particular noema, namely, its constituents reciprocally determining and qualifying each other, comes to be disenveloped, unfolded, and unraveled in the course of the perceptual process (*FC*, pp. 294 f.).

We claim that our account faithfully renders the phenomenal state of affairs: *The thing itself* appears under different aspects and from different sides, is manifest in its various properties and qualities, or, as we may say, *the internoematic system as a whole presents itself from the varying vantage points of its several members.* Finally, the indeterminateness by which every perceptual encounter is affected may also be accounted for in terms of Gestalt theory. If a Gestalt contexture is not yet completed but is still sufficiently established as to its generic style and type, its continuation, and, perhaps, its completion are subject to the condition of agreeing with, and fitting into, the generic and typical framework as established thus far. We may refer to the "law of good continuation" or "law of Prägnanz" as formulated by Wertheimer.[19] Elsewhere (*SPP*, p. 348), we have proposed the expression "principle of conformity to sense" (*Prinzip der Sinneskonformität*), a principle of which the law of good continuation is a special case.

PHENOMENOLOGICAL ORIGIN OF THE JUDGMENT OF PREDICATION

PASSING FROM PERCEPTUAL ENCOUNTER to predication, we shall follow Husserl's treatment of this transition as presented

19. Max Wertheimer, "Laws of Organization in Perceptual Forms," in *A Source Book of Gestalt Psychology*, comp. Willis D. Ellis (New York: Humanities Press, 1938), p. 83. See also Kurt Koffka, *Principles of Gestalt Psychology* (New York: Humanities Press, 1935), pp. 110, 171, 174 f.

in *Experience and Judgment.* Some of Husserl's analyses will be modified, others will be reinterpreted in the light of the results achieved in the preceding section.

In accordance with his general program, Husserl takes his departure from perceptual encounter, of which he distinguishes two kinds. One is "simple apprehension" (*schlichte Erfassung*), the other is "explicating contemplation" (*explizierende Betrachtung*).

In simple apprehension the thing is merely surveyed; it is perceived in a rather global way with little or no discernment of details (*EJ*, pp. 103 ff.). Husserl refers to the case of a vague perception, as when a visual object appears at the periphery of the field of vision so that hardly any of its properties are given with any distinctness. Repeatedly he calls the thing as given in simple apprehension an indeterminate substratum susceptible of undergoing perceptual determinations by explicating contemplation (*EJ*, pp. 113, 117, 206, 211). The notion of indeterminate substratum is reminiscent of the conception of the pure X or mere carrier of sense. While the latter terms do not occur in *Experience and Judgment*, the notion of a substratum, understood as pole of inherence, plays a predominant role. Apart from the criticism which we have formulated with respect to the notion of an indeterminate substratum, this notion is at variance with Husserl's emphatic insistence on every perceived thing's presenting itself in the light of a certain typicality or under the horizon of some preacquaintanceship (*EJ*, § 8; cf. *ibid.*, pp. 112, 127). In fact, however indistinct the perception of a thing may be, it appears at least as a spatial object, no matter how vaguely localized. On the level of perceptual encounter, the notion of an indeterminate substratum cannot even be admitted as a legitimate idealization, since the actualization of the ideal limit-case is, in principle, precluded by the essential nature of perceptual consciousness.

More adequate—we submit—is Husserl's description of simple apprehension in terms of the interest of the perceiving subject who aims at surveying the perceived thing in a global way rather than entering into, penetrating, and studying its details (*EJ*, p. 103). In elaborating somewhat this hint of Husserl, we first note that the comparative familiarity or unfamiliarity of the thing perceived, as well as the comparative distinctness or indistinctness of the perception of it, are hardly of importance in the present context. For a thing to be perceptually accessible it must exhibit some property or quality. Even when it is observed under the most unfavorable circumstances, the thing appears as having some spatial shape and being somehow colored, no matter how vague its shape and how unobtrusive its color. Regardless of the degree of distinctness or indistinctness of the perception, *in simple apprehension the perceiving glance does not stop at, still less focus on, the property or quality* which yields an entry into the thing perceived. Rather, *the perceiving glance passes through that property* which in a certain sense is transparent; *the glance is directed to the thing perceived in its globality.* Noematically expressed, *the thing appears as an undifferentiated unity,* none of the constituents of the perceptual noema having any prominence.[20]

Explicating contemplation presupposes simple apprehension and is accounted for by Husserl in terms of thematizing activities (see *EJ,* § 24c). In passing from simple apprehension to explicating contemplation, the thing as given in the former mode, the substratum S, understood in the sense of pole of inherence, remains "maintained in grasp." [21] At the same time, another thematizing glance comes to be directed to some property *p* of S, which has aroused perceptual interest. Both thematizing activities, however, do not occur merely simultaneously, side by side, so to speak. Between them an overlapping (*Überschiebung*) or a coincidence (*Deckung*) takes place, so that, while S is throughout maintained in grasp as the primary or principal theme, *p* is grasped as a subservient theme, subordinate to S. That is, *p* is not grasped as a theme in its own right but as a theme relative to the theme S—as something concerning S and, in a sense, dependent on S.[22]

In other words, *p* is grasped as a determination or an attribute of S. According to Husserl, the notions of substratum as such (*Substratgegenstand als solcher*) and attributes or determinations (*Bestimmungen*), as these notions are to be understood on the perceptual level, have their phenomenological origin in explicating contemplation (*EJ,* p. 114); S as given in simple

---

20. Husserl himself speaks, in this connection, of "undifferentiated unity" (*EJ,* p. 206).

21. Concerning "grasping," "holding in grasp," and modalities thereof, see *Ideas,* § 122; *EJ,* § 236.

22. Though this statement holds for "independent" and "nonindependent" parts alike, we here confine ourselves, for the sake of simplicity, to the latter. For this distinction, see *LI,* pp. 437 ff.

apprehension now becomes a substratum ready for, and requiring, determination by attributes. Such a determination takes place by means of a *synthesis*, with the attribute p, by virtue of the mentioned coincidence, being incorporated into S which, in turn, undergoes a modification, namely, an enrichment of sense and content.

Still more to clarify the point in question, let us consider Husserl's account of a continuing explicating contemplation which passes from the property p to another property, q. At the second step, S is still maintained in grasp as the principal theme. However, it is no longer maintained as it was at the first step, as a "pure" S, so to speak, but as $S(p)$, that is, as having undergone a first perceptual determination. The primary thematizing activity is directed to $S(p)$ as resulting from the first determination; the secondary thematizing activity is directed to q as a further perceptual determination. No thematizing activity is directed to p any longer. Still, p does not vanish from consciousness. It is still retained in grasp, but it is thus retained as incorporated into S, as sedimented on S, and not as a theme, not even a subordinate one.

For continuity of presentation, we now proceed to summarize Husserl's account af the phenomenological origin of the judgment of predication. According to Husserl (*EJ*, §§ 147 f.), predication is an activity which in some respects bears similarity, in other respects dissimilarity, to practical activity. All activity is motivated by and arises from a decision of the will. Whereas, in the case of practical activity, the volitional decision aims at the possession of some object, its modification, or the bringing about of a certain state of affairs, the goal of the specifically cognitive will—which motivates predication and, generally, all logical activity—is the generation and production of knowledge about an object, more precisely, knowledge as an abiding possession, available at any time and for everyone (see *FTL*, §§ 42 f., 73).

Perceptual encounter yields acquaintance with the thing perceived, but that acquaintance lasts no longer than the encounter itself. To be sure, circumstances permitting, the encounter may be repeated, the thing may be perceived again or be remembered. Such reactivation, however, is contingent on circumstances; and, furthermore, the acquaintance in question remains in principle a matter of the perceiving and remembering subject who cannot communicate it to others. The transformation of perceptual acquaintance into abiding knowledge, that is, knowledge in the proper sense, requires the generating production of specific entities, "categorial objects" (*Verstandesgegenständlichkeiten*)—in the first place, predicative judgments through which perceptual acquaintance is made a permanent acquisition which, by means of linguistic expressions, may be communicated and, hence, may become the possession of everyone, and which, finally, may motivate the reinstatement or the reactivation of perceptual encounter, on the basis of which a certain predicative judgment arises and by which it is validated.

Predication requires a specific attitude induced by the will to cognition. In this specifically cognitive attitude, the process of explicating contemplation is in a way recapitulated (*EJ,* § 50). Having performed the explicating contemplation, we again return to S, not as the principal theme still maintained in grasp, but as a theme *simpliciter,* more or less as it was grasped in the simple apprehension which underlies the explicating contemplation. The latter, still retained as having just been performed, is at the same time protended as repeatable. In other words, there is a tendency to pass to p again. Under the impact of the will to cognition, the transition from S to p is now effectuated actively. In explicating contemplation, p is incorporated into S by means of "passive coincidence" (*passive Deckung*), whereas there is now the intention to refer p to S in active way, by an active synthesis.[23] If this intention is fulfilled, both p and S undergo a transformation of sense. P, which had been a property found to inhere in the substratum S, acquires the logical sense of a predicate to be explicitly asserted about S—which, in turn, acquires the logical sense of the subject about which assertions can be made, while previously it had simply appeared as a carrier of attributes and properties. What in perceptual encounter is merely ascertained is, on the basis of an active transition from the subject S as *terminus a quo* to the predicate p as *terminus ad quem,* now explicitly asserted in a judgment of predication.

23. The difference between the thematizing activity which, according to Husserl, is involved in explicating contemplation and the activity here in play seems to depend on the cognitive will's being absent from the former case while intervening in the latter. This is the sense in which we interpret Husserl's distinction between "synthetic activity in general" and "activity of synthesis itself" (*EJ,* p. 207).

Predication undoubtedly rests on perceptual encounter, more particularly on what Husserl calls explicating contemplation, whose distinction from simple apprehension is here not challenged either. But whereas, according to Husserl, explicating contemplation arises from simple apprehension by virtue of a thematizing activity, we account for the difference under discussion in terms of noematic organization. In simple apprehension, as mentioned before, the perceptual noema is undifferentiated. On the contrary, in the case of explicating contemplation, the perceived thing, as it actually presents itself, appears as centered with regard to a certain property. One of the constituents of the pertinent noematic sense predominates over the others, or—as it may also be expressed—has special phenomenal weightiness (SPP, pp. 189–92). Because the organizational structure of the perceptual noema is that of Gestalt coherence, the internoematic system as a whole is "contained" and present in each of its members from whose vantage point it appears through a given perception. In explicating contemplation, the perceptual noema may be characterized as a *differentiated unity*. The differentiation is between the system of properties pertaining to the thing perceived, to the extent to which those properties actually play a role in the perception under consideration and taken in the very role they play, on the one hand, and, on the other hand, a particular property with regard to which the thing appears centered in its perceptual presentation.

Husserl describes the phenomenal state of affairs in question to the effect that, in and through encountering the properties, we become acquainted with the thing perceived as manifesting itself in its properties (EJ, pp. 113 f., 130 f.), and that every partial apprehension, namely, of a property, is at the same time a total apprehension of the thing as a whole (EJ, p. 117). While we fully endorse these descriptive formulations, our account differs in two respects from that of Husserl, who resorts to thematizing activity by means of which the property p is incorporated into S as substratum in the sense of inherence. In the first place, it is—we submit—S, understood as an internoematic system or the system of properties, which is incorporated in the particular property p, rather than the converse. Second, *what Husserl presents as the result of an operating activity is for us a matter of noematic structure and organization.* Differently expressed, *while Husserl conceives of explicating contemplation as a synthesis, we see in it a kind of analysis.* In fact, through successive acts of explicating contemplation, the thing perceived successively displays its various properties, being present in each one of them. Continual explicating contemplation proves a progressive analysis of the total system into its several members.

While absent from explicating contemplation, thematizing activity does play a role in predication—even a preeminent role. By granting that the will to cognition motivates that activity and sets it in motion, we establish no more than a condition, perhaps a necessary one, under which alone that activity may operate. Consequently, the very nature of the activity involved in predication requires definition and analysis. After the preceding discussion, we can no longer conceive of the activity of predication as recapitulation of explicating contemplation in the specifically cognitive attitude.

In explicating contemplation, the perceptual noema presents the structure of differentiated unity, containing two terms in unity. That is, the constituents of the noema may be considered as pertaining to one or the other of two terms. One term is the system of properties other than the one with regard to which the system is centered; the latter property is the second term. This differentiated unity or duality in unity is rendered explicit, thematized, or, to express it more properly, articulated. *Articulating thematization consists in dissociating the mentioned terms from, and opposing them to, one another.* By virtue of being thematized, the system of properties making up the first term acquires the logical sense of the *subject* about which assertions are made, when the system is explicitly and actively articulated into its members. Correspondingly, the second term, by being opposed to the system of which it is a member, acquires the logical sense of an asserted *predicate*. It must be remembered that all constituents of a perceptual noema qualify each other in thoroughgoing reciprocity and mutuality. In the present context, the property p, which becomes the predicate p in the way just described, is seen to qualify the other constituents. Its being qualified by the latter will presently be taken into consideration. Because of the mentioned dissociation, the act of predicative judging which arises on the grounds of, or may even be equated with, articulating thematization, is polythetic in contradistinction to perceptual encounter, which is essentially monothetic (*EJ*, p. 207). By articulating thematization, the differentiated unity of explicating contemplation, though not broken, is nevertheless modified. In its place, there is now a different kind of unity, which may be called "articulated unity."

Like the terms themselves, the connection between them must be thematized. This thematization is expressed by the copula "is," which denotes the specific unity of subject and predicate (*EJ*, pp. 208, 214). To state it in more detail, the copula expresses the relation of articulated unity which results when a property, becoming a predicate, is at the same time both dissociated from and explicitly referred to the system which comprises it. Whereas, in monothetic perceptual encounter, the table presents itself *as* brown, it is in the polythetic judgment of predication asserted to *be* brown. Moneta has very aptly formulated it: "the 'as' of perception . . . becomes the 'is' of predication." [24] The circumstance that some languages do, while others do not, have a special word for denoting the copula is immaterial in the present context. Undeniable and obvious though the importance of linguistic formulations is for purposes of communication, the first concern, even with regard to a theory of language, must be the phenomenological clarification of that which is expressed in linguistic formulations, namely, the noematic correlate of the act of judging.

Articulating thematization proves to be a special mental operation performed on a given perceptual situation, which thereby undergoes categorial formation. To that specific operation corresponds a specific noematic correlate, namely, the *state of affairs* (*Sachverhalt*) which is the *judgmental noema*, founded on, but different from, the perceptual noema.[25] Husserl has formulated the difference as that between what is judged, the "what is judged" (*das Geurteilte*), and that on which the judgment bears or to which it refers (*das Beurteilte*).[26] The latter denotes the thing perceived, the former the state of affairs which results from and is constituted by the categorial formation

---

24. Giuseppina C. Moneta, "The Identity of the Logical Proposition" (Ph.D. diss., Graduate Faculty of Political and Social Science, The New School for Social Research, 1969), p. 156.

25. *Ideas*, § 94; *FTL*, § 45; see also *LI*, pp. 579, 611, although the term "noema" is not used in this earlier work.

26. *Ideas*, § 94. William James makes a similar distinction between the "object" and the "topic" of thought (the "topic" corresponds to Husserl's "*Beurteilte*" and the "object" to "*Geurteilte*"), in *The Principles of Psychology* (New York: Henry Holt & Co., 1890), I, 275 f.

of the thing perceived by means of articulating thematization. As is to be expected in an inquiry into the phenomenological origin of the judgment of predication, our discussion has brought us before the state of affairs apprehended in the mode of originarity or, which amounts to the same, the judgment, understood in the noematic sense, in the mode not only of distinctness but also of clarity (*FTL*, §§ 16b, 16c), that is, the judgment as fulfilled. "Originarity" here refers to both the bodily presence of the thing in perceptual encounter and the manner in which the operation of articulating thematization is performed (*FTL*, p. 150, and app. II. § 2a).

As repeatedly emphasized, every constituent of a perceptual noema contributes to the qualification of the other constituents and is at the same time qualified by them. This is of consequence for the sense of perceptual properties as well as the corresponding predicates. Logicians have pointed out that, when a piece of cloth is judged to be blue, the intention is not to assert that it is a member of a class which also comprises certain kinds of ink, the eyes of certain persons, the sky as it appears on a cloudless day, the Mediterranean, and the like.[27] "Blue" does not, in this connection, have a general and conceptual sense but rather a generic, typical, even physiognomical one, denoting the specifically typical way which cloths have of being blue. Because of the presence of the properties of a perceived thing, the ones within the others, these properties prove to be thing-tied.[28] Katz has noted that primitive people, though not they alone, have the tendency to designate colors after the things whose properties or attributes they are.[29] Such a tendency strikingly manifests itself under pathological conditions.[30] In an orientation totally different from the phenomenological one, namely, from a phylogenetic

27. Charles Serrus, *Traité de logique* (Paris, 1945), p. 213.
28. As Merleau-Ponty says, "A colour is never merely a colour, but the colour of a certain object, and the blue of a carpet would never be the same blue were it not a woolly blue" (*Phenomenology of Perception*, p. 313).
29. *The World of Colour*, trans. R. B. MacLeod and C. W. Fox (London: Kegan Paul, Trench, Trubner, & Co., 1935), § 1.
30. Adhémar Gelb and Kurt Goldstein, "Über Farbennamenamnesie," *Psychologische Forschung*, VI (1924), 133 f.; and Kurt Goldstein, "L'Analyse de l'aphasie," *Psychologie du langage* (Paris, 1933), p. 480. See also the detailed discussion by Ernst Cassirer, *The Philosophy of Symbolic Forms*, trans. Ralph Manheim (New Haven: Yale University Press, 1957), III, 223 ff.

point of view, Pradines has emphasized that sounds as well as colors are primarily and fundamentally thing-tied, that is, they belong to things as their attributes and do not have the status of "pure qualities," a status given to them in the arts (painting and music) and in the sciences (physical optics and acoustics).[31] Pradines goes so far as to raise the question of whether those "pure qualities," which, according to him, are certainly not primary data, are *data at all* and not, rather, products of a special mental operation.[32] From the point of view of constitutive phenomenology, the operation in question proves to be that of ideation.

We cannot go along with Husserl when he maintains that, in the judgment of predication at least, the predicate contains an implicit, not yet thematized, reference to a general essence, e.g., redness (*EJ*, §§ 49, 80). The term "implicit" is here somewhat ambiguous. Husserl has explicitly rejected the view that the essence redness may, by an appropriate direction of attention, be "extracted" from the red color of a perceptually given object to be referred to in a predicative judgment, like "this rose is red," in a way more or less similar to that in which a thing appearing at the periphery of the field of vision may be made a theme by appropriately directing the perceiving glance (*LI*, Investigation II, chap. 3). On the other hand, the term "implicit" may be understood to refer to the perceptual basis underlying the apprehension of essences. For this apprehension, however, a special mental operation, namely, ideation, is required, whose study cannot be undertaken here. Husserl writes, "if I judge, *This paper is white,* then . . . the predicate acquires, over and above its own material content, a relation to the subject, *paper,* and engages significationally with the relatedness of the subject to subject-matter" (*FTL*, p. 299). According to the account here proposed, the predicate has its relation and relatedness to subject and subject matter, to begin with, or—as we have expressed it

31. *Philosophie de la sensation* (Paris, 1928), bk. I, chap. 6, § 2. See also the distinction which Merleau-Ponty makes between "colour-function" and "colour-quality" (*Phenomenology of Perception,* p. 305).

32. "La question est de savoir si ces états sensoriels sont primatifs ou seconds, et même dans la seconde hypothèse, s'ils sont *donnés,* ou s'ils ne sont pas *produits* par quelque opération mentale qui pourrait dépasser l'ordre de la sensation" (*Philosophie de la sensation,* p. 40).

—is tied to it, and the problem is rather how the predicate comes to be disengaged from its relation and relatedness so as to acquire a general and conceptual meaning.

Conclusion

OUR DISCUSSION has been confined within certain limits. Because of our concern with the phenomenological origin of the judgment of predication, we have, in studying it, kept as close as possible to its perceptual foundation, without considering the modifications it undergoes and the status it assumes when it is severed from that foundation and is taken in itself as, so to speak, a self-contained independent entity. Since our purpose is to lay bare the structure of predication in its essential purity, we have deliberately excluded from consideration all problems related to conceptualization and ideation, in order to avoid additional complications. For this very reason, it is not before the end of our discussion that we raise the question of whether, in a systematic study of the phenomenological origin of the forms of judgment, in a systematic "genealogy of logic" (the subtitle of *Experience and Judgment*), precedence should not be given to the judgment of subsumption, that is, the judgment of the form "this is an *S*" (e.g., "this is a rose"), over the judgment of predication. Judgments of subsumption—we submit—stand to simple perceptual apprehension in a relation analogous to that of judgment of predication to explicating contemplation. Obviously, an account of the judgment of subsumption requires a theory of conceptualization, as does the account of the transition from predicates expressing thing-tied properties to predicates with general and conceptual meaning.

Those limitations notwithstanding, we claim for our results symptomatic significance. In general, the transition from the perceptual to the logical realm ("logical" understood in the most inclusive sense) rests on, and is motivated by, predelineated and pretraced perceptual structures. *Mutatis mutandis*, the same holds for the transition from a lower to a higher level within the logical or conceptual realm. Again, the transition involves thematization of what is pregiven. However, thematization need not always be articulating thematization, which is but one kind or variety among others. At any event, because of the intervention of thematization as a special mental activity, in every such transition a jump or leap occurs, as most strikingly appears in the transition from the perceptual to the logical realm. Articulating thematization, e.g., though founded on and taking its departure from explicating contemplation, is as such not of the order of perceptual encounter. Moreover, to the intervening mental activity corresponds a specific noematic correlate which is founded on but different from that which pertains to the underlying level, whether perceptual or other. This new noematic correlate lends itself, in turn, to further mental activities' operating on it.

In fact, our analysis has traced the phenomenological origin of the state of affairs, the noematic correlate of the judgment of predication, as arising by means of articulating thematization of a perceptual situation encountered in explicating contemplation. However, it is the perceptual situation that is thematized, not the resulting state of affairs, which is constituted but is not itself thematized. For its thematization further mental operations are required (*LI*, pp. 796 ff.; *FTL*, §§ 42b, 48 f.; and *EJ*, § 58). Among the latter is the one called "nominalization," by means of which a categorical judgment is made a member of a disjunctive, hypothetical, etc., one, or a judgment like "the weather has been clement" is made part of a more complex one, e.g., "the fact that the weather has been clement has been most welcome to the vacationers" (*LI*, pp. 631 ff., 638 ff.; *Ideas*, § 119; *FTL*, pp. 69 f., app. I, §§ 1, 8 f.). Nominalization is likewise involved when the predicate of a judgment ("this rose is red") appears, in a subsequent judgment, as an attribute of its subject or is sedimented on the latter, for instance, "this red rose is fragrant" (*LI*, pp. 515 f., 627 ff.; *FTL*, § 13b, pp. 184, 275).

Within the logical realm, the notion of sedimentation has its legitimate place, while—as we have argued elsewhere[33]—perceptual modifications and alterations must be accounted for in terms of reorganization and restructuration. Accordingly, we have presented the difference between simple perceptual apprehension and explicating contemplation as a difference in noematic structure and organization, rather than resorting to a synthesizing activity, as Husserl does. Finally, a special case of thematization, entirely different from nominalization, is formali-

---

33. "The Phenomenology of Perception: Perceptual Implications," in *An Invitation to Phenomenology*, ed. James M. Edie (Chicago: Quadrangle Books, 1965). See also *FC*, pt. II, § 3b.

zation or algebraization.[34] Applied to judgments of predication, this operation leads from a concrete judgment or proposition, like "this table is brown," to the mere form of that judgment or, as it is called in contemporary logic, the propositional function, "this *S* is *p*" (*FTL*, § 12). All these operations and kindred ones, as well as conceptualization and ideation, are here mentioned as posing problems which arise on the horizon of the present inquiry but whose discussion and treatment do not fall within its purview.[35]

34. The notion of "formalization" in contradistinction to "generalization" has been central to Husserl's theory of logic and mathematics from the beginning. See especially *Philosophie der Arithmetik*, chap. 4; *LI*, pp. 236 ff., 241 ff., 482; *Ideas*, §§ 10 ff.; *FTL*, §§ 24, 27 ff., 87; and *Crisis*, §§ 9 f.

35. To complement and supplement the present study, see the author's essays "Substantiality and Perceptual Coherence, Remarks on H. B. Veatch: *Two Logics*," *Research in Phenomenology*, Vol. II (1972), and "On Thematization," *Research in Phenomenology*, Vol. IV (1974).

Index